CW01649869

'Geopolitics isn't just the manoeuvres of great powers and Castan Pinos highlights the geopolitics of peripheral conflicts by focusing on NATO's "humanitarian" intervention in Kosovo. An artful blend of regional expertise and political theory, Castan Pinos's latest book is a must-read for those interested in how geopolitics actually works.'

Steven M. Radil, Assistant Professor, Department of Geography, University of Idaho, USA

'Castan Pinos's study of the "collateral consequences" of NATO's intervention in Yugoslavia and the subsequent Kosovo's unilateral declaration of independence offers a timely and important examination into the ad hoc approaches to conflict resolution to one of the last open-ended conflicts in the Balkans. Challenging assumptions that Kosovo's statehood is sui generis, this work links moral imperatives for humanitarian intervention with strategic policies of *Realpolitik*.'

Michael Rossi, Lecturer, Department of Politics, Rutgers University, USA

Kosovo and the Collateral Effects of Humanitarian Intervention

Humanitarian intervention is rising ever higher in international relations discourse, with many publications exploring the nature, legality and success of these interventions. However, less attention is given to what happens after an intervention. This book looks in particular at the implications for territorial and border relations, exploring the case of Kosovo, which in many ways can be seen as a turning point in post-cold war international humanitarian intervention. The 1999 intervention has had significant consequences for Kosovo in terms of political transformations, territorial alterations and enclavisation, none of which was officially intended or foreseen when NATO intervened.

Two decades after NATO's intervention and a decade after unilaterally declaring independence, Kosovo continues to be confronted with daunting existential challenges that inevitably affect the stability of the region, border relations, and the credibility of the organisations operating within Kosovo, namely the UN, the EU and NATO. The book claims that not only is the political and territorial conflict far from being settled, but that the implications have gone beyond Kosovo, creating shock waves which have galvanised conflicts elsewhere. In effect, Kosovo has been used as a pretext, as a legitimation and as an inspiration for those who aspire to challenge the border status quo.

The book is primarily aimed at undergraduate and postgraduate students of International Relations and Political Science and as well as Border Studies scholars but will also appeal to researchers focusing on state-building, peace-building, humanitarian studies, nationalism/secessionism and Balkan studies.

Jaume Castan Pinos works as an Associate Professor at the Department of Political Science and Public Management, University of Southern Denmark. He holds a Ph.D. in International Politics (Queen's University Belfast, 2011). He is the Director of the European Studies Bachelor programme at the University of Southern Denmark. His academic interests are framed by ethno-territorial conflicts, sovereignty and political violence. He has conducted extensive research in Catalonia, North Africa and former Yugoslavia.

Routledge Borderlands Studies

Borderlands are spaces of transition between cultures, societies and states. Often, like in the case of the US and Mexico, they are understood as static territorial lines and buffer zones, subservient to the development of states and state territories. However, borderlands can also be fluid and ambiguous spaces, moulded by processes of economic and political integration or shifting geopolitical dividing lines. Moreover, borderlands cultures can be found far from borders, in cities, multicultural neighbourhoods and diasporic communities. They also exist as both future-oriented geographical imaginations and imaginaries with profound historical roots. Today, globalisation, integration and new transnational forms of communication change the complex interrelationships between state, society, space and borders. Consequently, borderlands become more and more places in their own right, reflecting broader supranational patterns of political, economic and social change.

With this series we encourage inter- and multidisciplinary investigation on borders and borderlands throughout the world. We engage with the political, social and historical richness of borderlands, reflecting their unique (geo)political and cultural significance in contexts of colonial rule, nation-building and integration. The Series will explore, among other things, shifting social and political relations and place-related identities that emerge in borderlands, as well as cross-border interaction and the historical memories of every-day life at borders. With this series, we will both contribute to the rich tradition of North American and European borderlands studies and provide a forum for new growing interest in research on borderlands in Africa, Asia and Latin America.

For more information about this series, please visit: www.routledge.com/Routledge-Borderlands-Studies/book-series/BORDERLAND

Post-Cold War Borders
Reframing Political Space in Eastern Europe
Edited by Jussi Laine, Ilkka Liikanen and James W. Scott

Kosovo and the Collateral Effects of Humanitarian Intervention
Jaume Castan Pinos

Kosovo and the Collateral Effects of Humanitarian Intervention

Jaume Castan Pinos

Routledge
Taylor & Francis Group
LONDON AND NEW YORK

First published 2019
by Routledge

2 Park Square, Milton Park, Abingdon, Oxfordshire OX14 4RN
52 Vanderbilt Avenue, New York, NY 10017

Routledge is an imprint of the Taylor & Francis Group, an informa business

First issued in paperback 2020

British Library Cataloguing-in-Publication Data
A catalogue record for this book is available from the British Library

Library of Congress Cataloging-in-Publication Data
A catalog record has been requested for this book

ISBN: 978-1-138-55217-3 (hbk)
ISBN: 978-0-367-66518-0 (pbk)

Typeset in Goudy
by Wearset Ltd, Boldon, Tyne and Wear

MIX
Paper from responsible sources
FSC™ C013985
FSC www.fsc.org

Printed in the United Kingdom
by Henry Ling Limited

To Séamus and Lola.
To all *victims of the conflict in Kosovo.*

Contents

Illustrations

Figures

Boxes

Acknowledgements

I would first of all like to thank all the people who kindly and generously agreed to be interviewed for this book. Without their contribution this book would not have been possible. I am particularly grateful to Gisela Gorbalán, for her everlasting friendship and her outstanding pictures which have been used to illustrate my arguments. I would also like to express my deepest thanks to Maja Perić and Sladjana and her family for their assistance and hospitality.

I owe a debt of gratitude to Katarina Budrik for reading and reviewing the book and providing me with ideas, suggestions and brightly sarcastic comments. Special thanks to Dr. Elisabeth Vetsergaard and Prof. Steen Bo Frandsen for putting their trust in me and in this project from the very beginning of my academic career. I would also like to thank the Routledge editors Helena Hurd and Leila Walker for their infinite patience and useful advice and the anonymous referees who peer-reviewed the manuscript.

Finally, I am extremely grateful to Noam Chomsky whose encouragement and kind words were the best motivation a writer can hope for.

Introduction

In a recent conversation with Noam Chomsky, we discussed how the concept of humanitarian intervention had been seriously misrepresented in the West. The point of this book is not so much to fundamentally redress this misrepresentation – that would be a prodigious task – but to provide the reader with elements to challenge the hegemonic discourses in relation to humanitarian intervention. To do so, this book problematises the notion of humanitarian intervention (HI) in light of the Kosovo case. More specifically, the aim is to evaluate, without shying away from controversy, the multiple ramifications of such intervention.

The title – *Kosovo and the Collateral Effects of Humanitarian Intervention* – is not coincidental. The term 'collateral' has a particularly intimate relationship with Kosovo, and, more specifically, with NATO's 1999 bombing campaign, framed as a humanitarian intervention, against Yugoslavia. NATO briefings and press conferences[1] at the time did use and abuse the term 'collateral damage'. For instance, William Cohen, U.S. Secretary of Defence at the time, in a statement which used this infamous expression ten times, bragged about the (disputable) fact that NATO's Operation Allied Force was 'the most precise and lowest-collateral-damage air campaign in history' (U.S. Department of Defense, 1999). The axiom, repeated *at nauseam* by NATO officials is of course a perverse euphemism with clear Orwellian connotations which attempts to conceal an inconvenient fact: civilian deaths caused as a result of NATO's bombs. Given its strong ties with Kosovo, it does make sense that this book's title includes the adjective 'collateral' to describe the side-effects of the humanitarian intervention in Kosovo.

There are a great many studies which examine the concept of humanitarian intervention, focusing *inter alia* on its desirability, legality, the importance of the moral imperative and human rights or on operational details (Holzgrefe and Keohane, 2003; Evans, 2009; Badescu, 2011; Hehir, 2012, 2013; Weiss, 2016; Bellamy and McLoughlin, 2018). This book intends to scrutinise an aspect which is generally neglected or at least not sufficiently inspected: *what happens after the intervention?* Thus the book concentrates on the aftermath of the NATO intervention in Kosovo, analysing its multi-faceted impacts: human, political, territorial, institutional, geopolitical, legal, regional, discoursive, etc. The analysis of the HI repercussions is a key question that must be addressed irrespective of the fact that we believe (or don't) in the legitimacy, or the imperative necessity, of such interventions.

The point of departure is that this practice has become a popular feature of International Relations in the post-Cold War period. Popular it is, yet deeply controversial. A glance at the HI literature shows that critics and supporters of such practice agree on very little if anything at all. This is rather unsurprising if we bear in mind that the subject is highly divisive and has enormous consequences for states but also for geopolitics and for regional (and global) power balances. In academia, HI has triggered heated discussions. Gareth Evans, a strong advocate of the practice, qualifies these discussions as a 'bitter debate, with the trenches dug deep on both sides' (2009, p. 285).

What is the point of focusing on Kosovo?

In the introduction to his book *Understanding the War in Kosovo*, Florian Bieber pointed out that Kosovo had received extraordinary attention among policy makers and academics (2003, p. 1). Kosovo's golden age, however, seems to be long gone and nowadays this territory has dramatically lost momentum, becoming a geopolitical periphery with little or no media attention. This, in turn, is coupled with a gradual disengagement by a myriad of international organisations (and states) which formerly displayed a high degree of eagerness towards the territory but that have, in recent years, been steadily reducing their personnel and their enthusiasm.

In recent years, the subsequent wars in Afghanistan, Iraq, Libya and Ukraine, the so-called Arab Spring, the threat posed by the Islamic State (IS) and the instability in the Korean peninsula or the South East China Sea have taken the focus away from this troubled territory in South-Eastern Europe. It should be noted that this book will be using the terms 'South-Eastern Europe' or 'former Yugoslavia' to refer to the region, deliberately avoiding 'Western Balkans', an ill-defined ahistorical concept recently constructed by the European Union that connotes paternalistic, EU-centric and post-colonial attitudes.

The reader may very legitimately be wondering about the need for a monograph focusing on Kosovo, a peripheral territory allegedly far from contemporary geopolitical fault lines. This question becomes even more valid when considering that the common perception is that unlike the fiascos of Iraq and Libya, the intervention in Kosovo went relatively well. On top of it, we may assume that Kosovo's disappearance from the international media focus probably denotes that the conflict is settled and stabilised. I, of course, profoundly contest these (mis)perceptions.

Kosovo matters for a wide range of reasons. For starters, the humanitarian intervention in Kosovo is far from being uncontroversial. As the book will argue it was illegal because it was not sanctioned by the UNSC, it did commit serious crimes itself, it did trigger more violations of human rights than it prevented, it probably aggravated the conflict and it has generated a repertoire of subsequent collateral effects. In addition, two decades after NATO's intervention and a decade after unilaterally declaring independence, Kosovo continues to be confronted with daunting existential challenges that inevitably affect the stability of the region, the border status quo of its neighbours, as well as the credibility of the organisations – namely the UN, the EU and NATO – that currently operate in Kosovo. The political and territorial conflict is therefore ongoing and far from being settled.

This book intends to fill a gap in the literature by addressing the collateral effects and the post-intervention idiosyncrasies in Kosovo. The 20 years that have gone by since NATO's *Operation Allied Force* in Kosovo provide us with sufficient perspective to scrutinise the (humanitarian) intervention, and most importantly, to analyse its territorial externalities. Interestingly, Kosovo's impact goes well beyond Kosovo as its shock waves have affected other conflicts such as Macedonia, Libya, Crimea and parastates in the post-soviet space. The argument which will be discussed at the end of this book is that the Kosovo legacy transcends Kosovo. In some occasions, this legacy has the potential to galvanise other conflicts, poison relations between states and be used as a pretext to commit illegal foreign interventions.

Indeed, Kosovo has also been used as a precedent for other secessionist conflicts and, unwillingly, has become a pawn in the global struggle for hegemony between Russia and the United States. Given this, it would appear that Kosovo and the numerous *problématiques* associated with it do not receive sufficient attention in the media, in academia and elsewhere. This book is intended as a humble contribution to redress this.

Chapter outline

The book is organised in six chapters, in addition to this introduction and a conclusion. The first chapter will briefly explain the territorial conflict that affected Kosovo prior to the NATO intervention in 1999. The chapter will also shed light on the nationalist narratives from both Serbs and Albanians and how these narratives clashed over Kosovo. The chapter will subsequently account for the different developments that led to the escalation of the conflict between the Yugoslav government and Albanian secessionists. The conflict, which had sovereignty and territoriality as its main driving factors, will be analysed through a theoretical framework based on the sequential escalation of secessionist conflicts. Kosovo's spiral of violence, the chapter claims, reached a point of no-return with the armed insurrection carried out by the Kosovo Liberation Army (KLA). The last part of the chapter will explore the main features of the KLA, its controversial 'moral hazard' strategy and its successful diplomatic efforts which led the U.S. and its European counterparts to consider them as a 'legitimate interlocutor'.

Following on from this, the second chapter will analyse the main factors leading up to NATO's Operation Allied Force. It will begin with a scrutiny of a major turning point, the Račak massacre, which paved the way to the Rambouillet non-accords. The chapter analyses Rambouillet in detail, examining the protagonists and the nature of the negotiations, paying special attention to their territorial and controversial military conditions (Appendix B). It will examine the failure of Rambouillet, which prompted NATO to carry out the 78-day bombing campaign that would shape Kosovo and arguably also the transatlantic organisation. The final part of the chapter problematises Operation Allied Force, examining the multifaceted reasons behind it and the numerous critiques it has been subject to by scholars, policymakers and those directly affected by it.

The aftermath of NATO's intervention in Kosovo will be examined in Chapter 3, focusing on the political and territorial collateral consequences unleashed by Operation Allied Force. The chapter will analyse the new power realities on the ground and the institutional architecture built by the UN mission in Kosovo (UNMIK). It also addresses the multifaceted challenges faced by UNMIK, including the development of local institutions of self-government and the arduous negotiations regarding Kosovo's 'final status'. The chapter will scrutinise the Ahtisaari report, which advocated for the controversial solution of 'supervised independence' as the only viable option. The final part of the chapter will show how the impossibility of achieving a negotiated solution prompted the Kosovo Assembly, with the support of its Western allies, to choose the unilateral path in the form of a unilateral declaration of independence (UDI) in February 2008.

Chapter 4 is an important pillar of the book in the sense that it delves further into the collateral effects of the 1999 intervention. The focus, in this case, will be on the post-Unilateral Declaration of Independence (2008) scenario and on the difficulties of the new Kosovo state in consolidating its international legal sovereignty, epitomised by its inability to join the UN. The chapter will argue that, as a result of this and despite its notable number of recognitions, Kosovo is unable to rid itself of its parastate status. The chapter will discuss that this is not the only factor curtailing Kosovo's sovereignty. Western actors, such as the U.S. and the EU, which played a fundamental role in terms of granting Kosovo statehood, are undermining Pristina's sovereignty by vigorously and persistently intervening in its internal affairs

Building on the arguments of Chapter 4, Chapter 5 will examine how some fundamental aspects regarding Kosovo's status remain unsettled. The focus will be on internal challenges, namely institutional instability of the north of the country, where Serb-dominated municipalities have traditionally resisted Pristina's rule. The chapter will claim that the EU's attempts to settle the dispute by advocating for the establishment of an autonomous Serb entity (Community of Serb Municipalities) and promoting the 'normalisation of relations' between Serbia and Kosovo have hitherto ended in a deadlock. The final sections of the chapter will examine how this political impasse, added to the lack of UN prospects for Kosovo, may open the door for 'alternative solutions' which entail further border transformations, for instance to the controversial prospect of Kosovo and Albania unification.

Finally, Chapter 6 will make the claim that the collateral effects triggered by humanitarian intervention in Kosovo did transcend Kosovo by focusing on how imperative non-intended consequences emanating from Kosovo have materialised in regions plagued by territorially-driven conflicts. One of the examples to illustrate this will be the 2001 armed conflict in neighbouring Macedonia, caused by an insurgency from a Macedonian–Albanian guerrilla force whose fighters and weapons came largely from Kosovo. In light of the cases of South Ossetia, Crimea and Catalonia, the chapter will discuss whether or not Kosovo constitutes a precedent. The core argument will be that while Kosovo constitutes an exceptional case in many regards, it has become a precedent due to discourse, practice and policy. In other words, Kosovo's legacy has indeed extended well beyond its borders.

A short note on methodology

This book is based on primary and secondary material. The primary sources include 20 qualitative interviews that the author conducted in the period 2012–2018 with local political and governmental figures in the region, officers from international organisations operating in Kosovo (UN, OSCE and EU), journalists, civil society as well as former internally displaced persons/refugees. Some of the interviewees play or have played a major political role in the post-intervention period in Kosovo.

For instance, one of the interviewees is the UN Special Representative of the Secretary-General for Kosovo (2004–2006), Søren Jessen-Petersen, who was determinant in advancing Kosovo's 'supervised independence' status. Another key actor is Kosovo government's political advisor Bashmir Xhemaj who, as a prominent member of Kosovo's Foreign Ministry, has directly negotiated independence recognitions with several states. The Archdeacon of Dečani, Father Sava, a former member of several political institutions in Kosovo, who is famous for providing shelter to thousands of refugees regardless of their ethnicity during (and after) the conflict, has also collaborated with the book. Some interviewees (nine), from organisations such as the OSCE, EU, EULEX and UNMIK, have preferred to remain anonymous due to the sensitivity of the matters discussed. The vast majority of interviews have been carried out in person in Kosovo and Serbia.

Notes

1 General Marani, for example, expressed at a press conference justifying the airstrikes that

> although we put all our effort in avoiding *collateral damage*, things like this can happen and in fact they happened. Over so many bombs dropped, so much activity, then I would say that our efforts to prevent *collateral damage* are quite successful.
>
> [emphasis added by author] (NATO, 1999)

Bibliography

Badescu, C. G. (2011). *Humanitarian Intervention and the Responsibility to Protect: Security and Human Rights*. Abingdon: Routledge.

Bellamy, A. and McLoughlin, S. (2018). *Rethinking Humanitarian Intervention*. London: Palgrave Macmillan.

Bieber, F. (2003). 'Introduction', in F. Bieber and Ž. Daskalovski (eds) *Understanding the War in Kosovo* (pp. 1–12). London: Frank Cass Publishers.

Evans, G. (2009). 'The Responsibility to Protect: An Idea Whose Time Has Come … and Gone?'. *International Relations*, 22(3): 283–298.

Hehir, A. (2012). *The Responsibility to Protect. Rhetoric, Reality and the Future of Humanitarian Intervention*. London: Palgrave Macmillan.

Hehir, A. (2013). *Humanitarian Intervention: An Introduction*. London: Palgrave Macmillan.

Holzgrefe, J. and Keohane, R. (2003). *Humanitarian Intervention: Ethical, Legal and Political Dilemmas*. Cambridge: Cambridge University Press.

NATO (1999, 28 April). 'Press Conference by Mr Jamie Shea and General Giuseppe Marani'. Retrieved from: www.nato.int/kosovo/press/p990428b.htm

U.S. Department of Defense (1999). 'Joint Statement on the Kosovo After Review'. Retrieved from: http://archive.defense.gov/Releases/Release.aspx?ReleaseID=2220

Weiss, T. (2016). *Humanitarian Intervention. Ideas in Action*. Cambridge: Polity Books.

1 From secessionist challenge to armed insurgency

Examining the spiral of violence in Kosovo prior to 1999

In order to comprehend the transformations experienced by Kosovo in the post-1999 context, it is imperative to shed light on the conflictual background prior to the 'Operation Allied Force' NATO intervention. It goes beyond the scope of this book to provide a comprehensive historical analysis of the roots of the conflict between Serbs and Albanians. It is, however, important to gain some understanding of the context in which the conflict between Kosovo's secessionists and the Yugoslavian central government took place. With the purpose of accomplishing this, Buchanan's (2003) 'sequential escalation of secessionist conflicts' will be used as a theoretical framework.

Before this, the chapter will briefly discuss the causes and nature of the conflict in Kosovo. The central argument is that this territory is of paramount importance for understanding the disintegration of Yugoslavia. It is often argued that Kosovo constitutes the first and the last act of the Yugoslavian crisis (Castan Pinos, 2015, p. 223). Some go as far as to claim that 'it is not an exaggeration to say that the locus of Yugoslavia's demise was in Kosovo' (Pesić, 1996, p. 16). What seems clear is that before wars of different intensity broke out in Slovenia (1991), Croatia (1991) and Bosnia (1992), leading to the collapse of the Socialist Federal Republic of Yugoslavia (SFRY), the former Serbian province of Kosovo experienced serious political turmoil which was from the very early stages of an ethno-territorial nature. In 1986, in a statement that would turn out to be premonitory, an anonymous Western diplomat interviewed by the *New York Times* asserted that: 'Kosovo is Yugoslavia's single greatest problem. They [SFRY] can pay off their huge debt, but Kosovo defies solution' (Kramm, 1986a). These concerns were replicated by the then president of the Socialist Republic of Serbia, Ivan Stambolić,[1] who stated that: 'we have to say how dangerous the Kosovo problem is to the integrity of our country.... It is the most delicate problem we have ever had' (Kramm, 1986b). In a similar vein, Balkan history Professor Stevan Pavlowitch claimed in 1988, two years after the *New York Times* articles and three years before the first armed conflict in Yugoslavia, the ten-day war in Slovenia, that Kosovo was Yugoslavia's most explosive problem (1988, p. 78). It is therefore essential to scrutinise the causes of the conflict in Kosovo not only for the sake of understanding the dynamics in this particular former Serbian province but also because of its seemingly protagonist role in the collapse of Yugoslavia.

The roots of an old complex conflict

Causes and competing narratives

To a certain extent, Kosovo established a path-dependence symbiotic relationship with other conflicts in Yugoslavia. On the one hand, it contributed to fuelling nationalist discourses at the embryonic phase of the crisis, particularly amongst Serbs, and on the other, the territory became susceptible to conflict and secession in the mid-1990s, when every single Yugoslavian republic but Montenegro[2] had achieved independence. In other words, Kosovo acted as a catalyst for other territorially-driven conflicts in Yugoslavia but was, at the same time, poisoned by the virulence of the neighbouring crises. According to Malcolm, the growing fear by the Slovenian and Croatian elites of a federal presidency controlled by Serbs is pivotal to understand Yugoslavia's disintegration (1998, p. 344). Interestingly, as will be argued below, this accumulation of power in the late 1980s by Serbs in general, and Milošević in particular, is deeply rooted in Kosovo.

The last U.S. ambassador to unified Yugoslavia, Warren Zimmerman, described amidst the escalation of hostilities between the Kosovo Liberation Army (KLA) and the Yugoslavian security forces, his views on the nature of the conflict in Kosovo:

> The competing claims of Serbs and Albanians in Kosovo have been hopelessly tangled in the webs of history and myth. In its essence, however, the main issue is as simple as it is intractable. The Serbian claim to hegemony is based primarily on the historical/cultural principle: the Jerusalem argument. The Albanian claim to independence is based largely on the demographic principle–the majority argument. Since these claims are mutually incompatible, there is little reason to think that Kosovo will be easy to solve.
>
> (Zimmerman, 1998, pp. 5–6)

In addition to concluding with a clearly pessimistic note, Zimmerman's remarks provide us with very useful clues to reaching a better understanding of the Kosovo imbroglio. The first, and perhaps most important, is that we are essentially dealing with a classic example of a conflict over sovereignty between two national projects trying to impose their rule over a particular territory. This idea, which is implicit rather than explicit in Zimmerman's quote, is in alignment with Sahin's perspective on the sovereignty roots of the conflict (2015, p. 62). This view is also shared by Visoka who contends that the Kosovo conflict is primarily related to self-determination and statehood (2017, p. 14). The sovereignty/territorial nature of the conflict spells trouble according to Horowitz, who argues that 'the powerful ideology of self-determination helps explain the emergence of a political environment hospitable to territorially divisive claims' (1981, p. 166).

The weight of the sovereignty factor is also highlighted by Pavlowitch (1988, p. 93) fretful rhetorical question amidst the Constitutional crisis in Kosovo which would lead to the revocation of its autonomy: 'if Albania were to ... become an attractive proposition, could Yugoslavia keep Kosovo as a semi-colonial problem, at best of the Northern Irish, at worse of the Algerian type?'. It is important to note that unlike other conflicts in the former Yugoslavia, religion did not play a central role in Kosovo because, among other factors, it is not a pivotal component of Albanian nationalism[3] (Babuna, 2000, p. 67).

Simply put, Kosovo presents all the attributes of an ethno-territorial conflict of competing legitimacies. These competing legitimacies, one of them centrifugal and the other centripetal, construct opposing narratives to support their particular causes. As Daskalovski asserts, the 'rights' of particular groups over territory 'are based on a complex interpretation of a combination of historical, legal and demographic' factors (2003, p. 14). Similarly to most debates over sovereignty and territory, the Kosovo case is characterised by incompatible and deeply divided perceptions which reinforce the zero sum nature of the conflict. Simply put, there is a direct correlation and incompatibility between gains, territorial or otherwise, of one ethnic group and losses of the other.

It is worth succinctly exploring the arguments on both sides. The Serbian standpoint, on the other hand, focuses as Zimmerman claims, on historical and cultural elements. The importance of Kosovo for Serbian history is generally underlined as one of the core arguments to justify the Serbian character of Kosovo, not least due to the fact that the medieval Serbian 'state' emerged in this territory. From a constructivist perspective, this could be seen as the manufacturing of history so that it fits the current goals of a particular political project. This is in no way unique to the Serbian case as most nations/states rely on national myths to justify their existence, depict their past glory and serve as an inspiration for the collective destiny of the nation. The use of history is coupled with more poetic claims that Kosovo is the cradle or the heart of the Serbian nation. This sentence was popularised by Slobodan Milošević in the late 1980s and is currently reproduced by political movements and football fans as well as religious or cultural organisations. In a nutshell, it could be argued that the phrase currently belongs to the mainstream Serbian national discourse.

Architectural heritage is also being used as an element supporting the Serbian claims over Kosovo. Krstić-Brano claims that the hundreds of mostly medieval cultural monuments spread around the territory constitute 'the basis for ascertaining the Serbian historical territories and thereby also the rights of the Serbian ... peoples on these territories' (2004, p. 54).

It comes, therefore, as little surprise that this reasoning tends to be referred to as the Jerusalem argument. The critique of the argument focuses on the fact that claiming that Kosovo is the 'Jerusalem' of the Serbs constitutes an exaggeration because Kosovo does not have the role of 'holy place' for (Orthodox) Christianity, as Jerusalem does for Judaism (Malcolm, 1998, p. xxxi).

Last but not least, these arguments are often accompanied, in a quasi-mystical manner, by the 1389 myth, where a Serbian Prince (Lazar Hrebeljanović) commanding a Christian army was defeated by the Ottoman Sultan (Murad I) at the battle of Kosovo Polje. The defeat of 1389 played a

Figure 1.1 Serbia map (pre-Kosovo independence declaration).

Source: UN Geospatial Information Section.

fundamental role as a resurrected *lieu de memoire* and myth, which was particularly useful to fuel the Serbian nationalist discourse due to its sacrificial nature. According to Jakica, 'the story of the Kosovo Battle developed into national mythology where the deeds of the Serbian knights served as examples of national moral values and a national ethos' (2010, p. 163).

Thus, in the very last years of the SFRY songs, poems and books glorifying the Kosovo Polje battle proliferated. Unsurprisingly, Milošević commemorated the 600th anniversary of the battle with a speech which is often considered controversial at the fields of Kosovo Polje, a few miles outside Pristina. According to *The Economist*, it was a 'stirringly virulent nationalist speech' which echoed his primitive nationalism (1999). It certainly depicted Serbs as historical victims, containing passages of sacrifice and parallelisms between 1389 and 1989 with premonitory sentences such as '[S]ix centuries later, now, we [Serbs] are being again engaged in battles and are facing battles. They are not armed battles, although such things cannot be excluded yet' (Milošević, 1989). While it is true that the speech was unprecedentedly nationalist for a Yugoslav Communist leader, it is also true that the speech had elements of praise for Serbia's diversity and multiculurality, which in no way seem to be inspired by irrational ultranationalism.[4]

In addition to the historical and cultural arguments, the Serbian perspective also uses the classic argument used by all host states when facing a threat of a secessionist nature: the legal card. The Serbian government, as well as Serbian scholars, have claimed that Kosovo's secession cannot be considered legal for the very reason that the independence of this territory would flagrantly violate Article 8 of the Serbian constitution which stipulates that '[T]he territory of the Republic of Serbia is inseparable and indivisible' (Government of the Republic of Serbia, 2006). In order to legally alter Serbia's borders or territory, the argument claims, the current constitution would have to be amended. Behind this argument lies the principle of territorial integrity, which Serbia has continuously advocated since the eruption of the conflict.

Kosovo Albanian secessionists, on the other hand, primarily frame their arguments along the lines of self-determination and demographics. The use of the demographic argument is far from staggering if we consider that according to recent data Albanians constitute approximately 87 per cent of the population,[5] whereas Serbs account for less than 8 per cent (ECMI, 2013a; ECMI, 2013b). To this, we should add that an overwhelming majority of Albanians in Kosovo supported and support secession from Yugoslavia/Serbia: 93 per cent of Kosovo Albanians believed independence was 'a good thing' in 2008 (Damjanović and Chapman, 2010), the year that the Kosovo Assembly unilaterally declared it. Given such astounding numbers, it appears to be logical that Kosovo Albanian secessionists embraced the principle of self-determination. This principle is interpreted by stateless territories or breakaway regions as the right of a nation to decide its own destiny. In other words, it corresponds to the citizens of a particular nation, not the administrative entity that currently rules it, to determine its political future. This principle is also claimed by other secessionist movements worldwide from (Iraqi) Kurdistan to Abkhazia or indeed Catalonia. In these cases, similarly to the Kosovo conflict, the principle of self-determination and territorial integrity clash in a seemingly irreconcilable manner.

It must be noted that the Serbian myths connected to Kosovo are accompanied by counter-myths from the Albanian narrative, where (Kosovo) Albanians establish a link between them and the Illyrians (Ingimundarson, 2007, p. 98) with the similar purpose of upholding their rights and legitimacy over Kosovo. The problem of such connection is that as Malcolm argues, connecting the dots between Albanians and Illyrians 'is like trying to solve an equation with too many unknowns' (1998, p. 31), not least because there is no written text in Illyrian. A more severe critique comes from Serbian authors who point out the huge gap between the Illyrians' extinction (sixth century) and the appearance of the term Albanian (eleventh century), adding that 'there is no reliable scholarly evidence of the continuity between Illyrians and present-day Albanians' (Bataković, 2012, p. 21). At any rate, what is relevant about Albanian and Serbian myths is that they reveal the emphasis by both sides on claiming both autochthonousness and ownership over the territory through the national manufacturing of history.

The Kosovo Albanian narrative also uses more recent historical arguments, less mythical, to uphold their claim. One which deserves particular attention is the denunciation of the Serbian 'occupation' of Kosovo in 1912, shortly after gaining its independence and in the midst of the collapse of the crumbling Ottoman Empire. The 'military occupation' of what Albanians perceived to be an 'Albanian land' was, according to Kola, accompanied by a strategy to portray Albanians as inferior beings who were incapable of self-governing themselves and to *Serbianise* Kosovo (2003, pp. 11–13). The modern acquisition of Kosovo by Serbia, which was materialised at the Conference of London (1912–1913), led to an armed conflict between Kosovo Albanian militias, who opposed the integration into Serbia, and the Serbian army and paramilitary forces (Schwegler and Ripley Smith, 2012, p. 353). It also meant that the to-be-born Principality of Albania (officially recognised in 1913) would be politically disunited to a territory which had a considerable Albanian majority.[6]

Interestingly, both sides trade blame regarding ethnic cleansing and *Albanisation* or *Serbianisation* respectively of the territory in different periods of history. The Albanian narrative, for instance, emphasises the ethnic expulsions with the aim of altering the ethnic balance of Kosovo carried out by the Serbian government in the period between 1912 and 1941, when according to their account 300,000 Albanians were forced to leave and 14,000 Serbs were brought to Kosovo (Daskalovski, 2003, p. 19). This is, according to Stefanović, due to an authoritarian policy carried out by the Kingdom of Yugoslavia aimed at national homogeneity through the

Figure 1.2 Kosovo map.

Source: UN Geospatial Information Section.

expulsion of Albanians (2005, p. 480). This trend was consolidated during the first decades (1950–1966) of Tito's rule of the SFRY, when 100,000 Albanians migrated to Turkey (Malcolm, 1998, p. 322). The crux of the matter is, of course, to establish whether this migration was caused by economic reasons or it was connected to political persecution and discrimination.

Likewise, a grievance of forced expulsion is also present in the Serbian narrative. Former Serbian Prime Minister and Yugoslavian President, Vojislav Koštunica, estimates that 100,000 Serbs (and Montenegrins) were ethnically cleansed from Kosovo by ethnic Albanian National Socialist battalions such as the SS *Skanderbeg* and the *Balli Kombëtar* in the period 1941–1945 (2002, p. 15). In a period when Kosovo was occupied by Fascist Italy and temporarily united with Albania (1941–1943), the Fascist-inspired Albanian government[7] and organisations like *Balli Kombëtar* were able to carry out their political plans of *Albanising* Kosovo through a campaign of mass assassinations and successful ethnic cleansing of Serbs and Montenegrins (Vickers, 1999; Bataković, 2012). Finally, Serbian scholarship points out that during the SFRY period, particularly in the 1960s and 1970s decades, there was a significant exodus of Serbs and other Slavs (nearly half of the population) as a result of campaigns of intimidation by ethnic Albanians (Krstić-Brano, 2004, pp. 86–87). The significant reduction of Serbs, the argument claims, is not due to economic reasons but to a phenomenon labelled as 'departure under pressure'. Forced departure coupled with historical ethnic cleansing and the situation of vulnerability of the Serbian community in the post-1999 context would explain the fact the small number of Serbs in Kosovo nowadays (around 8 per cent).

Summing up, both sides highlight (and conceal) particular past events that are advantageous (or disadvantageous) to their narratives through a strategy of historical cherry-picking. Both Albanians and Serbs have been victims and perpetrators of ethnic cleansing, sectarian killings, forced religious conversions and compulsory linguistic assimilation in Kosovo. The main factor, therefore, does not seem to be the ethnic group (Serb or Albanian) but the position of power of a particular group over the other. That being said, it is important to note that these two antagonistic accounts may obscure and neglect the fact that there were long periods of peaceful coexistence between both communities. There is an analytical peril which we could categorise as the sectarian trap, in other words, using sectarianism as the main vehicle to explain conflict.

This has often been the case with journalistic reports that have a tendency to reduce a complex situation to a binary explanation based on ethnoreligious hatred which is depicted as permanent and 'historical', instead of contextual, contingent and largely constructed. As Sluglett claims 'sectarianism … can be used by the lazy superficial observer as a kind of portmanteau explanation for everything, from the Balkans to Iraq' (2016, p. 44). One of the main weaknesses of this approach is that it ignores that populations, in our case Serbs and Albanians, have enjoyed large periods where violence and hostility were not prevalent. In addition, despite the fact that Serbs and Albanians can be distinguished by distinct non-mutually intelligible languages,[8] these divisions have not always been completely clear-cut due to centuries of mutual contact and 'ethno-linguistic assimilation in both directions' (Malcolm, 1998, p. xxix).

Transcending the sectarian narrative without ignoring it, Pavlović argues that the expansionist desires of adjoining states (Serbia and Albania) with their grand territorial projects of establishing greater Serbia and greater Albania are pivotal factors that explain the instability in Kosovo (2013, p. 50). Tentatively, we may conclude that local coexistence between different communities in Kosovo, and elsewhere, is particularly vulnerable to state projects which view homogenisation as a national priority and diversity as an existential threat. Such local coexistence is, as we will see in future chapters, also susceptible to geopolitical power struggles.

The patterns of secessionist conflict escalation in Kosovo

Drawing inspiration from a wide range of cases including Sudan, Eritrea, the Iraqi Kurdistan and Kosovo, Allen Buchanan establishes a sequential pattern of events that are common and characteristic in conflicts of a secessionist nature:

> pressures from a minority group eventually result in the state agreeing to an intrastate autonomy arrangement; the state breaks the agreement; in response to the broken autonomy agreement autonomists become secessionists; and then the state violently attempts to suppress the secession.
>
> (2003, p. 221)

The Kosovo case, however, requires additional stages subsequent to the 'state violently attempts to suppress the secession' phase. These additional elements could be categorised as: armed secessionist insurgency, (humanitarian) intervention by foreign powers (Chapter 2) and finally internationally supported institution-building (Chapter 3) leading to the establishment of a quasi-state or parastate (Chapter 4).

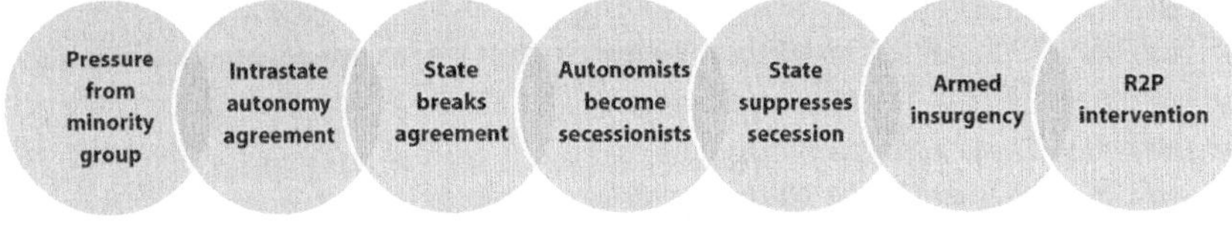

Figure 1.3 Patterns of secession.

Source: elaborated by author based on Buchanan (2003, p. 221).

This section will complete Buchanan's sequential pattern by filling each of the phases with relevant details connected to the Kosovo case. Doing so will be particularly relevant not only because it will help us make sense of the conflict using a theoretical secessionist framework but also due to the fact that it will shed light on the recent historical background of the conflict thus providing us with food for thought for understanding its gradual escalation.

1 *Pressure from minority group*: One of the first manifestations of (bottom-up) Kosovo Albanian nationalism occurred in November 1968, when demonstrations emerged in several cities populated by Albanians in the province of Kosovo as well as in Macedonia. Similarly to other protests in Belgrade, Zagreb and Sarajevo, these protests epitomised youth anger against undemocratic policies and crowed dorms (Fichter, 2016, p. 107). Unlike the protests in other Yugoslavian cities, the demonstrations in towns populated by Albanians had a secessionist flavour. In addition to demanding the status of a republic for Kosovo, Albanian activists had unequivocally territorial claims. According to Çeku, the protesters demands included 'self-determination with the right of secession' as well as the 'union of the Albanian-inhabited territories with Kosovo' (2015, p. 236). This mass movement echoed some of the claims of much more marginalised groups such as Adem Demaçi[9]'s *Revolutionary Movement for Albanian Unity*, whose aim was the creation of a Greater Albania based on a Stalinist ideology (Maliqi, 1996, p. 140). Whether the protests emerged locally through a bottom-up process or, on the contrary, they were institutionally instigated by the leader of the People's Socialist Republic of Albania, Enver Hoxha, remains a contested, open, and heated debate.
2 *Intrastate autonomy agreement*: In 1969, shortly after the pro-secessionist protests by Albanian activists, Kosovo was granted a new constitution, a supreme court and a new university, the University of Pristina (Rogel, 2003, p. 171). This can be interpreted as a concession to Albanian nationalists by Tito but also, through a geopolitical prism, as a positive outcome of the policy of *rapprochement* developed by Yugoslavia and Albania in the period 1966–1971 (Bataković, 2012; Çeku, 2015). Furthermore, consolidating the decentralisation trend initiated by the 1968 and 1971 constitutional amendments, the 1974 Yugoslav Constitution provided Kosovo with the status of an autonomous province, making Kosovo 'one of eight official units of the Yugoslav federation' (Rogel, 2003, p. 171). This recognition of self-rule, however, fell short of explicitly recognising Kosovo as a Yugoslav republic and consequently did not go far enough for the most uncompromising elements of the Albanian nationalist movement. This comes as little surprise because the fact that Kosovo did not manage to become a republic effectively meant that it did not have the self-determination right recognised. Kosovo

was, therefore, practically a de facto republic but lacked the *de jure* status.

At any rate, the Constitution empowered Kosovo (and more specifically Kosovo Albanians) by, for instance, establishing legislative, judicial, and executive institutions as well as by providing equal status to the Albanian language in the province (Graczyk and Giannakos, 2006, p. 147). In addition, Kosovo was granted a constitution in 1974, which defined the Kosovo Assembly as the most prominent institution in the autonomous province (Pavlović, 2013, p. 56). Serbian policymakers,[10] such as former Yugoslav President Dobrica Ćosić, and scholars have been blatantly critical of the Constitution arguing that it planted the seeds for the future disintegration of Yugoslavia (Bataković, 2012, p. 110). Serbs perceived that Albanians were being privileged whereas they were being discriminated against because their minorities in the republics of Bosnia-Herzegovina and Croatia did not enjoy any degree of autonomy of federal recognition. The Serbian perspective is that the Constitution irresponsibly empowered the autonomous provinces of Kosovo (and Vojvodina), and by doing so, it disempowering Serbia's central institutions by, for instance, making them susceptible to the two province's veto on sensitive matters. Krstić-Brano epitomises this view with his claim that the Constitution 'paved the way for Albanian separatism and the concept of the ethnically pure Kosovo' (2004, p. 168).

3 *State breaks agreement*: Florian Bieber claims that 1981 represents a milestone for the conflict over Kosovo (2003, p. 2). Bieber's assertion is unsurprising considering the fact that in 1981 an explosive cocktail of co-constructive negative dynamics which included demands for further autonomy by Kosovo Albanians, discrimination claims by disempowered Kosovo Serbs and calls for recentralisation amongst Serbs (scholars, policymakers and civil representatives alike) emerged. The 1981 crisis very much resembles that of 1968 in the sense that it erupted as a result of street protests by students who originally had socio-economic grievances related to unemployment and education, not territorial or constitutional affairs. A crucial difference, nonetheless, is that the charismatic figure of Tito was no longer present as the Yugoslavian President had died a year earlier. In other words, one of the fundamental pillars of state unity and a primary source of regime legitimacy for Yugoslavia was no longer a part of the picture. As the demonstrations gained momentum and spread throughout the province, however, the nature of the protests gradually evolved into manifestly secessionist gatherings with similar slogans to those of 1968: '"Kosovo–Republic", "We are Albanians – not Yugoslavs" and "Unification with Albania"' (Malcolm, 1998, p. 334). The ghost of secessionism did resonate loudly in the ears of the official party, the League of Communist of Yugoslavia, which reacted through a document labelling the demonstrations as 'aggressive, ruthless, brutal and devastating actions with the scope of

forming the Republic of Kosovo, which would secede from Serbia and Yugoslavia' (cited by Pavlović, 2013, p. 61). The response of the Yugoslavian authorities did not limit itself to condemnations and declarations of disapproval. The 1981 protest in Kosovo triggered a harsh response from the government (Petrović and Stefanović, 2010, p. 1077), which included the deployment of the Yugoslavian National Army (JNA), the declaration of the state of emergency, the arrest of around 2,000 activists and the death of nine people (Pavlowitch, 1988, p. 86), as a result of the confrontation between protesters and security forces.

At this stage, it is worth mentioning that one of the crucial debates for scholars of secessionism is whether autonomy and decentralisation contribute to ameliorate territorially-driven conflicts (Horowitz, 1985), or on the contrary, they aggravate them by perpetuating conflict and, eventually, facilitating secession (Anderson, 2004). It has been argued that the introduction of ethno-federalist policies was particularly detrimental in terms of disintegration for socialist states like Yugoslavia (Petrović and Stefanović, 2010, p. 1073). In the case of Kosovo, it seems that the provision of autonomy was utterly unsuccessful in resolving territorial rifts between Kosovo Albanians and the Yugoslav government. When autonomy was suspended in 1989, an event which could be seen as a point of no return in terms of conflict escalation, both parties blamed the other. Buchanan uses the Kosovo case to highlight the difficulty of determining which actor is ultimately responsible for reaching that conflictual zenith:

> There is no doubt that Serbia, under Milošović's leadership, unilaterally revoked Kosovo's autonomy in 1989. But there is dispute about who violated the terms of the autonomy agreement first. According to those who supported the revocation of autonomy, the Kosovar Albanians had abused their right of autonomy, by using the Kosovar Communist Party as a corrupt patronage system that excluded Serbs and by engaging in violent attacks on Serbs.
>
> (Buchanan, 2003, p. 221)

As mentioned above, this fear of Albanian dominance and particularly of being driven out of the province was a constant for minorities in Kosovo such as Serbs and Montenegrins in the 1980s. Their grievances and demands were mostly connected to the discrimination they suffered and by the demands of protection of their security and rights. The existential anxiety and anguish experienced by Serbs in Kosovo, particularly in the 1980s, is confirmed by a (Serbian) former Internally Displaced Person and current returnee from Eastern Kosovo.[11] The gradual decline of the Serbian population since the 1960s, when it dropped from 27.5 per cent to less than 15 per cent (Vladisavljević 2004, p. 783), contributed to trigger the fear of disappearance, or at best insignificance, amongst many Serbs in Kosovo. This fretfulness explains the eruption of a Serbian civil society movement, in the mid-1980s, which would soon acquire tremendous political importance. The movement could also be interpreted as the consequence of a growing politicisation of Serbs in Kosovo.

The movement consisted of a loosely connected network of activists in Serbian settlements in Kosovo (Pavlović, 2013, p. 68). Their modus operandi was primarily participation in meetings of official political organisations, different forms of political protests, promoting petitions and, in their late stages, lobbying policy-makers so that they would endorse their cause. Initially, the protests were semi-tolerated by the party apparatus, though some of their leaders were jailed and some of their protests violently repressed by the security forces. Eventually, their demands became the official policy of the party (Vladisavljević, 2004; Pavlović, 2013) and, as is common in these contexts, this led to their demise as a social movement.[12]

The Kosovo Serb movement experienced a rapid transformation from a local conflict to a national *cause célèbre* which mobilised the support of Serbian intellectuals and policy-makers and challenged the non-ethnic approach of the communist cadre. The defining moment of this transformation took place in April 1987, when a mid-rank cadre from the communist party, Slobodan Milošević, was sent to Kosovo to deal with the conflictual situation in the province. Originally, the visit did not include any meeting with the Kosovo Serb movement but in an unprecedented move in socialist Yugoslavia, he decided to go off-script and he met with them and listened to their demands and grievances[13] (Pavlović, 2013, p. 68). The importance of that day is highlighted by Geoffrey Nice, the Deputy Prosecutor at the trial of the former Yugoslavian and Serbian President at the International Criminal Tribunal for the Former Yugoslavia (ICTY), who affirmed that the participation in that meeting 'either reflected or created or stimulated the accused's interest in the pursuit of power' (ICTY, 2005, p. 36012). Kosovo Serbs were indeed the main fuel used by Slobodan Milošević to boost his political career by exploiting the Serbian nationalist card in Kosovo (Vladisavljević, 2004). As British historian Noel Malcolm (1998, p. 341) puts it, Kosovo catapulted Milošević from a 'little-known Party *apparatchik*' to a famous, powerful (and demagogic) political leader. The relationship was one of mutual dependence: the movement needed him to get the institutional support that they were craving for and, in turn, he needed them to enhance his political career. Two crucial effects could be identified; the first is the *ethnification* of political cleavages in Kosovo, and the second is the consolidation of Kosovo as a federal matter.

The 1987 events lie at the core of the political crisis which culminated in the revocation of Kosovo's autonomy two years later, in 1989.

Kosovo was no longer a local issue but had now reached the central stage. The consequences of this were multi-faceted and significant. The most visible and spectacular, perhaps, was the organisation of mass rallies focusing on the situation of Kosovo Serbs in Belgrade and other Serbian cities outside of Kosovo. More importantly, prominent Albanian figures in the Kosovo Communist party, Azem Vllasi and Kaqusha Jashari, were dismissed and the Kosovo's autonomous powers were gradually dismantled through amendments to the Serbian constitution, leading to the final revocation of the autonomy in March 1989 (Malcolm, 1998, pp. 342–344). In practical terms, this meant that the Serbian Assembly assumed control over Kosovo's police, courts, economic policy, etc. (Trix, 2010, p. 362). One of the important consequences of this was the fact that the Kosovo police was disbanded and a police force directly controlled by Belgrade was deployed. The balance of power between Serbs and Albanians had dramatically shifted. As Snyder (2000, p. 204) puts it, referring specifically to the Kosovo case: 'all sides suffered in cycles of aggression and retaliation, and all sides engaged in strategies that seem to have been self-defeating'. In the late 1980s, it was the Serbs turn to retaliate, a retaliation which would subsequently prove to be unambiguously self-defeating. In the short run, however, this move empowered Serbia's position not only in Kosovo but also vis-à-vis the other republics of Yugoslavia.

4 *Autonomists become secessionists*: Political decisions frequently come accompanied by embedded consequences, and choices of a territorial nature tend to be no exception. The suspension of autonomy, which was the visible feature of a more general policy aimed at disempowering Albanians in Kosovo, rapidly transformed autonomists or federalists into secessionists by confirming the secessionist narrative of *we told you so, there is no possible accommodation for Albanians in Yugoslavia*. This pattern, which is very evident in the Kosovo case, is by no means exceptional in conflicts of a secessionist nature. This, perhaps, signals a point of no-return for secessionist crises because after autonomists cross the Rubicon it is very unlikely that they will return to their previous moderate convictions. This generates a polarised milieu, where there is little room for compromise and, as a result, the potential future scenarios are reduced to victory, defeat…or, as it will be analysed in detail in Chapter 4, to the creation of an entity which navigates in a legal limbo; a parastate.

In the case of Kosovo, this point of no-return was arguably reached in 1989, when the autonomy was suspended. That same year, a political party, the Democratic League of Kosovo (LDK) was founded by the charismatic leader, Ibrahim Rugova, along with fellow members of the Kosovo-Albanian elite. The transformation of the party from autonomist to secessionist was remarkably fast-paced: from demanding real autonomy in early 1990 to having equal rights to other Yugoslav republics some months later to downright secession in 1991 (Babuna, 2000, p. 76). That being said, it is possible that the secessionist aims were present from the beginning, at least at a latent state, but were concealed due to tactical reasons. In view of the U.S. Special Envoy to Kosovo (1998–1999), Christopher Hill, 'Rugova's aim was complete independence, nothing less' (2014, p. 124). In his appearance at the ICTY, where he offered his testimony in the Milošević trial, Rugova stated, omitting the initial autonomist goals, in unambiguous terms that the main priorities for his party were the establishment of democracy in Kosovo as well as the creation of an independent republic (ICTY, 2002, p. 4192). This is a very significant step for two reasons. First, because of the weight of the LDK, which had a considerable amount of power-it did hold the Presidency of the shadow government-and enjoyed great support amongst the Kosovo Albanian community. Second, Rugova's statement is remarkable because the LDK is often perceived as a moderate force in the Kosovo (Albanian) nationalist movement, compared to other more radical actors, which will be scrutinised below.

In other words, the bridges had arguably been burned and accordingly the possibility for returning to a status quo characterised by an autonomous regime seemed remote to say the least. As argued in the above paragraph, in these high stakes situations, the room for negotiation is rather limited and the options are constrained to maximalist outcomes. This apparently insurmountable impasse is summarised by Bataković: 'the opposing attitudes of Serbs and Albanians, with their leaders Slobodan Milošević and Ibrahim Rugova … entrenched in their uncompromising positions, blocked the various mediation efforts of European or American representatives' (2012, p. 130).

In this context, the LDK issued a 'Constitutional Declaration', which asked for the creation of a 'Republic of Kosova'[14] with the same rights as other Yugoslav republics, and which was endorsed by the Kosovo Albanian members of the Assembly in July 1990 (ICTY, 2002, p. 4193). As a result of this, some days after the declaration, the Kosovo Assembly, one of the last vestiges left of the autonomy, was formally yet only 'temporarily' suspended by the Serbian government. Whilst Serb scholars have interpreted that revocation as a necessary step to impede the creation of an ethnically pure (Albanian) independent Kosovo (Krstić-Brano, 2004, p. 168), for Albanians this suspension is viewed as a trigger of an apartheid system aimed at excluding and marginalising Albanians (Maliki, 2012, p. 46). The LDK response pointed once again towards further escalation of the crisis: in September 1990 in the town of Kačanik, Kosovo MPs formally approved the independence declaration and its new constitution (ICTY, 2002, p. 4193). Far from capitulating or disappearing, the pro-secession Albanian movement led by the LDK engaged in diplomatic contacts with Western institutions and organised a clandestine self-determination referendum in September 1991, which, according to their estimates gathered 99 per cent of support with a turnout of 89 per cent of registered voters (Trix, 2010, p. 362).

Amidst this rapid tit-for-tat escalation of the secessionist conflict, also in 1991, Ibrahim Rugova and his supporters developed what was going to be known as 'parallel institutions' or 'shadow government', boycotting federal institutions dominated by Serbs (Dietrich, 2010, p. 295) and de facto creating independent governmental structures. Rugova became the President of the parallel institutions in Kosovo's in 1992, after winning the – not recognised by Serbia/Yugoslavia – presidential and legislative elections. Interestingly, these parallel institutions operated as some sort of social balm, prompting a provisional appeasement of Kosovo. Both Serbian and Albanian authors (Bataković, 2012; Maliki, 2012) agree in arguing that this bizarre social peace is an indication that such parallel institutions were tolerated, to a certain extent, by Belgrade because among other factors they allowed the Serbian President to concentrate his efforts in 'solving the Serbian question in other parts of Yugoslavia' (Maliki, 2012, p. 47). It did also mean that with Albanians boycotting the official elections in Serbia, with the loyal Kosovo Serb votes Milošević was able to secure most of the Kosovo seats for the Serbian Parliament.

Rugova's aims, nevertheless, were to overcome the 'parallel institutions' status quo. The strategy he pursued to achieve his secessionist objective has been conceptualised as a three-fold policy where the main foundations were: (a) non-violence; (b) internationalisation of the cause; and (c) systematic denial of Serbian legitimacy in Kosovo (Malcolm, 1998, p. 348). We can therefore identify elements of civil disobedience and non-violent resistance against oppression and discrimination which have generated comparisons with Gandhi. It has been argued that he enjoyed some sort of democratic legitimacy after winning successive 'parallel' elections lacking, however, real power (Wolff, 2003, p. 80) to implement the changes that he was advocating. Despite the fact that Rugova attempted to gain recognition from European states as well as the U.S. or alternatively become a UN protectorate (Bugajski, 1995, p. 153), his efforts were unsuccessful as he did not manage to obtain a single recognition[15] for Kosovo's unilaterally declared independence nor the UN engagement. To make matters worse, in what would be one of the biggest blows to his political career, in 1996 the European Union (in the aftermath of the Dayton agreement) officially recognised the Federal Republic of Yugoslavia (Wolff, 2003, p. 80), slamming the door on any potential independent Kosovo state. The conclusion seemed to be crystal clear; gaining sympathy from an international audience by using Gandhian methods had proven to be insufficient to realise his national aspirations (Babuna, 2000, p. 77). For an Albanian secessionist in the mid-1990s, the picture was gloomy; the vast majority of seceding territories in Yugoslavia had achieved independence, most of them through force. Kosovo, on the other hand, and despite its overwhelming Albanian majority, was still a part of the crumbling federation. The failure of Rugova's non-violent resistance strategy triggered the emergence of critiques and alternatives not only to his rule but, more significantly, to the territorial status quo.

Armed secessionist insurgency: the Kosovo Liberation Army

Due to its significance for this book's argument, the armed rebellion carried out by Albanian secessionists against the central (Yugoslavian) state deserves its own independent section. This phenomenon is particularly relevant because it directly touches upon the core central theme of this book. In effect, the secessionist armed rebellion triggered an iron fist response from the Milošević administration which, in turn, was the main *casus belli* behind NATO's intervention. In other words, without the armed campaign of the Kosovo Liberation Army[16] (KLA), it is very unlikely that this internal conflict, which had experienced some isolated low-violence incidents until 1998, would have escalated into a fully-fledged war between a state and a coalition of states under the umbrella of NATO. Whereas most secessionist conflicts experience the previous phases described by Buchanan, only a few of them end up with a full scale intra-state war. According to the data from the Conflict Eurobarometer out of 44 secessionist conflicts identified worldwide in 2016, 28 involved some degree of violence and only two were of a 'high intensity' degree, that is, only two out of 44 had escalated into a war (Heidelberg Institute for International Conflict Research, 2017, p. 19).

The relationship of the group with the LDK has been, putting it mildly, tumultuous. At first, the party and Rugova himself attempted to deny its existence and, when this was no longer possible, they portrayed its members as bandits, collaborators and undercover agents of the Serbian police who were 'trying to draw innocent Kosovar Albanians into a trap that would be sprung, extinguishing all that he had worked for' (Perritt, 2008, p. 15). The relationship between both groups has oscillated between serious feuds, including political assassinations, to *rapprochement* contexts characterised by *bonne entente*. The latter is illustrated by the recognition of the KLA as a legitimate organisation, in July 1998, by the parallel institutions set up by Rugova and his party in 1990. Acting perhaps inspired by the old saying 'if you can't beat them, join them', Rugova stated in 1998 that such recognition of legitimacy should have been done 'long ago' (Johnstone, 2002, p. 234). Supporters of the armed rebellion in Kosovo such as Pettifer and Vickers argue that 'the time for peaceful solutions was passing away' in the late 1990s because the gap between the LDK and the realities in Kosovo was widening (2007, pp. 95–96).

In this context of discontent amongst some sections of the Kosovo Albanian community, a new actor emerged: the Kosovo Liberation Army (KLA). The group was formed in 1991, conducted its first operation in 1993 when it killed two Serbian police officers in central Kosovo, and officially announced its creation in 1996 (Vickers, 1998, p. 292). The KLA, which was officially disarmed and disbanded after the NATO operation in 1999, can be conceptualised as an 'ethnic Albanian organisation'. It has been claimed that its roots can be traced back to the university protests of 1981 (Pokalova, 2010, p. 440), however, as will be argued below, we could also conjecture that the KLA has deeper roots. Its ethno-nationalist liberation struggle managed to attract members not only from Kosovo, but also from Albania, from the Albanian diaspora and from other states in the region with Albanian minorities, such as Macedonia.

Ideology-wise, the group was characterised by its ambiguities and seemingly irreconcilable contradictions, as Hedges put it in a *Foreign Affairs* article: 'the KLA splits down a bizarre ideological divide, with hints of fascism on one side and whiffs of communism on the other' (1999, p. 26). It is therefore tremendously difficult to establish parallels between this particular organisation and other armed secessionist groups in Western Europe like the Basque Homeland and Freedom (ETA), the Provisional Irish Republican Army (PIRA) or even with armed groups in Croatia, like the Croatian Defence Council (HVO). Unlike the former, which were never able to conquer or control territory, the KLA was able to exert control over a significant part of Kosovo in 1998, the year that it initiated its armed struggle campaign.

The KLA needs to be understood in the Albanian historical context of the twentieth century, which is characterised by a hermetic Stalinist regime in Albania proper for most of the second half of the twentieth century and Nazi oriented guerrillas like the Albanian SS Skanderbeg division during World War II. The different factions of the KLA were representatives of this amalgamation of distinct ideological traditions. The glue that brought coherence to the organisation was Pan-Albanian nationalism. This idea is shared by Judah who claims that Albanian nationalists were not concerned with 'Communism, Stalinism or any other 'ism' (1999, p. 9). They wanted to believe that one day Kosovo would no longer be part of Yugoslavia'. While the KLA, like most Albanian separatists, did not frame the conflict in religious terms (Babuna, 2000, p. 67), it has been alleged the group received weapons, training and financial assistance from Islamic groups based in the Middle East (Chomsky, 1999, p. 30).

Ambiguity is also, to a certain extent, pertinent in terms of its territorial aims. It is often argued that the main objective of the KLA was to free Kosovo from Serbian rule and to achieve independence for this territory (Pettifer and Vickers, 2007; Koktsidis and Dam, 2008). This assertion, however, may not be fully accurate, or at least not fully encompassing, in light of the oath that KLA fighters had to swear when joining the group:

'As a member of the Kosovo Liberation Army, I hereby swear that I will fight for the liberation of the occupied territories of Albania and their unification' (cited by ICTY, 2009, p. 2450). The use of the plural form 'territories', instead of territory, and the explicit mention to 'unification' denotes that there were ulterior motives to Kosovo's independence. This double aim is also reproduced in KLA communiqués such as the one on 4 January 1998, where the group announced the launch of 'the armed struggle for the liberation of Kosovo and its unification with Albania' (cited by Moore, 1998). The ultimate aim seems to be to create or recreate the old nationalist aspiration of Greater Albania, which included Albania proper plus Kosovo, some small valleys in Southern Serbia, large parts of North-West Macedonia, Northern Greece and Southern Montenegro. This Greater Albania project will be further discussed in Chapters 5 and 6.

Even though the KLA had intensified its attacks in 1997, its official 'war declaration' against the Yugoslavian state did not take place until January 1998 (see Moore, 1998). By early 1998, they had managed to force the withdrawal of the Serbian security forces from some areas, eventually being able to control around a third of the territory in Kosovo (Babuna, 2000, p. 77), which constituted no-go areas for governmental forces. It must be noted, nonetheless, that these areas were rural, mostly around the Drenica Valley in central Kosovo, and that the KLA did not succeed in establishing control of any city or even large village (Pettifer and Vickers, 2007, p. 114). There are very dissimilar estimations with regard to KLA manpower – while some claim that in 1998 the group had around 10,000 fighters (Bekaj, 2010, p. 22) others elevate their number of militants to 30,000 (Curtis, 2010, p. 238). Milošević responded to this fully-fledged armed secessionist insurgency with a massive counter-offensive which brought up to 50,000 members of the security forces (from the Yugoslav army, the Serbian Ministry of Interior police and the Special Anti-Terrorist Unit) to the province (Koktsidis and Dam, 2008, p. 169). Despite this, in June 1998, the KLA increased its attacks against Serbian security forces in what Crawford labels as a 'provocateur strategy' by the KLA (2001, p. 507). Such a quasi-suicidal step was rewarded by NATO with a clear threat in the form of military drills in neighbouring Albania and Macedonia. The menacing character of the exercise was made explicit by British Defence Minister George Robertson who warned Milošević, in the wake of the drills, that 'very serious options can be put in place at a very early date' and therefore the Yugoslavian President should not 'ignore the message coming from NATO. The message is clear an unambiguous – Belgrade, think again' (cited by CNN, 1998).

Despite the rhetorical threats, by September 1998, the governmental forces had retaken *manu militari* all the areas formerly controlled by the KLA (Krstić-Brano, 2004, p. 237). However, as recent conflicts in the Middle East and elsewhere have shown, military victories do not necessarily lead to successful outcomes. It could be argued that such disproportionate response by the Serbian government did not contribute to win the hearts and minds of the local Kosovo Albanians. On the contrary, it did play very well for the KLA's narrative of victimhood, which portrayed an operation aimed at them as a war on Albanians in Kosovo. As a result of the brutality of the operation, which included, dozens of civilian casualties, many Kosovo Albanians became radicalised (Human Rights Watch, 2001, p. 99). That being said, some voices were critical with that perspective and pointed out that the level of repression was substantially lower than in Bosnia –there had been 700 people killed in Kosovo (many of them militants) since the beginning of the conflict– and that the use of force by Serbian/Yugoslav forces was 'relatively restrained' (Kuperman, 1998). In the same vein, George Robertson, the British Secretary of Defence at the time (who would later become Secretary General of NATO) admitted, during a parliamentary committee hearing, that up until January 1999 'the KLA were responsible for more deaths in Kosovo than the Yugoslav authorities had been' (cited by House of Commons, 1999). In any case, perhaps unknowingly and certainly unwillingly, such anti-terrorist operations constituted the best source of legitimacy for the KLA and a pretext for a reinvigorated international pressure on Belgrade.

On 23 September 1998, the United Nations Security Council (UNSC) passed a resolution which decried 'the excessive and indiscriminate use of force by Serbian security forces and the Yugoslav Army which have resulted in numerous civilian casualties' and called for a ceasefire, a negotiation between the government and the KLA and for international monitoring of the conflict (UNSC, 1998). The resolution explicitly called for Yugoslavian forces to 'cease all action by the security forces affecting the civilian population' (UNSC, 1998). In the aftermath of this resolution, the U.S. steeped up its pressure on the Milošević administration with the architect of the Dayton Agreement in Bosnia, Richard Holbrooke, visiting Belgrade to play the coercive diplomacy card and, in particular, with the threat issued by NATO on 12 October for a potential air campaign if the Yugoslav President did not comply (Pevehouse and Goldstein, 1999, p. 541). The coercive pressure mechanism prompted the desired effect and a ceasefire came into effect with a large contingent of Serbian troops leaving Kosovo (those deployed after February 1998) and 2,000 monitors from the Organization for Security and Co-operation in Europe (OSCE) being deployed (Chomsky, 1999, p. 33) in the province through the Kosovo Verification Mission (KVM). However, unlike Dayton, the peace deal brokered by Holbrooke was a complete blunder. Shortly after the Serbian withdrawal, the KLA exploited the cease-fire in their own advantage and reoccupied the areas abandoned by the governmental troops while, at the same time, resuming their attacks against them (Kuperman, 2008, p. 66). Needless to say, such developments triggered the return of the Serbian counter-terrorist operation, burying the short cease-fire in the dustbin of history. As will be discussed in the next chapter, the resumption of Serbian counter-terrorist operation led to a controversial massacre, another failed negotiation and eventually to NATO's intervention in March 1999.

The reasons behind the KLA's astounding success

One of the most fascinating aspects of the KLA is its outstanding success, unprecedented for the vast majority of similar guerrilla/terrorist groups. Koktsidis and Dam provide a list of factors which, in view of the authors, contribute to explain the rapid and spectacular materialisation of some of their primary objectives: in the short-run withdrawal of Yugoslavian security forces in the mid-term creation of a Kosovo state, or at least, a par-astate. Their list includes seven decisive factors:

1 Well-prepared rebellion
2 Limitations and mistakes by rivals
3 Cheap weaponry from Albania
4 Effective guerrilla tactics
5 Crackdown sparking large scale revolt
6 Learning from mistakes
7 Support from NATO and the West

(Koktsidis and Dam 2008, pp. 167–171)

It is worth critically scrutinising some of these causes. With the aim of simplifying this categorisation, it would be possible to group factors 1, 4 and 6 in a single and more encompassing category: resorting to an insurgency based on guerrilla tactics. According to Pettifer and Vickers, in the months prior to NATO's intervention: 'A KLA group might occupy ground for a time, only to retreat when superior Serb forces arrived on the scene and then reoccupy it when the Serbs left' (2007, p. 114). This is by no means startling when we consider situations where an insurgent group faces a military superior enemy. In fact, this strategy reproduces with astounding accuracy the classic tactics of guerrilla warfare laid out by Chinese Chairman Mao Zedong: 'when guerrillas engage a stronger enemy, they withdraw when he advances; harass him when he stops; strike him when he is weary; pursue him when he withdraws' (1937/2005, p. 46). Factor 2 has been analysed above; the KLA benefited from the lack of concrete results from the LDK's non-violent approach. The LDK's crisis aggravated with the Serbian military crackdown (factor 5), which the KLA was able to instrumentally use to gather support for their violent campaign. Factor 3 is significant and perhaps not fully developed by the authors.

In 1997, as Koktsidis and Dam explain, an unprecedented financial and political crisis affected neighbouring Albania with the result of nearly 2,000 dead and the quasi-collapse of the Albanian state (2008, p. 167). It could be argued that Albania became a failed state or fragile state – that is, a state that cannot fulfil its most basic duties. As a result of the turmoil, in the first half of 1997 half a million Kalashnikovs and 200,000 semi-automatic weapons were looted from arms deposits in Albania, a large percentage of which ended up at the hands of KLA militants (Koktsidis and Dam, 2008,

p. 167). What the authors do not fully address is the fact that Northern Albania, an area of the country that borders Kosovo, had become a lawless territory where local mafias were able to operate freely and the KLA was able to establish a training base for its fighters. The Albanian army was conspicuously absent from the border areas (Vickers, 2013, p. 32) thus paving the way for the consolidation of a safe haven for the KLA, just across the border from Kosovo. The KLA used its safe haven in Northern Albania to smuggle weapons to Kosovo, to train its fighters but also according to the EU Special Investigative Task Force (SITF) to run a network of detention facilities where heinous crimes were committed (Marty, 2011, pp. 13–15)

Despite the importance of the factors mentioned above, there is one element in Koktsidis and Dam list which is especially important in explaining the KLA's success: support from NATO and the West. Without the assistance of the transatlantic organisation it seems very unlikely that the KLA would have been able to oust Serbian forces from Kosovo and materialise its secessionist aims. An inevitable question at this stage is: did the KLA leadership genuinely believe that its desperate offensives of 1998 and 1999 had any chance of prospering and that their final outcome would be the capitulation of the Serb/Yugoslavian security forces? A hypothetical answer to the question is that the strategic goal of the KLA was not victory, which was hardly attainable given the disproportionate military imbalance between the two warring parties, but instead fierce retaliation by the Yugoslavian government.

Such governmental reprisal would trigger an international response, as did occur at the end of the war in Bosnia, which would ultimately benefit the KLA's cause. This idea, as twisted as it might appear at first glance, is supported by a wide range of scholars. Selver Sahin, for instance, supports this hypothesis by arguing that the ultimate aim of the KLA was Belgrade's retaliation in order to force a foreign intervention (2015, p. 67). Likewise, Krstić-Brano asserts that 'The KLA leaders knew that military actions would not lead them to victory in Kosovo and invested every possible effort to create conditions convenient for military intervention by NATO' (2004, p. 239). In the same vein, Johnstone maintains that, through its 'strategy of provocation' based on assassinating Serbian security forces, the KLA exposed ethnic Albanian villages to reprisals because 'civilian victims would help to bring in NATO' (2002, p. 235). This KLA provocation–Serbian atrocities–foreign intervention formula was also confirmed by U.S. intelligence reports (Gellman, 1999).

Alan Kuperman, who labelled the KLA rebellion as suicidal, applies the economic concept of moral hazard – defined as reckless risk-taking behaviour due to risk protection insurances – to the crisis of a political nature between a non-state actor and a state (2008, p. 50). Kuperman's central point is that the prospect of foreign (humanitarian) intervention encourages insurgent groups to rebel against a government by increasing their chances for success while reducing the costs of a rebellion (2008,

p. 51). The moral hazard constitutes one of the fiercest critiques of humanitarian intervention, alleging that it aggravates conflicts that would otherwise not escalate without the prospect of foreign interference. Kuperman's description of one of the potential scenarios that may occur due to the moral hazard phenomenon perfectly describes the KLA formula: 'rebels will attack state officials deliberately intending to provoke retaliation against their own group's civilians, to attract international intervention that they deem necessary to attain their political goals' (2008, p. 51). For this formula to succeed, however, it was essential to be on good terms with the hegemon at the time and, as it will be shown below, this was not always the case.

The U.S. role and the terrorist label

The discussion on whether or not the group constituted a terrorist organisation is futile for the very reason that, like in most cases, this exercise of labelling is determined by the political allegiances of the subject who defines it. As seems obvious, for central governments framing a secessionist group as a terrorist organisation is tremendously useful because, by doing so, it conceals the ethno-territorial nature of the conflict placing the emphasis instead on security related issues or, more cynically, in the fight against global terror (Pokalova, 2010, p. 429). Conversely, for secessionist groups engaged in political violence it is crucial to avoid the terrorist label so that they can present themselves as a legitimate actor both internally as well as internationally. The long and rather unsuccessful struggle to define the term undertaken by intergovernmental organisations and states makes it particularly complicated to escape the old interpretivist axiom that 'one man's terrorist is another man's freedom fighter'.

At any rate, terrorism is the epitome of political and politicised labels and, as such, it generates a variability of interpretations (Bhatia, 2005, p. 7) that very often obscure a genuine debate on the causes and consequences of political violence. Instead of engaging in the Gordian knot of labelling the KLA as a terrorist organisation or otherwise, what is useful and doable is, on the one hand, analysing the primary targets of the group, and on the other examining how the organisation was perceived by other actors. In this analysis of perceptions, it will be particularly enlightening to examine the rapid transformation of U.S. views towards the organisation.

The KLA explicitly stated that sociocultural monuments and civilian populations would not be attacked and defined its legitimate targets as the following: the military and police apparatus of the Yugoslavian state, the volunteers and paramilitaries and Albanian 'traitors' who were guilty, in the eyes of the KLA, of collaborating with the state (Bekaj, 2010, p. 17). In short, with the exception of the third group – 'Albanian traitors' which could potentially open the door for arbitrariness and the execution of political rivals – the rest of the targets of the KLA could be seen as 'legitimate' in the sense that they focused on what they perceived as an 'occupying force'.

Figure 1.4 The KLA flag in Southern Mitrovica (2017).
Source: Gisela Gorbalán.

This official declaration of legitimate targets is, however, contested by several authors and international organisations, including the Special Investigation Task Force (SITF) set up by the European Union. It has been argued that, in addition to 'legitimate targets', the KLA targeted civilians, both Albanian and Serbs, and bombed refugee camps housing Serbian refugees who had been expelled from Croatia and Bosnia as early as 1996 (Curtis, 2010, p. 238). Critics claim that one of the purposes of the KLA was to disrupt contacts between moderates from both communities by assassinating those who were seen as bridges and thus aggravating the conflict (Johnstone, 2002, p. 234). Far from the romanticised version of the group that characterised the dominant Western discourses during the conflict, the group suffered several PR blows in recent years that have tainted the once pristine image of the KLA. These image setbacks have come from institutions, which could hardly be considered as Serbian propagandists, such as the German foreign intelligence service, Bundesnachrichtendienst (BND), the United Nations Mission in Kosovo (UNMIK) and an EU sponsored investigative commission (SITF).

Wikileaks published a classified intelligence report from the BND which identified key figures of the KLA (who have later reached the highest positions of power in Kosovo) as the main figures of organised crime, including drug-trafficking, in Kosovo, before, during and after the war (cited by

Wikileaks, 2008). According to a UNMIK investigation, between 100 and 300 people (mostly Serbs) were kidnapped and transported to facilities in Northern Albania where they were assassinated and their organs extracted and used for illegal trafficking. The investigation concludes that KLA militants played an active role in the transport of the victims and that 'the transports and surgical procedures were carried out with the knowledge and/or active involvement of mid-level and senior KLA officers' (cited by France24). These very serious criminal allegations, which have emerged from leaked documents, were confirmed by the Chief Prosecutor of the SITF, Clint Williamson who unambiguously concludes that:

> certain elements of the KLA intentionally targeted the minority populations with acts of persecution that included unlawful killings, abductions, enforced disappearances, illegal detentions in camps in Kosovo and Albania, sexual violence, other forms of inhumane treatment, forced displacements of individuals from their homes.... This effectively resulted in the ethnic cleansing of large portions of the Serb and Roma populations from those areas in Kosovo.
>
> (Williamson, 2014, p. 2)

These unlawful acts, which will be analysed with further detail in the next chapter, lead us to a necessary reflection concerning the perception of the group by its primary international backer: the United States.

When the KLA began its armed campaign in 1998, the U.S. administration lacked a coherent approach towards it, suggesting that there were radically different voices and opinions within the administration. U.S. diplomat and envoy to the Former Yugoslavia in the Clinton Administration, Robert Gelbard, stated, during a trip to Belgrade and Pristina, in February 1998 that the KLA was undoubtedly a terrorist group, and after meeting two of its members, he added that 'I know a terrorist when I see one and these [KLA] men are terrorists' (cited by Hill, 2014, pp. 124–125). There are contradictory versions regarding the KLA designation as a Foreign Terrorist Organisation by the U.S.: while some claim that it was listed and removed twice from the list (Napoleoni, 2004, p. 34) others argue that it never entered the list (Phillips, 2012, p. 87). The fact of the matter is that the name of the group does not appear on the list, not even as a de-listed organisation on the webpage of the U.S. Department of State (2017).

It has been argued that Gelbard's remarks were troublesome for the U.S. Department of State since they came at time where the Clinton administration was trying to build bridges with the KLA and to present it as a 'legitimate interlocutor' (Phillips, 2012, p. 86). The transformation of the KLA into a legitimate force occurred with unprecedented diligence and hastiness if we consider that as early as the summer of 1998, some months after Gelbard's comments, the KLA command structure was being reorganised and restructured with the assistance of U.S. military Private Military

Contractors (Pettifer and Vickers, 2007, p. 175). Actions came accompanied by words in this case and in 1999, in the wake of NATO's intervention any sign of ambiguity had dissipated as the words from the State Department Deputy Spokesman, James B. Foley, unmistakeably suggest:

> the United States is moving quickly to help transform the Kosovo Liberation Army from a rag-tag band of guerrilla fighters into a political force Washington clearly sees it as a main hope for the troubled province's future.... We believe that we have a lot of advice and a lot of help that we can provide to them [KLA].
>
> (Cited by Craig and West, 1999)

The statement above denotes that the policymakers in the Clinton administration that were more enthusiastic to intervene in Kosovo had won their internal battle against their more sceptical counterparts. This move was not uncontroversial bearing in mind the heinous crimes (including war crimes) committed by the KLA. Additionally, considering that officials of the Clinton administration had, only a few months earlier, accused the KLA of being a terrorist organisation the rhetorical turn is astounding, to say the least. One potential explanation for such hasty legitimisation baptism of the KLA is that a humanitarian intervention by a defence organisation which is composed of democratic states cannot be justified if the main beneficiary is a designated terrorist organisation. In addition to becoming a legitimate interlocutor, one of the chief successes of the KLA was the fact that they had managed to convince Washington that their national cause was NATO's cause (Johnstone, 2002, p. 230). Their diplomatic triumph was far from being translated into a military or even a significant political victory. Their strategy, based on the moral hazard approach, had to be stepped up to convince their new international partners that a foreign intervention was the only way to solve an otherwise intractable conflict.

Notes

1 Stambolić was assassinated in 2000 by eight members of the Serbian Special Operations Units. It is believed that the order came directly from Slobodan Milošević.

2 Montenegro did not achieve independence until 2006, after narrowly voting in favour of secession in an agreed referendum with Belgrade.

3 Albanians are religiously divided between Muslims (Sunni and Bektashi), Christians (Catholic, Orthodox and others) as well as non-religious. The rationale is that since religion is a divisive element, Albanian nationalism does not use this component to frame its narrative.

4 See for instance the sentence:

> [S]erbia has never had only Serbs living in it. Today, more than in the past, members of other peoples and nationalities also live in it. This is not a disadvantage for Serbia. I am truly convinced that it is its advantage.... Citizens

of different nationalities, religions, and races have been living together more and more frequently and more and more successfully.

(Milošević, 1989)

5 The remaining 5 per cent is represented by smaller communities such as Roma, Bosniaks, Turks, Gorani, Ashkalia, Egyptians. Due to their small numbers, these minorities do not play a significant role when it comes to territorial debates.

6 According to Albanian authors 'there were hardly any Serbs' in Kosovo in 1912 (Kola, 2003, p. 12), whereas Serbian scholars claim that according to Austro-Hungarian statistical data that there were 230,300 Albanians and 187,200 Slavs (60 per cent of them Serbs and the rest Muslims and Catholics) in the former Ottoman province in 1903 (Bataković, 2012, p. 74).

7 The Albanian Prime Minister (1941–1943) Mustafa Merlika-Kruja stated in 1942 that:

> [W]e should endeavor to ensure that the Serb population of Kosovo should be removed as soon as possible.... All indigenous Serbs who have been living here for centuries should be termed colonialists and as such, via the Albanian and Italian governments, should be sent to concentration camps in Albania. Serbian settlers should be killed.
>
> (cited by Schwegler and Ripley Smith, 2012, p. 354)

Such statement clearly indicates that the assassinations and ethnic cleansing of Serbs during World War II were institutionally supported and strongly embedded in Albanian governmental policies.

8 Both languages are Indo-European but Serbian or Serbo-Croatian is a Slavic language and Albanian is considered to be an isolated branch of the Indo-European family.

9 Demaçi, who spent 28 years in prison, is considered to be one of the key figures of the Kosovo pro-secession movement.

10 The reluctance of Serbian policymakers towards the constitution is illustrated by the fact that only a few months after its approval, the presidency of Serbian asked for it to be revised with the aim of reinforcing Serbia's rule over its autonomous provinces (Pavlović, 2013, p. 60).

11 Sladjana Miletić, author interview, Peć, 31 July 2012.

12 Manuel Castells argues that it is difficult for social movements to remain autonomous and vigorous after they engage in institutionalisation processes (Castells, 2010, p. 249).

13 At the 24 April meeting with representatives from the Kosovo Serb movement, Milošević pronounced its famous sentence 'You will not be beaten again' phrase, after thousands of Kosovo Serb protesters had been beaten up by the local police force.

14 In Albanian, 'Kosovo' is known as 'Kosova'. The book will refer to the territory as 'Kosovo' due to the fact that it is the most common term in English.

15 Sometimes it is wrongly claimed that Albania recognised Kosovo's independence in the early 1990s. This, however, is inaccurate because as Wolff (2003, p. 83) points out such support came in form of verbal declarations but never materialised through the formal procedural channels.

16 'Ushtria Çlirimtare e Kosovës' or UÇK in Albanian.

Bibliography

Anderson, L. M. (2004). 'Exploring the Paradox of Autonomy: Federalism and Secession in North America'. *Regional and Federal Studies*, 14(1): 89–112.

Babuna, A. (2000). 'The Albanians of Kosovo and Macedonia: Ethnic identity superseding religion'. *Nationalities Papers*, 28(1): 67–92.

Bataković, D. (2012). *Serbia's Kosovo Drama*. Belgrade: Cigoja.

Bekaj, A. R. (2010). 'The KLA and the Kosovo War: From Intra-state Conflict to Independent Country' in *Transition Series, Resistance/Liberation Movements and Transitions to Politics*. Berlin: Berghof Center. Retrieved from: www.berghof-conflictresearch.org/documents/publications/transitions8_kosovo.pdf

Bhatia, M. (2005). 'Fighting words: naming terrorists, bandits, rebels and other violent actors'. *Third World Quarterly*, 26(1): 5–22.

Bieber, F. (2003). 'Introduction', in F. Bieber and Ž. Daskalovski (eds) *Understanding the War in Kosovo* (pp. 1–12). London: Frank Cass Publishers.

Buchanan, A. (2003). *Justice, Legitimacy, and Self-Determination: Moral Foundations for International Law*. Oxford: Oxford University Press.

Bugajski, J. (1995). *Ethnic Politics in Eastern Europe: A Guide to Nationality Policies, Organizations and Parties*. New York: M. E. Sharpe.

Castan Pinos, J. (2015). 'The Challenge to Territorial Integrity, Kosovo and beyond', in C. Gaitanides (ed.), *Diversity in Europe* (pp. 220–236). Baden-Baden: Nomos Verlagsgesellschaft.

Castells, M. (2010). *The Information Age: Economy, Society and Culture. Volume II: The Power of Identity*. Oxford: Blackwell Publishing Ltd.

Çeku, E. (2015) 'The Kosovo Issue and Albano–Yugoslav Relations, 1961–1981'. *Diplomacy and Statecraft*, 26(2): 229–248.

Chomsky, N. (1999). *The New Military Humanism. Lessons from Kosovo*. London: Pluto Press.

CNN (1998, 11 June). 'NATO making plans for military action in Kosovo'. Retrieved from: http://edition.cnn.com/WORLD/europe/9806/11/nato.kosovo/

Craig, L. E. and West, J. (1999, 31 March). 'The Kosovo Liberation Army: Does Clinton Policy Support Group with Terror, Drug Ties? From 'Terrorists' to 'Partners''. *United States Senate, Republican Policy Committee*. Retrieved from: https://fas.org/irp/world/para/docs/fr033199.htm

Crawford, T. (2001). 'Pivotal Deterrence and the Kosovo War: Why the Holbrooke Agreement Failed'. *Political Science Quarterly*, 116(4): 499–523.

Curtis, M. (2010). *Secret Affairs: Britain's Collusion with Radical Islam*. London: Serpent's Tail.

Damjanović, V. and Chapman, J. (2010). 'Two Years In, Kosovo Albanians More Sober on Independence'. *Gallup*. Retrieved from: www.gallup.com/poll/125978/two-years-kosovo-albanians-sober-independence.aspx

Daskalovski, Ž. (2003). 'Claims to Kosovo. Nationalism and Self-Determination', in F. Bieber and Ž. Daskalovski (eds) *Understanding the War in Kosovo* (pp. 13–30). London: Frank Cass Publishers.

Dietrich, F. (2010). 'The Status of Kosovo – Reflections on the Legitimacy of Secession'. *Ethics and Global Politics*, 3(2): 123–142.

ECMI (2013a). 'Community Profile: Serb Community'. *European Center for Minority Issues*. Retrieved from: www.ecmikosovo.org/uploads/Serbcommunity1.pdf

ECMI (2013b). 'Community Profile: Albanian Community'. *European Center for Minority Issues*. Retrieved from: www.ecmikosovo.org/uploads/Albanian.pdf

Fichter, M. (2016). 'Yugoslav Protest: Student Rebellion in Belgrade, Zagreb, and Sarajevo in 1968'. *Slavic Review*, 75(1): 99–121.

France24 (2003). 'Issues with the Chief Prosecutor's visit meeting with the Director DOJ UNMIK' *UNMIK* CRX-103. Retrieved from: www.france24.com/static/infographies/documents/kosovo_house_2003.pdf

Gellman, B. (1999, 18 April). 'The Path to Crisis: How the United States and Its Allies Went to War', *Washington Post*. Retrieved from: www.washingtonpost.com/archive/politics/1999/04/18/the-path-to-crisis-how-the-united-states-and-its-allies-went-to-war/52533b73-cf3e-4e21-a771-8f1806bc0577/?utm_term=.f25f5ea4f8f3

Government of the Republic of Serbia (2006). 'Constitution of the Republic of Serbia'. Retrieved from: www.srbija.gov.rs/cinjenice_o_srbiji/ustav_odredbe.php?id=217

Graczyk, D. A. and Giannakos, S. A. (2006). 'The Face of Kosovar Albanian Nationalism: A Violent and Volatile Transformation of the Balkan Political Landscape'. *Mediterranean Quarterly*, 17(4): 142–159.

Hedges, C. (1999). 'Kosovo's next Masters'. *Foreign Affairs*, 78(3): 24–42.

Heidelberg Institute for International Conflict Research. (2017). *Conflict Barometer 2016*, 25: 1–202.

Hill, C. R. (2014). *Outpost: A Diplomat at Work*. New York: Simon and Schuster.

Horowitz, D. L. (1981). 'Patterns of Ethnic Separatism'. *Comparative Studies in Societies and History*, 23(2): 165–185.

Horowitz, D. L. (1985). *Ethnic Groups in Conflict*. Berkeley: University of California Press.

House of Commons (1999, 24 March). 'Select Committee on Defence Minutes of Evidence. Examination of Witnesses (Questions 380–399)'. Retrieved from: https://publications.parliament.uk/pa/cm199899/cmselect/cmdfence/39/9032403.htm

Human Rights Watch (2001). *War Crimes in Kosovo*. New York: Human Rights Watch.

ICTY (2002). 'Case IT-02-54, Prosecutor v. Slobodan Milošević', pp. 4188–4307. Retrieved from: www.icty.org/en/content/ibrahim-rugova

ICTY (2005). 'Case IT-02-54, Prosecutor v. Slobodan Milošević', pp. 35298–36042. Retrieved from: https://web.archive.org/web/20060623152824/www.un.org/icty/transe54/050209IT.htm

ICTY (2009). 'Case IT-05-87/1, Prosecutor v. Vlastimir Đorđević', pp. 2423–2488. Retrieved from: www.icty.org/x/cases/djordjevic/trans/en/090318IT.htm

Ingimundarson, V. (2007). 'The Politics of Memory and the Reconstruction of Albanian National Identity in Postwar Kosovo'. *History and Memory*, 19(1): 95–123.

Jakica, L. (2010). 'The Problem of Resurrection of Kosovo Mythology in Serbian Popular Culture'. *Transcultural Studies*, 6(1): 161–170.

Johnstone, D. (2002). *Fools' Crusade. Yugoslavia, NATO and Western Delusions*. London: Pluto Press.

Judah, T. (1999). 'Kosovo's road to war'. *Survival*, 41(2): 5–18.

Koktsidis, P. and Dam, C.T. (2008). 'A Success Story? – Analyzing Albanian Ethno-Nationalist Extremism in the Balkans'. *East European Quarterly*, 42(2): 161–190.

Kola, P. (2003). *The Search for Greater Albania*. London: C. Hurst and Co. Publishers.

Koštunica, V. (2002). *Entre la force et le droit: chroniques du Kosovo*. Lausanne: Éditions L'Age d'Homme.

Kramm, H. (1986a, 28 April). 'In one Yugoslav province Serbs fear the ethnic Albanians'. *New York Times*. Retrieved from: www.nytimes.com/1986/04/28/world/in-one-yugoslav-province-serbs-fear-the-ethnic-albanians.html

Kramm, H. (1986b, 27 July). 'Minorities are uneasy in Yugoslav province'. *New York Times*. Retrieved from: www.nytimes.com/1986/04/28/world/in-one-yugoslav-province-serbs-fear-the-ethnic-albanians.html

Krstić-Brano, B. (2004). *Kosovo. Facing the Court of History*. New York: Humanity Books.

Kuperman, A. (1998, 9 October). 'NATO Move May Widen War'. *USA Today*. Republished and retrieved from: www.brookings.edu/opinions/nato-move-may-widen-war-letter-to-the-editor/

Kuperman, A. (2008). 'The Moral Hazard of Humanitarian Intervention: Lessons from the Balkans'. *International Studies Quarterly*, 52(1): 49–80.

Maliqi, S. (1996). 'The Albanian Movement in Kosova', in D. A. Dyker and I. Vejvoda (eds) *Yugoslavia and After: A Study in Fragmentation, Despair and Rebirth* (pp. 138–154). Abingdon: Routledge.

Maliqi, S. (2012). 'Why the Peaceful Resistance Movement in Kosovo Failed', in R. Hudson and G. Bowman (eds) *After Yugoslavia. Identities and Politics within the Successor States* (pp. 43–76). New York: Palgrave Macmillan.

Malcolm, N. (1998). *Kosovo: A Short History*. New York: New York University Press.

Marty, D. (2011). 'Inhuman treatment of people and illicit trafficking in human organs in Kosovo'. *Council of Europe*, Doc. 12462. Retrieved from: www.sitf.eu/images/110107CoEReport.pdf

Miletić, S., author interview, Peć, 31 July 2012.

Milošević, S. (1989). 'Solobodan Milošević Kosovo Polje Speech, 28 June 1989'. Retrieved from: www.slobodan-milosevic.org/spch-kosovo1989.htm

Moore, P. (1998, 9 January). 'Yugoslavia: Tensions Rise in Montenegro And Kosovo' *Radio Free Europe Radio Liberty*. Retrieved from: www.rferl.org/a/1087706.html

Napoleoni, L. (2004). 'The new economy of terror: how terrorism is financed', in A. P. Schmid (ed.) *Forum on Crime and Society*. New York: United Nations Office on Drugs and Crime.

Pavlović, M. (2013). 'Kosovo under autonomy, 1974–1990', in C. Ingrao and T. A. Emmert (eds) *Confronting the Yugoslav Controversies* (pp. 49–80). West Lafayette, IN: Purdue University Press.

Pavlowitch, S. K. (1988). *The Improbable survivor. Yugoslavia and its Problems 1918–1988*. London: C. Hurst and Co. Publishers.

Perritt, H. H. (2008). *Kosovo Liberation Army, the inside story of an insurgency*. Chicago: University of Illinois Press.

Pesić, V. (1996). 'Serbian Nationalism and the Origins of the Yugoslav Crisis'. *United States Institute of Peace*, WP Peaceworks 8: 1–40.

Petrović, A. and Stefanović, Đ. (2010). 'Kosovo, 1944–1981: The Rise and the Fall of a Communist 'Nested Homeland''. *Europe-Asia Studies*, 62(7): 1073–1106.

Pettifer, J. and Vickers, M. (2007). *The Albanian Question: Reshaping the Balkans*. New York: I. B. Tauris.

Pevehouse, J. and Goldstein, J. (1999). 'Serbian compliance or defiance in Kosovo? Statistical analysis and real-time predictions'. *Journal of Conflict Resolution*, 43(4): 538–546.

Phillips, D. (2012). *Liberating Kosovo: Coercive Diplomacy and U. S. Intervention*. Cambridge, (MA: The MIT Press.

Pokalova, E. (2010). 'Framing Separatism as Terrorism: Lessons from Kosovo'. *Studies in Conflict and Terrorism*, 33(5): 429–447.

Rogel, C. (2003). 'Kosovo: Where It All Began'. *International Journal of Politics, Culture, and Society*, 17(1): 167–182.

Sahin, S. (2015). *International Intervention and State-Making. How the Exception Became the Norm*. Abingdon: Routledge.

Schwegler, U. and Ripley Smith, L. (2012). 'Ethno-political Conflict in Kosovo: Cultivating Trust in Serbian–Albanian Post-conflict Peace building', in D. Landis and R. Albert (eds) *Handbook of Ethnic Conflict* (pp. 349–377). London: Springer.

Sluglett, P. (2016). 'Deadly Implications: The Rise of Sectarianism in Syria', in M. Beck *et al*. (eds) *The Levant in Turmoil. Syria, Palestine, and the Transformation of Middle Eastern Politics* (pp. 39–55). London: Palgrave Macmillan.

Snyder, J. (2000). *From Voting to Violence. Democratization and Nationalist Conflict*. New York: W. W. Norton & Company.

Stefanović, Đ. (2005). 'Seeing the Albanians through Serbian Eyes: The Inventors of the Tradition of Intolerance and Their Critics, 1804–1939'. *European History Quarterly*, 35(3): 465–492.

The Economist (1999, 3 June). 'What next for Slobodan Milosevic?' Retrieved from: www.economist.com/node/210238

Trix, F. (2010). 'Kosova: resisting expulsion and striving for independence', in S. P. Ramet (ed.) *Central and Southeast European Politics since 1989* (pp. 358–376). Cambridge: Cambridge University Press.

United Nations Security Council (1998). *Resolution 1199: The Situation in Kosovo (FRY)*. Retrieved from: http://unscr.com/en/resolutions/1199

U.S. Department of State (2017). 'Foreign Terrorist Organizations'. Retrieved from: www.state.gov/j/ct/rls/other/des/123085.htm

Vickers, M. (1998). *Between Serb and Albanian. A History of Kosovo*. London: Hurst.

Vickers, M. (1999). *The Albanians*. New York: I. B. Tauris.

Vickers, M. (2013). *Tirana's Uneasy Role in the Kosovo Crisis 1998–1999*, in K. Drezov, B. Gokay, M. Waller *Kosovo: The Politics of Delusion* (pp. 30–36). Abingdon: Routledge.

Visoka, G. (2017). *Shaping Peace in Kosovo: The Politics of Peacebuilding and Statehood*. Cham: Palgrave Macmillan.

Vladisavljević, N. (2004). 'Grassroots Groups, Milosevic or Dissident Intellectuals?'. *Nationalities Papers*, 32(4): 781–796.

Wikileaks (2008). 'Bundesnachrichtendienst Kosovo Intelligence Report, 22 February 2005'. Retrieved from: https://wikileaks.org/wiki/BND_Kosovo_intelligence_report,_22_Feb_2005

Williamson, C. (2014). 'Statement by the Chief Prosecutor of the Special Investigative Task Force, 29 July 2015', *Special Investigative Task Force*. Retrieved from: http://sitf.eu/images/Statement/Statement_of_the_Chief_Prosecutor_of_the_SITF_EN.pdf

Wolff, S. (2003). 'The limits of Non-Military International Intervention: A Case Study of the Kosovo Conflict', in F. Bieber and Ž. Daskalovski (eds) *Understanding the War in Kosovo* (pp. 77–98). London: Frank Cass Publishers.

Zedong, M. (1937/2005). *On Guerrilla Warfare*. New York: Dover Publications.

Zimmerman, W. (1998). 'The Demons of Kosovo'. *The National Interest*, 52: 3–11.

2 Coercive diplomacy

Humanitarian intervention and its controversies in Kosovo

Perhaps the most contested, controversial and yet crucial event of the conflict in Kosovo was the Račak massacre, also known as the Račak operation, which took place on 15 January 1999. The alleged killing of 45 civilians, all of them ethnic Albanians, by Serbian Security Forces represents a turning point which transformed a local insurgency/counterinsurgency low-level conflict into an inter-state war waged by a multinational organisation (NATO) against a sovereign state, the Federal Republic of Yugoslavia, on humanitarian grounds.

Prior to concentrating on the particulars of Račak, it is imperative to provide some background details on the context which led to it. As stated in the previous chapter, the attempts led by Richard Holbrooke to negotiate a ceasefire between the Yugoslavian government and the secessionist insurgent group of the Kosovo Liberation Army (KLA) failed abruptly. The diplomatic success of the *Dayton architect* in Bosnia did not reverberate in Kosovo. The compromise proposed by Holbrooke was based on the conditions laid out by the UNSC Resolution 1199 and was characterised by straightforward conditions: the Yugoslavian government ought to allow NATO to monitor their airspace, a 2,000 strong OSCE unarmed verification mission (Kosovo Verification Mission) was to be deployed in Kosovo, and the government had to engage in political dialogue over the political future of Kosovo with ethnic Albanians (Bouckaert, 1999, p. 67).

The ceasefire was tremendously weak from its very inception and the belligerent parties only accepted it reluctantly. The most difficult condition to palate for the Yugoslavian administration was the partial withdrawal of the Yugoslavian/Serbian Security Forces from Kosovo. This was also the most contentious demand due to the fact that, in the opinion of the Yugoslav government, the KLA could potentially seize the opportunity to consolidate its control of territory. In fact, those fears were not completely unfounded bearing in mind that the troop pull-out was indeed used by the KLA in order to take advantage of the ceasefire to reorganise and resume their campaign of violence allowing them to recapture some of the territories they had lost prior to the ceasefire (Crawford, 2001, p. 513). Western diplomats, including Secretary of State Madeleine Albright, issued explicit warnings to the KLA leadership not to utilise the ceasefires for territorial or military gains. An anonymous diplomat explicitly stated in the *New York Times* that: '[T]hey've [KLA] been told not to start trouble because we are not going to bail them out' (cited by O'Connor, 1998).

In the end, the KLA ignored the Western request for restraint and violated the ceasefire brokered by Holbrooke. This hypothesis is supported by statements from the KLA itself as well as by documents from NATO, the UN (UNSC, 1999a) and the OSCE (1999). A KLA military commander, Agim Çeku, admitted in a BBC documentary that 'the cease-fire was very useful for us, it helped us to get organised, to consolidate and grow' (cited by BBC, 2000). Similarly, former KLA commander and current Kosovo Prime Minister Ramush Haradinaj acknowledged that 'we were interested to be able to breathe so to speak for a period of time. Actually, the agreement was life saving for the KLA'. (cited by Hamzaj, 2000, p. 115).

According to a confidential report from NATO's North Atlantic Council (NAC), the KLA was 'the main initiator of violence' because it 'launched what appears to be a deliberate campaign of provocation' (cited by BBC, 2000). In a similar vein, a joint statement addressed to the UN Secretary General written by the Russian Foreign Minister, Igor Ivanov, and U.S. Secretary of State Madeleine Albright blamed the KLA for 'provocations [which] have contributed significantly to the renewed deep tensions in Kosovo. The United States and the Russian Federation condemn such provocations and demand they end immediately' (UNSC, 1999a). Finally, the OSCE recognises that '[T]here were frequent small-scale ambushes against MUP [Serbian Interior Ministry Police] forces by the UCK [KLA] during the first two-and-a half months of 1999, clearly breaching any conceptions of a cease-fire' (1999).

This has led several authors to conclude that NATO and the U.S. did not effectively use their influence to contain the KLA and force it to comply with the agreement (Crawford, 2001; Gibbs, 2015). Turning a blind eye to the KLA ceasefire violations resulted, in the end, in the total derailment of the so-called Holbrooke-Miloševic Agreement, thus paving the way for a yet more violent escalation between the belligerent parties. As soon as the ceasefire collapsed, the Milošević administration responded with a revamped counterinsurgency, which involved the return of thousands of Yugoslavian security forces to the province, aimed at retaking the territory lost to the KLA during the truce.

Račak: The contested *casus belli*

The Kosovo Verification Mission

Interestingly, this renewed offensive took place at a time, December 1998/ January 1999, when the Kosovo Verification Mission (KVM) was deployed in the area. The legitimacy and legality of the mission stems from UNSC

Resolution 1199 which called for the establishment of a diplomatic observation mission in Kosovo, allocating the task initially to the 'European Community' (UNSC, 1998). Eventually, it was the Organisation for Security and Cooperation in Europe (OSCE) which took the responsibility. The main task of the mission was to ensure that the Yugoslav forces would comply with the UNSC Resolution 1199 and abide with the Holbrooke ceasefire. The OSCE mission was composed of up to 2,000 *verifiers* who were unarmed but who, contrary to some ill-informed media reports, were not civilians but mostly retired military personnel from the organisation's member states (Bellamy and Griffin, 2002, p. 13).

At the insistence of the head of the mission, William Walker, the OSCE-led mission did not limit itself to supervise the ceasefire, as stipulated in the mandate which emanated from the Security Council. Instead, Walker established a division dedicated exclusively to human rights which 'monitored, reported and verified human rights violations throughout the [Kosovo] province' (Walker, 2000, p. 134). Even though this division was not legally sanctioned and went beyond the KVM mandate, supporters argue that provided that the human dimension is an essential attribute of the OSCE, and the Helsinki Final Act, all missions carried out by the organisation must incorporate a human rights focus (Bellamy and Griffin, 2002, p. 16). The Human Rights division of the KVM published an impressive document *Kosovo/Kosova as seen as told* detailing a large number of human rights violations, occurred in Kosovo during the deployment of the mission (OSCE, 1999). The crux of the matter is whether this humanitarian emphasis had ulterior motives, that is, if its main objective was to 'prepare the ground', morally speaking, for a potential intervention against Yugoslavia. According to several sources from international organisations working in Kosovo this was the case, that is, the KVM's chief objective was to gather information and collect data about massacres perpetrated by the Yugoslav forces in order to build a case to justify a potential NATO intervention.[1]

This harsh allegation by officers from international organisations is not the sole critique addressed at the KVM. As a matter of fact, the mission was marred by controversy from the very beginning. For instance, one of the most vocal critics, Diana Johnstone, points out that Washington pushed hard to appoint an American diplomat, William Walker, as head of the mission creating uneasiness amongst Europeans (2002, p. 237). Walker himself admits that the mission triggered severe animosity between Americans and their European partners: 'European resentments, suspicions, and uneasiness vis-à-vis the United States were ever-present' (2000, p. 133). Through an *ad hominem* critique, Noam Chomsky questions the integrity of Walker arguing that the former U.S. Ambassador in El Salvador had been directly involved in supporting the state terror perpetrated by the Salvadorian government in the late 1980s and that Walker had eagerly denied the atrocities (otherwise well documented) committed by what Chomsky refers to as a U.S. 'client state' (1999, p. 41).

The mission, which was defined by Walker as an instrument to bring peace and stability to a 'badly troubled corner of Europe', is unprecedented by OSCE standards: its 2,000 strong team meant that it was nearly ten times larger than the second biggest OSCE mission until that point (Walker, 2000, p. 128). While they deem the mission as a watershed for the OSCE in terms of consolidating its role as a peacekeeping organisation, Bellamy and Griffin pinpoint some of the KVM weaknesses: namely the fact that the mission lacked a 'properly coordinated system of mandate formulation' because the organisation was not involved in setting up the agreement 'on which its mandate was based' (2002, p. 22). In practical terms, one of the negative consequences stemming from this was the fact the KLA was not included in the ceasefire agreement and, therefore, unlike the Yugoslav forces it was not formally subjected to the ceasefire demands.

Partly – but not *only* – as a result of this imbalance, the mission was heavily criticised for being biased, favouring the KLA. The head of the mission, William Walker, is singled out as one of the *evidences* of the lack of neutrality of the KVM.[2] In a nutshell, his assessment of the situation was that 'the violations, deliberate and province-wide, were committed by a government against an ethnic minority comprising a 90 per cent majority of Kosovo's population' (Walker, 2000, p. 136). It could be argued that the picture is incomplete since Walker fails to identity or at least to mention the gross violations of human rights conducted by the other belligerent party, the KLA guerrilla. As explained in Chapter 1, these crimes, which included kidnappings, the assassination of civilians and participation in criminal activities among others, were meticulously detailed in the EU's Special Investigative Task Force report[3] in 2014 (Williamson, 2014). An OSCE officer with vast experience in Kosovo has stated that the raison d'être of the KVM was fully justified not least because the 'International Community was fed up with Milošević's abuses' but that its implementation showed a serious lack of impartiality.[4] To justify his point, the officer claims that

> the [KVM] mission played a reckless role seeing what they wanted to see and ignoring what they did not want to see. It deployed on the ground fully supporting the Albanians and buying into the KLA narrative and this meant among other things neglecting their multiple criminal enterprises, including organ trafficking.[5]

Dragiša Djoković, former point of contact with the OSCE in Mitrovica and former member of the Serbian Parliament (2001–2012), claims that the KVM systematically ignored the complaints by Serbs regarding assassinations committed by the KLA.[6] He goes even further to accuse the mission of collaborating and supporting the KLA armed group: 'the [KVM] mission was officially established to facilitate peace but in fact it was helping the KLA by providing them with information and logistics'.[7] This idea is also articulated and replicated by Mark Curtis who makes the bold claim that the KVM verifiers 'were in reality CIA agents' who provided the KLA with 'US military training manuals and field advice on fighting the Yugoslav army' (2010, p. 244). Proving the veracity of such a shocking statement is a sensitive and quasi-unfathomable task that goes well beyond the scope of this book. What seems clear is that the OSCE *verifiers* were viewed with the utmost suspicion by Belgrade, which had only consented to their presence due to the threats and ultimatums issued by the U.S. and its NATO allies.

The Račak killings and its conflicting narratives

This distrustfulness became yet more obvious in the most definitive moment for the KVM, in the small village of Račak[8] in January 1999, when the mission hit the world spotlight. Due to its significance, it is necessary to go into the particulars of the case. According to the KVM reports, three Serbian police officers had been ambushed and killed by the KLA in the village of Dulje, a few kilometres west of Račak on 8 January and, two days later, another member of the Serbian security forces perished as a result of a KLA ambuscade (OSCE, 1999). In this context, a combined operation from the Serbian security forces, the Special Police Unit (PJP), the Yugoslav Army and the Interior Ministry Police (MUP), launched an antiterrorist operation in the area to dismantle the KLA cell responsible for the recent attacks. Unprecedentedly, foreign media outlets, as well as the KVM, had been granted access to the area where the governmental counteroffensive was taking place (Bellamy, 2002, p. 114). This media invitation by the Yugoslav authorities has been used by sceptics to argue that the Serbian police 'did not seem to have anything to hide' (Parenti, 2000, p. 106).

Up until that point, there is no major contradiction between the different versions of the story. After 15 January, however, the two different accounts become entirely irreconcilable. Simply put, the core disagreement between the two perspectives lies in whether the dead bodies belonged to KLA fighters, as Serbian officials claim, or whether they were innocent civilians assassinated in cold blood by the Serbian Security forces.

According to the Serbian official version, Račak constitutes an impeccably well executed antiterrorist operation. The Serbian Interior Ministry issued a statement the very same day stating that '[S]everal dozen terrorists were killed in the clashes with the police. Most of them were in uniforms bearing the insignia of the ethnic Albanian terrorist organisation calling itself the Kosovo Liberation Army (KLA)' (cited by BBC, 1999a). The communiqué also claimed that security forces had been able to seize a large number of weapons (including 36 automatic rifles), ammunition and telecommunications equipment (BBC, 1999a). A very similar version of the events has been recently supported by Goran Radosavljević, former commander of the PJP, who regards the operation as fully legitimate and successful. Radosavljević explains that it followed the pattern of any conventional battle with an insurgent group:

> [A]s we approached Racak, the terrorist group started firing at us from the village itself, from the trenches, bunkers, and other fortifications, using automatic weapons, RPGs and mortars, but the police managed to break them up.... The [KLA] terrorists had a far greater number of casualties.
>
> (Cited by B92, 2017)

After the operation, the Serbian forces withdrew from Račak, allowing the KLA to re-enter the area (Herman and Peterson, 2000, p. 118). The following day, on 16 January, OSCE verifiers arrived to the town to gather evidence, talk to witnesses, and to exhaustively document what had occurred the previous day (OSCE, 1999). Amidst this investigation, they found 40 corpses in different locations.[9] William Walker, the head of the KVM, provides a perspective which entirely differs from the Serbian version. According to Walker, '[T]he dead were mostly elderly men, all in peasant work clothes, and had died where they were discovered. The evidence of deliberate execution was overwhelming' (2000, p. 141). Walker expressed in similar terms, shortly after visiting the site in front of a plethora of international journalists that 'from what I personally saw I do not hesitate to describe the event as a massacre, a crime against humanity' (cited by Bird and Steele, 1999).

A possible critique regarding Walker's bold statement where he assertively claimed that it constituted 'a massacre' and 'a crime against humanity' is that such a declaration was hasty, emotionally-driven and issued before any proper forensic investigation took place; in other words, it was too premature to determine whether that was a massacre or the result of a bloody battle between the KLA and Serbian security forces. A further criticism of Walker's role could be the fact that he called General Wesley Clark, NATO's Supreme Allied Commander Europe[10] (SACEUR) at the time, the very day when he visited the scene, to inform him about his conclusions on the Račak killings (Clark, 2001, p. 158) and arguably to put pressure on the transatlantic organisation to act.

Several correspondents, in particular from the French media, questioned the official version of events by introducing elements of doubt and scepticism. Christophe Chatelet, from *Le Monde*, points out that the Albanian (and OSCE) version of the story leaves many questions unanswered, seems too good to be true and is contradicted by the accounts from the Associated Press TV journalists (Chatelet, 1999). Further, Renaud Girard, from *Le Figaro*, implied that the KLA could have piled up the dead bodies to create an execution scene and, by doing so, transform a military defeat into a political victory (cited by Johnstone, 2002, p. 242). In very similar terms, Parenti claims that the KVM frame of the Račak events decisively contributed to transforming a 'military defeat into a propaganda victory' for the KLA (2000, p. 107).

This version, which Bellamy labels a conspiracy theory (2002, pp. 118–119), has also been hinted at by forensic expert and head of the EU team investigating the Račak massacre, Helena Ranta. The expert, in a TV interview, reproduced at the ICTY Slobodan Milošević trial, affirmed that

> [Y]ou could say that the entire scene in the little valley had been staged. I am aware of that because this is actually a possibility. Our initial investigation results suggest this, as do the later forensic examinations we conducted on the spot in November 1999.
>
> (ICTY, 2003, p. 17709)

It would appear, therefore, that this dialectical Gordian Knot could only be resolved scientifically rather than politically. With the aim of clarifying the events in Račak scientifically, two investigations were carried out. The first one, conducted by Yugoslavian forensics, supervised by Belarusian experts, took place a few days after the massacre and emphatically concluded that 'not a single body bears any sign of execution.... The bodies were not massacred' (cited by BBC, 1999b). A second investigation, under a mandate from the EU, was carried out by a group of Finnish forensic experts. The first results of the investigation came to light through the head of the team, Helena Ranta, who issued a report on 17 March which constituted a personal comment rather than an official authorised communication by the EU Forensic Team (cited by Krieger, 2001, pp. 197–198).

Far from ending the venomous clash of narratives or being fully illuminating, Ranta's comments added more fuel into the fire and generated even further speculation. On the one hand, in her report, Ranta claims that '[N]o indication of removal of badges or insignia was evident.... It is highly unlikely that clothes could have been changed or removed.... There were no indications of the people other than being unarmed civilians' (Ranta cited by Krieger, 2001, pp. 197–198). This is interpreted by Bellamy as an endorsement of the KVM perspective (2002, pp. 114–120). However, this is far from evident for the very reason that the report also states that '[M]edico-legal investigations cannot give a conclusive answer to the question whether there was a battle or whether the victims died under some other circumstances' (Ranta *et al.* cited by Krieger, 2001, pp. 198–199). In addition, there is no mention that the dead had been shot at close range. This points to the direction that the report is inconclusive to say the least. Nevertheless, the report was used as unequivocal evidence that the Serbian security forces had committed a massacre against civilians in Račak.

All in all, it must be noted that NATO's 'Operation Allied Force' began a week after the publication of Ranta's report. A more comprehensive scientific piece of forensic investigation was published in 2001, two years after NATO's intervention, by three members of the Finnish forensic team in the journal *Forensic Science International*. This academic article concluded that out of the 40 bodies delivered to the forensic team, 39 were male and there was only a single female. There was a wide range of age groups: one was a younger than 15, three were older than 65 and the rest (36) were adults (Rainio *et al.*, 2001, p. 178). The paper also concludes that all the victims had died as a result of 'varying numbers of gunshot injuries', ranging from a single gunshot wound to 20, and more significantly, only one single case of close-range discharge was found (Rainio *et al.*, 2001, p. 179). The authors conclude by stating that unrealistic expectations cannot be imposed on forensic experts and that it is not within their scope to determine whether the victims were militants or civilians: '[D]etermination of reasons for events, their political and moral meanings, or the connection of victims to political or other organisations are questions which lie beyond the scope of forensic science' (Rainio *et al.*, 2001, p. 184).

The scientific forensic analysis, therefore, did not clarify fundamental issues such as the status of the dead but it did seem to put into question the hypothesis that the victims had been shot at close range and the claim, made by President Clinton among others, that women and children had been executed in Račak.[11] At any rate, the article was published two years after NATO's intervention and had no impact whatsoever in terms of policy-making. It is therefore possible to argue that the international intervention, prompted to a large extent by Račak, was not based on the scientific results of the forensic analysis.

Račak, the turning point

As the previous paragraphs have shown, the controversy surrounding the Račak massacre is significant. There is, however, crucial common ground. The two contradictory narratives concur with the fact that this event was a 'turning point' in the Kosovo conflict. This very term is used over and over by both those who embrace the official KVM version as well as by those who view it with the utmost scepticism. The *Washington Post*, for instance, stressed that 'the killings at Račak ... outraged the international community and became the turning point in the year-long conflict between the security forces and the Kosovo Liberation Army' (Smith, 1999). Similarly, for the charismatic Green Party MP and German foreign minister at the time, Joschka Fischer, Račak was a turning point which showed that appeasement was no longer an option (cited by Hoffman, 1999).

This 'turning point' expression cannot be understood *in vacuo* but needs to be put in the context of a major policy shift by Western powers. According to Bahador '[A]t the U.S. State Department, the shift in policy began to germinate almost immediately after the massacre' (2007, p. 151). This policy shift was solidified at the NATO council meeting called by Javier Solana, at the request of Wesley Clark, on 19 January (Clark, 2001). It could be argued that Račak empowered those within NATO who were more enthusiastic about a NATO campaign and who were ready to use 'all necessary means' to quash the Milošević administration. A figure that deserves particular attention in that regard is Madeleine Albright, the U.S. Secretary of State at the time, who played a pivotal role in persuading, on some occasions even coercing,[12] fellow U.S. practitioners as well as European counterparts that war was the only way.

Albright's view, which can be conceptualised as pre-emptive humanitarianism, is epitomised by her remarks: 'we should not wait as long as we did on Bosnia to have dreadful things happen; that we could get it ahead of the curve' (cited by Gellman, 1999). Albright's perspective is indeed highly influenced by a perception that the West's inaction in Bosnia contributed to mass violations of human rights and massacres by the Serbo-Bosnian forces. Kosovo, appeared, therefore, as an opportunity to atone and expiate the sins and *mauvaise conscience* caused by Western passivity in Bosnia: '[W]e are not going to stand by and watch the Serbian authorities do in Kosovo what they can no longer get away with doing in Bosnia' (Albright cited by Erlanger, 1998). More cynically, it could be argued that Albright was instrumentalising a conflict of a very different nature in order to pursue a war-oriented agenda in Kosovo.

Albright's belligerent approach was by no means hegemonic or consensual amidst her colleagues at the U.S. administration or amongst her allies in NATO. In fact, on 15 January, the same day that the Račak battle/killings occurred, she suffered a staggering political defeat at the White House National Security Council (NSC), when her proposal to push for airstrikes was rejected by the so-called *minimalists*, Defense Secretary William Cohen, national security advisor Sandy Berger and General Hugh Shelton, Chairman of the Joint Chiefs of Staff (Barthe and David, 2007, p. 94). President Clinton remained unconvinced and sided with the *minimalists*. Four days later, however, and due to the events in Račak – or more precisely due to the way they were framed[13] – there was a Copernican turn in terms of policy towards Yugoslavia, allowing Albright and the hawks to gain decisive momentum and galvanising support for their cause. In view of Gellman, 'Racak transformed the West's Balkan policy as singular events seldom do' (1999) by convincing the Clinton administration that the time for talking was over and that action – that is war – was required. Simply put, the *minimalists* within the Clinton administration had been politically defeated by the hawks.

This emphasis on Kosovo by the U.S. administration came at a time when President Clinton was seriously challenged on the domestic front by an impeachment process, on charges of perjury and obstruction of justice, originally connected to scandals of a sexual nature. At a time when the Račak issue was being discussed at the NSC (15 January and 19 January 1999) the President's lawyers were presenting their defence arguments at the Senate impeachment trial (19–21 January). This temporal overlap has raised speculations as to whether the decision to engage so actively in this remote Serbian province was triggered by domestic politics (Scolino and Bronner, 1999) rather than by purely humanitarian motives or even geopolitical concerns. According to this perspective, the Kosovo intervention would have played an instrumental role, as some sort of smokescreen, in distracting the media and public attention from an incendiary sexual scandal to a military operation aimed at protecting suffering civilians.

In this favourable context, on 19 January, the same day that the NATO council gathered in Brussels, the NSC met at the Situation Room, where Albright wheeled out an old proposal initially developed by Alexander Vershbow, the U.S. NATO ambassador. Vershbow's plan, outlined in the classified document 'Kosovo: Time for Another Endgame Strategy' advocated for Kosovo to be turned into an international protectorate with UN approval and with the presence of 30,000 NATO troops guaranteeing its security (Bellamy, 2002; Bahador, 2007). This is particularly significant for this book and for its main theme because for the first time, at least at a top official level, steps were taken in the direction of inducing territorial transformations in Kosovo. In addition, this would suggest that the border modifications did not only occur *a fortiori*, as a result of the NATO intervention, but that these redrawings had been previously envisioned and even engineered at the highest levels of the Clinton administration.

The ultimate incarnation of the connection between Račak and the intervention is epitomised by President Clinton's news conference at the White House, on 20 March, four days before NATO's air campaign, where he explicitly mentioned the Račak killings, twice, to justify the imminent bombing of Yugoslavia:

> We should remember what happened in the village of Racak back in January, innocent men, women and children taken from their homes to a gully, forced to kneel in the dirt, sprayed with gunfire – not because of anything they had done, but because of who they were.... Our firmness is the only thing standing between them [Serbian security forces] and countless more villages like Racak.
>
> (Cited by *New York Times*, 1999)

Clinton's explicit mention of Račak at such crucial time, four days prior to the start of the bombing, suggests that the incident was used as a convenient *casus belli* by the U.S. and its allies. Sceptical authors have bluntly argued that the Račak massacre was a set up in order to subsequently be exploited for warmongering elements within NATO (Herman and Peterson, 2000, p. 119). However, the link between the Račak killings and the NATO intervention is not entirely straightforward but rather indirect. That is due to the fact that Račak did not directly lead to the NATO air campaign but to the so called Rambouillet negotiations. These gatherings between the Contact Group[14] and the warring parties (the Yugoslavian government and the KLA) paved the way to the humanitarian intervention carried out by the transatlantic organisation. According to the U.S. and to a lesser extent its European allies' perspective, after Račak the room for manoeuvre appeared to have been reduced to two outcomes: NATO intervention or international negotiations, which would provide a lasting and stable solution to the conflict. In the end, the diplomatic solution triumphed. It was, however, a very *sui generis* type of diplomacy which has been illustrated by Parenti with an oxymoron – 'diplomatic aggression' (2000, p. 107).

The Rambouillet (dis)accords

Rambouillet's background

As explained in the previous section, the mood after Račak amongst Western policymakers was that something had to be done to push for a negotiated solution in the Kosovo conflict and to put an end to what they viewed as Milošević's policy of slaughter in this Serbian province. The general feeling was that they, particularly the U.S. diplomats, were running out of patience. Račak was, according to their perspective, the straw that broke the camel's back.

On 28 January, NATO's Secretary General at the time, Javier Solana, called for a 'political settlement under the mediation of the Contact Group' and stated, coercively, that '[W]e are ready to act, if necessary. The parties must seize this opportunity. It is the only way to overcome the Kosovo conflict' (NATO, 1999a). It has often been pointed out that Rambouillet was based on a strategy where diplomacy was coupled with threats and therefore the term 'coercive diplomacy', used by scholars and policymakers alike, appears to be fairly accurate (Bellamy, 2000; Clark 2001; Barthe and David, 2007). Such settlement had to include, according to Solana's statement, two ingredients which would become essential in most of the drafts used for the Kosovo conflict: a) ample autonomy for Kosovo and b) respect for Yugoslavia's sovereignty and territorial integrity (NATO, 1999a). The latter condition is significant because it denotes that, at least officially, NATO had no intentions of implementing or encouraging any border modification in (what was left of) Yugoslavia. The ultimatum tone was eminently clear as Solana explicitly mentioned that the initiative would be backed by NATO's military capabilities.

A day later, a Contact Group meeting in London called for an end to the violence through a political settlement and summoned the warring parties (the Yugoslavian government and the KLA) to a negotiation meeting on 6 February in the castle of Rambouillet, France (Office of the High Representative, 1999a). Rambouillet was framed as the *last chance* to find a negotiated solution. The negotiations were co-chaired by two European diplomats, French foreign minister Hubert Vedrine and British Foreign Secretary, Robin Cook, and were going to be arranged by the Contact Group itself. In addition, the international negotiating team also included the U.S. Secretary of State, Madeleine Albright, the Italian, German and Russian Foreign Ministers as well as three negotiators[15] known as the 'Negotiating Troika'. It has been claimed that the Contact Group was far from united, in particular over two crucial matters: the territorial integrity of Yugoslavia and the use of force against Yugoslavia. At one end, France and particularly Russia were seen as anti-interventionists and on the other extreme, the U.S. and the UK appeared as the actors more ardently pushing for intervention and showing more *flexibility* in terms of Yugoslavia's territorial integrity (Bellamy, 2000, p. 105).

The initiative was fully backed by the UN Security Council which, once again, repeated the mantra of 'substantial autonomy' for Kosovo combined with the 'commitment to the sovereignty and territorial integrity of the Federal Republic of Yugoslavia' (UNSC, 1999b). At first glance, the framework of the negotiations may appear similar to those of Dayton, which brought the war in Bosnia to an end. However, as it will be argued below, while Dayton was characterised by a balanced equidistance from the international parties, the same cannot be said about Rambouillet, where there are many aspects which appear outlandish and conceivably biased.

Not least due to the explicit threat against one of the parties, NATO's North Atlantic Council warned the Yugoslavian side that 'NATO Secretary General may authorise air strikes against targets on FRY territory' (NATO, 1999b) if it failed to comply. Due to the existence of such grave threats against Yugoslavia, some authors have questioned whether Rambouillet can be labelled as an accord or agreement. For instance, according to Layne,

> At Rambouillet the Yugoslavians were 'negotiating' with a gun to their head. Indeed, the United States and the West Europeans were not negotiating with Belgrade at all; Belgrade was presented with an ultimatum and given the choice of signing or being bombed.
>
> (2000, p. 16)

This ultimatum idea will be further explored below.

The composition of the delegation deserves to be put under critical scrutiny. On the Yugoslavian side, the delegation was led by the Vice-president of Serbia, Ratko Marković. Milošević refused to attend personally as he had done in Dayton four years earlier. Officially, this was due to the fact that he feared being arrested on counts of war crimes. Bellamy offers an alternative explanation by pointing out that the Yugoslavian President's absence was a calculated move aimed at undermining the political weight of the summit in order 'to make the talks as meaningless as possible' (2000, p. 103). Belgrade's goals were straightforward: to defend Yugoslavia's territorial integrity and to avoid a deployment of foreign troops in Kosovo. The delegation included not only policymakers from Serbia proper but also representatives from Kosovo's ethnic minorities[16] to demonstrate that the Kosovo Albanian delegation was not fully representative of the province' ethnic complexity and allegedly to show sensitivity towards national communities. It has been argued, however, that as the talks were reaching critical importance and the discussions were becoming substantial, the

Yugoslavian delegation began replacing the initial *straw men* with negotiating experts (Weller, 1999; Wolff, 2003).

The composition of the Kosovo Albanian delegation was even more puzzling and controversial. It was comprised of independent international experts and the leaders of the main secessionist parties: Ibrahim Rugova, the head of the LDK and Rexhep Qosja, leader of the opposition party United Democratic Movement (Krstić-Brano, 2004, p. 254). There were also five members of the KLA guerrilla force, including its leader Hashim Thaçi. Surprisingly, the latter and not Rugova, who was the (shadow) Kosovo President and who had gained international reputation through his non-violent civil disobedience struggle for independence, was designated as the head of the Kosovo Albanian delegation. According to Marc Weller, a scholar who served as a legal adviser to the Kosovo delegation at Rambouillet, the reason for such an odd choice was that Rugova's associates were outnumbered by the KLA members and sympathisers of the insurgent group and, consequently, the majority of the delegation voted for Thaçi to lead the Kosovo Albanian negotiating team (Weller, 1999, p. 227).

At any rate, Rambouillet consolidated the marginalisation, at an international level, of Rugova and his party and the consolidation of Thaçi and his armed fighters not just as a legitimate actor but as *the actor* representing the Kosovo Albanians. This protagonist role given to the KLA, a group deemed as a terrorist organisation by Belgrade, has been considered as a deliberate affront to the Yugoslavian delegation (Johnstone, 2002, p. 244). In fact, initially the KLA had refused to participate in Rambouillet on the grounds that there was no provision that included a legally binding referendum or indeed independence for Kosovo (Bellamy, 2000, p. 104). Eventually, as a result of pressures from Western diplomats and the Albanian government, the group agreed to participate in the peace conference.

The arduous (non)negotiation

Prior to the commencement of the Rambouillet conference, the Contact Group presented the two parties with a short document specifying the elements which would be non-negotiable. These basic principles were meant to represent the red lines which could not be crossed as well as some sort of negotiating guidelines intended at setting up the agenda. These basic elements were analogous to the conditions laid out by Solana some days earlier: a high degree of autonomy and self-governance for Kosovo and respect towards the FRY sovereignty and territorial integrity, coupled with calls for an immediate cessation of violence and a peaceful resolution of the conflict (ICTY, 2008, p. 21570). As in Dayton, in Rambouillet Western states had taken the lead through decisive actions and commitment in order to regulate and mediate in conflicts in the former Yugoslavian space.

Amidst an atmosphere of pessimism to the extent that it was feared that the talks could potentially collapse even before they commenced, negotiations in Rambouillet began on 6 February (Judah, 1999). The *modus operandi* was simple: the international negotiators provided the parties with different documents and annexes related to constitutional, economic, humanitarian assistance issues etc. and the parties had to come up with amendments and proposals. Those matters were seen as relatively uncontentious, at least compared to the issue of the international peacekeeping force brought up by Madeleine Albright who pressured the Serbs by

Box 2.1: Appendix B from the Interim Agreement for Peace and Self-Government in Kosovo

6 a. NATO shall be immune from all legal process, whether civil, administrative, or criminal.

b. NATO personnel, under all circumstances and at all times, shall be immune from the Parties' jurisdiction in respect of any civil, administrative, criminal, or disciplinary offenses which may be committed by them in the FRY. The Parties shall assist States participating in the Operation in the exercise of their jurisdiction over their own nationals.

[...]

7 NATO personnel shall be immune from any form of arrest, investigation, or detention by the authorities in the FRY. NATO personnel erroneously arrested or detained shall immediately be turned over to NATO authorities.

8 NATO personnel shall enjoy, together with their vehicles, vessels, aircraft, and equipment, free and unrestricted passage and unimpeded access throughout the FRY including associated airspace and territorial waters. This shall include, but not be limited to, the right of bivouac, maneuver, billet, and utilisation of any areas or facilities as required for support, training, and operations.

9 NATO shall be exempt from duties, taxes, and other charges and inspections and custom regulations including providing inventories or other routine customs documentation, for personnel, vehicles, vessels, aircraft, equipment, supplies, and provisions entering, exiting, or transiting the territory of the FRY in support of the Operation.

10 The authorities in the FRY shall facilitate, on a priority basis and with all appropriate means, all movement of personnel, vehicles, vessels, aircraft, equipment, or supplies, through or in the airspace, ports, airports, or roads used. No charges may be assessed against NATO for air navigation, landing, or takeoff of aircraft, whether government-owned or chartered. Similarly, no duties, dues, tolls or charges may be assessed against NATO ships, whether government-owned or chartered, for the mere entry and exit of ports.

11 NATO is granted the use of airports, roads, rails, and ports without payment of fees, duties, dues, tolls, or charges occasioned by mere use.

Source: cited by Le Monde Diplomatique, 1999

insisting that these foreign troops presence in Kosovo was a non-negotiable point (Bellamy, 2000, p. 109). This so-called military part of the agreement (Appendix B), which was handed to the delegations in the final days of the negotiations, is enormously controversial because it literally calls on Belgrade to surrender its sovereignty to NATO with unrealistic and even humiliating demands.

In short, what Appendix B was demanding was unrestricted passage through Yugoslavia, not simply the province of Kosovo. In addition, it stipulated that NATO forces would enjoy immunity and they would even be exempted from taxes and fees. In other words, it granted NATO a military occupation of the entire territory of Yugoslavia, requiring an unconditional humiliating capitulation. General Wesley Clark, NATO's former Supreme Allied Commander in Europe, claims paternity of the polemic appendix: 'My staff and I were involved in drafting the military agreements for the Rambouillet negotiations' (2001, p. 162).

Bearing in mind the uncompromising character of the demands laid out in Appendix B, Rambouillet can hardly be deemed a 'negotiation'. Critiques of these imbalanced demands can be found in abundance in the literature, even amongst Western policy-makers. The deputy British Defence Minister,[17] John Gilbert, asserted that 'certain people were spoiling for a fight in NATO at that time.... I think the terms put to Milosevic at Rambouillet were absolutely intolerable; how could he possibly accept them; it was quite deliberate' (Gilbert, 2000). Former U.S. Secretary of State, Henry Kissinger, labelled the Rambouillet text as a 'provocation, an excuse to start bombing' (cited by Bancroft, 2009). John Pilger's critique summarizes the Yugoslav delegation dilemma: 'the peace negotiations [in Rambouillet] were stage-managed, and the Serbs were told: surrender and be occupied, or don't surrender and be destroyed' (1999). The counterargument is that the FRY administration accepted practically identical provisions during the Dayton negotiations, only four years earlier, and those similar provisions did not represent an obstacle to sign the peace agreement which ended the war in Bosnia (Bellamy, 2000; Clark, 2001).

In parallel with the Serbian hesitancy to accept the content of Appendix B, it is often ignored that the Kosovo delegation was particularly reluctant to sign the agreement due to the fact that it did not include any mention of a referendum of independence for the province. Albright, who played a crucial role behind the scenes, was particularly adamant in trying to convince the KLA members that the agreement would include a clause incorporating the 'wishes of the people of Kosovo' (Bellamy, 2000, p. 110). This euphemistic formula, which concealed Kosovo's right to self-determination, was as far as the U.S. could go without compromising the non-negotiable element of Yugoslavia's sovereignty. In spite of her industrious efforts, Albright did not manage to convince the Kosovo delegation, prior to the deadline, on 23 February. The Kosovo Albanian signature was essential for a wide variety of reasons. In the words of Crawford:

> Rambouillet was an offer the KLA could not refuse, a negotiation they could not sit out. If they did, they would hand NATO and especially the United States such a smashing embarrassment that the West would wash its hands of Kosovo.
>
> (1999, p. 519)

The stakes were as high as they could possibly be. If the KLA-led delegation refused to sign, NATO's plan, defined by Clark as 'a non-forced entry of 25,000 to 30,000 NATO troops into Kosovo after a peace settlement' (2001, p. 163), could not be put into practice.

The Serbian delegation seemed closer to signing, at least the political part of the agreement, but preferred to wait until the details of the implementation of the accords (Weller, 1999, p. 233). This seeming lack of concrete success did not impede the Contact Group from issuing an enthusiastic statement, on 23 February, where they stated that 'a political framework is now in place', highlighting that the parties had reached consensus in many areas related to Kosovo's self-governance and the development of democratic institutions for this territory (Office of the High Representative, 1999b). They did fail to mention, nevertheless, that neither of the two parties had signed the 'Interim Agreement for Peace and Self-Government in Kosovo' accords. The final discussion, which would have to address the most sensitive part of the negotiation, that is, the implementation of the agreement, was postponed to 15 March.

From that day until 18 March the parties met in Paris, where they were expected to sign the documents discussed in Rambouillet. With the Serbian delegation unwilling to accept the so-called military provisions, it has been claimed that the meeting in Paris was aimed at convincing the KLA-led delegation to sign the agreement (Johnstone, 2002, p. 246). In that regard, it was fundamental to address the main concern from the Kosovo Albanian delegation, namely, the absence of references to a self-determination referendum or independence. The formula chosen to accommodate their wishes was purposely vague. In an amendment of the Interim Agreement for Peace and Self-Government in Kosovo, which appears at the end of the document, it is stipulated that: '[T]hree years after the entry into force of this Agreement, an international meeting shall be convened to determine a mechanism for a final settlement for Kosovo, on the basis of the will of the people' (cited by *Le Monde Diplomatique*, 1999). In the end, Washington's coercive insistence, led by Albright, bore fruit and the Kosovo Albanian delegation reluctantly agreed to sign.

Mark Weller, a negotiator working for the Kosovo Albanian delegation points out that the vagueness of the statement above was dissipated with verbal pledges: '[T]he delegation of Kosovo obtained certain assurances that this formula actually establishes a legal right to hold a referendum of the people of Kosovo' (1999, p. 245). Due to such assurances, the KLA-led delegation finally signed the accords and issued a statement, aimed at its members and supporters, where they clarified that 'after the expiry of the three-year interim period, the people of Kosovo will express their will at a referendum'[18] (cited by Krstić-Brano, 2004, p. 259). The formula of using euphemisms and acrobatics-driven semantics such as 'final settlement' or 'future status' was going to be reproduced in future texts such as UNSC Resolution 1244.

The absence of *cursed* terms such as 'self-determination', 'referendum' or 'independence' is explained by the fact that their presence would have contravened a vital condition of the non-negotiable elements issued by the Contact Group at the very beginning of the Rambouillet talks: the FRY territorial integrity. With the perspective of time, it is possible to argue that terms such as *final settlement* and *future status* did subtly pave the way for the bordering effects and transformations in Kosovo. In other words, the embryo of these crucial border and territorial transformations was produced in Rambouillet/Paris. In a more immediate fashion, the non-agreement during these bizarre negotiations led to war.

Indeed, when NATO's Secretary General at the time, Javier Solana, stated on 23 March, five days after the Rambouillet (non-agreed) accords that 'all efforts to achieve a negotiated political solution to the Kosovo crisis having failed, no alternative is open but to take military action' (NATO, 1999c) it was crystal clear that NATO was determined to attack Yugoslavia. The idea that transpires from Solana's statement is that of 'last resort', which at first glance further enhances the legitimacy of the intervention. It could be argued, however, that with the imposition of a humiliating and unrealistic 'military appendix' the bar was deliberately set too high and hence aimed at making a Yugoslavian signature impossible. By refusing to accept the accords, the Yugoslavian delegation would appear as the main obstacle and as the irredentist saboteurs of the negotiation. Given the nature of the military appendix, detailed above, it appears that the underlying reasons behind Rambouillet's collapse are perhaps more complex than simply due to Serbian intransigence. At this stage, it is worth remembering that the Yugoslavian delegation had accepted most points from the political part of the agreement. This brings us, once again, to the critics' hypothesis that Rambouillet was from its outset designed to fail so that NATO could have a pretext to start the bombing and implement 'Operation Allied Force'. Failure in Rambouillet, it appears, may have been a self-fulfilling prophesy.

Operation Allied Force

NATO's war

NATO's bombing of Yugoslavia, named 'Operation Allied Force', was, poetically speaking, the transatlantic organisation baptism by fire; that is, the first time it went to war since it had been established 50 years earlier.[19]

It has been labelled, perhaps with excessively flamboyant language, as 'the most intense and sustained military operation to have been conducted in Europe since the end of World War II ... as well as the first major combat operation conducted for humanitarian objectives' (Lambeth, 2001, p. 219). On 24 March, NATO initiated a 78-day campaign of uninterrupted bombing against the FRY. The idea was that it would not to be a military conflict *in strictu sensu* but an intense and short air campaign which would persuade Milošević to capitulate and accept the terms and conditions of Rambouillet (Daalder and O'Hanlon, 2000, p. 101). It would soon become clear to all parties that this assumption was erroneous and that 'Operation Allied Force' was nothing short of war.

According to NATO figures, over 1,000 aircraft from 13 of its members at the time 'flew 38,400 sorties, including 10,484 strike sorties. During these sorties, 23,614 air munitions were released' (ICTY, 2000). Human Rights Watch (HRW) estimated that approximately 500 civilians were killed (both in Serbia proper and Kosovo) as a result of NATO airstrikes, whereas Yugoslavian governmental sources elevated the figure to at least 1,200 direct civilian casualties (HRW, 2001). The targets, defined by NATO as intentional or legitimate, included the following: 'military forces; security forces; command and control facilities; the integrated air defense system; military-industrial infrastructure; the media and broadcasting system; supply routes; lines of communication; bridges; government ministries; and refineries' (Fenrick, 2001, p. 495). The U.S. Department of Defense, at the end of the

Figure 2.1 Bombed Serbian Ministry of Defence (2017).

Source: Gisela Gorbalán.

war, in June 1999, claimed to have inflicted crucial damage to Yugoslavia's military and infrastructure: NATO claimed to have destroyed 100 per cent of the country's oil production, 70 per cent of road bridges, 65 per cent of ammunition production capacity, 220 armoured personnel carriers, 450 artillery pieces and 120 tanks (cited by Cordesman, 2000, pp. 144–145).

This apparent stunning victory led some not only to embrace NATO's campaign as some sort of inspiring glorious victory but also to believe, perhaps too uncritically, in the limitless might of airpower and the advent of a new paradigm based on 'distance warfare'. John Keegan, for instance, enthusiastically claimed that:

> There are certain dates in the history of warfare that mark real turning points.... Now there is a new turning point to fix on the calendar: June 3, 1999, when the capitulation of President Milosevic proved that a war can be won by airpower alone.
>
> (1999)

The conclusions of a suppressed U.S. Air Force report, however, dilute this assertion by stating that they only found evidence of 58 confirmed destroyed targets (artillery, tanks and armoured carriers) in Kosovo, which is in stark contrast with the over 700 initially claimed by NATO (Barry, 2000). The strikingly low figures of the suppressed report resemble those of the Yugoslavian Army, whose commander in Kosovo, Nebojsa Pavković, claimed to have used plentiful decoys and dummy tanks to fool NATO's bombs (Norton-Taylor, 2000).

There are some additional details that must be taken into account. First, the operation was not free of internal rifts, most notably Greece, which has historical, cultural and religious links with Serbia. Those disagreements, however, were mostly kept internally and never had the potential to undermine NATO's military strategy. The formula was similar to the European Union's opt-outs: those who did not concur with the operation opted-out from participating without sabotaging the overall project. It should also be noted that the United States carried most of the weight of the operation: they conducted 60 per cent of the sorties and 80 per cent of the air strikes (Independent International Commission on Kosovo, 2000, p. 92).

The rationale behind Operation Allied Force

The immediate and manifest objectives of the intervention are laid out in President Clinton's speech shortly after the bombing began. According to Clinton, the main aims of the intervention are: 'to protect thousands of innocent people in Kosovo ... to prevent a wider war ... and, if necessary, to seriously damage the Serbian military's capacity to harm the people of Kosovo' (U.S. Government Publishing Office, 1999). Interestingly, as will be further analysed in the following paragraphs, Clinton also mentions, as an objective, the need 'to demonstrate the seriousness of NATO's purpose'. This opens the door to speculations that the aims of Operation Allied Force were not only simply connected to the case itself but also to internal or institutional matters related to NATO and its existential survival in the post-Cold War context.

One of the thorniest aspects of NATO's war against Yugoslavia over Kosovo is its legality or rather its lack of it. That should hardly come as a surprise given the fact that NATO's intervention did not have UNSC authorisation to act unilaterally against Yugoslavia. Enthusiasts of the intervention claim that NATO had based their actions on several UNSC resolutions: namely, 1160, 1199 and 1203 (Daalder and O'Hanlon, 2000, p. 102). However, those resolutions – which called for the establishment of an arms embargo against Yugoslavia (1160), the cessation of hostilities by both parties and demanded that they engaged in a meaningful dialogue – did not justify in any way or shape a unilateral act of aggression against a sovereign state which inevitably contravened the UN Charter. Intervention supporters point out that despite the fact that there was no explicit endorsement, there was no condemnation either for a proposed Russian resolution criticising 'NATO's aggression' was only supported by three out of the 15 members of the UNSC (Hehir, 2012, p. 36).

Critics, on the other hand, argue that NATO's intervention is not even contemplated in the transatlantic organisation own foundational 1949 treaty whose Article 5 states that an armed attack against one of its members may trigger a collective response by the others. Indeed, the Washington treaty does not envision out of area operations or actions against third parties under any other pretext than self-defence. It is worth remembering that Yugoslavia had not attacked or threatened any NATO member but instead was involved in an internal conflict which included an armed insurrection by a group, the KLA, which had been deemed a terrorist organisation by the U.S. envoy to former Yugoslavia in 1998 (see Chapter 1).

The legal burden is one of the biggest stones in NATO's shoes when it comes to the Kosovo intervention. In order to circumvent it, at least rhetorically, the formula 'illegal but legitimate' has often been used. For instance, the Independent International Commission concluded that Operation Allied Force was 'illegal but legitimate' because it liberated the majority of Kosovo's population from Serbian oppression and because all negotiating options had failed (Independent International Commission on Kosovo, 2000, p. 4). Furthermore, Operation Allied Force' blatant violation of legality is justified on the grounds that 'decisions on humanitarian intervention ... cannot be allowed to depend on Chinese or Russian acquiescence in the UN Security Council' (Hyde-Price, 2008, p. 40). As Chapter 6 will explain, justifying unilateral – and therefore illegal – humanitarian interventions in such a careless fashion can have a counter-productive effect as other states (i.e. Russia in Georgia) may make use of these perilous precedents.

The NATO intervention has been hyperbolically romanticised by some of its supporters, such as former Czech President Václav Havel who argued that 'this is probably the first war that has not been waged in the name of "national interests," but rather in the name of principles and values' (1999). Havel's words reverberate in the statements issued by policymakers engaged in the operation. Javier Solana, for instance, speaks of a 'moral duty' to stop the violence and 'bring an end to the humanitarian catastrophe' in Kosovo in his very first statement after the bombing commenced (NATO, 1999d). In a similar vein, President Clinton triumphantly expressed, a few days after the end of the intervention, a statement which is sometimes associated with a Kosovo-born *Clinton Doctrine*: 'whether within or beyond the borders of the country, if the world community has the power to stop it, we ought to stop genocide and ethnic cleansing' (CNN, 1999).

The core idea behind the intervention in Yugoslavia is, in Wheeler's terms, that 'for the first time' a group of states acting without the UN umbrella, had decided to violate the sovereignty of a state 'on humanitarian grounds' (2001, p. 113). Kosovo triggered and generated a debate, still ongoing and unresolved 20 years on, which is of paramount importance for states, territory, borders, human rights, sovereignty and intergovernmental organisations: should external actors intervene to protect vulnerable communities within a sovereign state? In this debate, humanitarian intervention (HI) or the Responsibility to Protect (R2P) seem to inexorably clash with the concept of sovereignty. Those who are more inclined to embrace the R2P thesis often view sovereignty as an obstacle to tackle violations and as a shelter for those who commit them. Henry Shue, for instance, openly argues for limiting sovereignty because it allows moral wrong-doers to act immorally, providing 'unlimited indulgence by permanent members of the Security Council for genocidal states' (2004, p. 20). Going a step further, Evans, one of the chief proponents of R2P, asserts that historically, sovereignty has acted as 'a license to kill' for states and that the UN enforces this paradigm with articles in its Charter (mainly Article 2) that protect and legalise such 'right' (2009, p. 16). Conversely, the strict legal interpretation would contend that a war waged illegally 'remains a violation of international law, even if it leads to normatively desirable outcomes' (Habermas, 2005, p. 19).

Indeed, this debate directly appeals to the UN and its Security Council through a dilemma which is seemingly irreconcilable and certainly problematic for this intergovernmental organisation. On the one hand, bypassing the Security Council through unilateral humanitarian interventionism undermines the UN Charter as well as global stability, peace and security. On the other hand, inaction by the UNSC may prompt gross human rights violations which, in turn, can also potentially put into question the very legitimacy and authority of the UN. At any rate, without UNSC authorisation an armed intervention inevitably constitutes a unilateral act and as such defies the very legal foundations of the international system. As bluntly put by Chomsky '[W]ithout Security Council authorisation, then, NATO has no more right to bomb Serbia than Saddam Hussein had to "liberate" Kuwait' (2008).

Critiques

Operation Allied Force has been subject to a repertoire of critiques from a wide range of angles. One of the most significant, the question of its lack of legality, has been scrutinised above. The current section will shed light on the rest of the critiques: namely, the national interest of intervening states; humanitarian militarism; the controversial collaboration with the KLA; the moral hazard; mistakes and collateral damage of the bombing campaign; and the 'Pandora's box'. The latter critique, which is related to opening the door to precedents by triggering further unilateral humanitarian operations, will be addressed in Chapter 6.

The first criticism stems from the realist tradition of International Relations and can be formulated through a question which thus far has not been addressed: was the intervention in Yugoslavia purely humanitarian and conducted solely on the grounds of values and morality, as Havel romantically suggests, and therefore free of national interests? According to the realist school that would be either deceitful, based on wishful thinking or, even worse a rhetorical trick, for states act according to their national interest not otherwise. A classic realist, Edward Carr, contends that universal moral principles and values are 'not principles at all, but the unconscious reflections of national policy based on a particular interpretation of national interest at a particular time' and, consequently, states clothe their national interests in the guise of a 'universal interest' (1939/2001, p. 80). The core idea is that states only intervene in conflicts when their national interests are at stake and, according to this perspective, humanitarian intervention potentially offers a framework or pretext in which sovereignty can be violated with relative impunity in the name of moral arguments.

The question at this point is which national or material interests could Kosovo offer to NATO? Perhaps the first and most obvious is the fact that it allowed the transatlantic organisation to redefine and broaden its mission, in other words, it allowed NATO 'to become a proactive force beyond the territory of the member states' (Carpenter, 2000, p. 175). Indeed, after the end of the Cold War, with the implosion of its arch-rival, the Soviet Union, NATO found itself in a very onerous situation and its very survival was under threat. In this context, it was, as Kenneth Waltz claims, in the interest of the U.S. 'to extend the life of a moribund institution' in order to safeguard and perpetuate its hegemony (2000, p. 20). David Gibbs concurs with Waltz and openly questions the altruistic intentions of the interveners arguing that instead their chief motivations were connected to consolidating U.S. hegemony in Europe through 'the primary institutional embodiment of that hegemony': NATO (2009, p. 172).

It could be therefore argued that Kosovo appeared as a suitable test to justify the continuation of the transatlantic organisation by adopting the self-appointed function of regional crisis manager. Poetically put, Operation Allied Force can be understood as a crucial step in the context of NATO's soul-searching process over its future (Sperling and Webber, 2009, p. 495). Another endogenously-driven factor is the 'credibility' of the organisation, that is, the need not to appear weak or incapable to address crises in its vicinity. As mentioned above, in his address to the nation on the same day the operation began, President Clinton explicitly refers to 'demonstrat[ing] the seriousness of NATO's purpose' as the first objective of NATO's mission in Kosovo, adding concernedly that inaction 'would discredit NATO' (U.S. Government Publishing Office, 1999).

Former British PM, Tony Blair, who was a fundamental key player in NATO's war against Yugoslavia, attempted to reconcile the two elements (moral principles and national interest) by arguing that NATO's actions were

> guided by a more subtle blend of mutual self-interest and moral purpose in defending the values we cherish. In the end values and interests merge. If we can establish and spread the values of liberty, the rule of law, human rights and an open society then that is in our national interests too. The spread of our values makes us safer.
>
> (Cited by Kaiser and McGuire, 1999)

The attempted reconciliation between national interest and moral purpose is also accompanied with a link between humanitarian intervention and the promotion of a particular ideology.

A relevant question, addressed by Burke, is whether Blair's arguments, which were also reproduced by Clinton, Michael Ignatieff and other policy-makers and scholars, create a new interventionist doctrine based on preventive war and unilateral humanitarianism (2005, p. 74). Some authors have coined more pejorative terms to describe this doctrine, such as 'humanitarian militarism' or 'humanitarian imperialism'. David Chandler emphasises that while the terms 'humanitarian' and 'militarism' would have been oxymoronic in the past, after the Kosovo war they had become a tautology (2001, p. 698). Similarly, Jean Bricmont contends that the case of Kosovo illustrates how humanitarianism and human rights can serve as a pretext to advance militaristic and imperialistic agendas (2006).

This is precisely Chomsky's central argument in his renowned manuscript *The New Military Humanism. Lessons from Kosovo*, where the U.S. linguist argues that this 'new humanism' underpinned by the Clinton Doctrine and overhauled by the intervention in Kosovo hides the old strategy of pursuing power 'under the cloak of good intentions' (1999, p. 11). The metaphor of 'old wine in new [moral and humanitarian] baskets' summarises this critique. The idea suggested by NATO's SACEUR at the time, General Wesley Clark, that the transatlantic organisation had used coercive diplomacy combined with 'armed forces to impose the political will of the NATO nations on the Federal Republic of Yugoslavia' (Clark, 2001, p. 418) certainly contributes to fuel critical discourses of 'humanitarian militarism' and 'humanitarian imperialism'.

Further, it is often neglected that, as explained in the previous chapter, NATO's intervention relied on an insurgent group, the KLA, which had been considered a terrorist organisation by the U.S. envoy to the Former Yugoslavia, Robert Gelbard, as its local partner during the bombing campaign. The legitimisation of the group was a hasty process and included, among other levels of coordination the fact that: '[O]fficers in the Kosovo Liberation Army would also be sent to the United States for training in transforming themselves from a guerrilla group into a police force or a political entity' (Perlez, 1999). Amongst Serbs, this co-operation is judged in very harsh terms. According to a Kosovo Serb MP in Belgrade, 'NATO was clearly supporting the KLA, it chose sides. NATO acted as the KLA logistic assistance. They [KLA] did not have an air force and they did not need one because NATO was the KLA's air force'.[20]

It must be noted that, as seen in the previous chapter, the KLA strategy was based on the moral hazard logic, in other words, on committing assassinations of officials, provoking the Yugoslav security forces so that they reacted disproportionately. The rationale was that this would attract international attention which could eventually lead to foreign intervention forcing the withdrawal of the Yugoslav army and the Serbian police forces. Looking back, it seems obvious that the KLA gamble worked out very successfully. The problem, nevertheless, is that, as Hehir notes, this strategy was 'clearly responsible for the deaths of many civilians who, it is reasonable to conclude, would not have died had the KLA not wished to provoke a humanitarian intervention' (2008, p. 111).

Another concern regarding the intervention is that it did not alleviate the conflict but it aggravated it with a dramatic surge in terms of killings and displacement of ethnic Albanians (Chomsky, 1999; Gellman, 1999; Parenti 2000). The UN Special Rapporteur for Human Rights in the Former Yugoslavia, Jani Dienstbier, stressed that

> [B]efore [NATO's 1999] bombing, Albanians were not driven away on the basis of ethnic principle. In the summer and autumn of 1998, many were victims of the brutal war between the Yugoslav army and the Kosovo Liberation Army. The persecution was not persecution of the Albanian people but the prosecution of the opposition by an authoritarian regime. It is only after the beginning of bombing that brutal ethnic cleansing erupted.
>
> (Cited by Radio Liberty, 1999)

Empirical evidence shows that, in effect, the situation dramatically deteriorated for Kosovo Albanians after Operation Allied Force began.

According to the UNHCR, there were 200,000 refugees and 260,000 internally displaced persons (IDP's) prior to NATO's intervention (UNHCR, 1999a). Though Albanians accounted for the majority of displacements, it is also estimated that 30 per cent of Serbs had also left the province fleeing the conflict and KLA persecution. After the bombing, the figures skyrocketed with over 850,000 refugees[21] and several hundred internally displaced living in dire conditions (UNHCR, 1999b). In terms of deaths, from 1998 to March 1999, during the internal conflict between Yugoslav security forces and the KLA, from 1,500 to 2,000 people (civilians and combatants) perished in Kosovo (HRW, 2001, p. 109). The final death toll is considerably higher; it is estimated to range from 10,000 to 12,000 people killed (Independent International Commission on Kosovo, 2000, pp. 94–96). Bearing in mind those figures, from 80 per cent to 87.5 per cent of the victims died during or after Operation Allied Force.

This would indicate that the vast majority of the victims died during Operation Allied Force, which arguably prompted the President of Yugoslavia, Slobodan Milošević to step up his repressive campaign not just against the KLA but also against ethnic Albanians in general, causing an exodus which affected the majority of ethnic Albanians in the province. According to Humans Rights Watch, the operation carried out by the Yugoslavian security forces after the bombing combined elements of counterinsurgency with systematic ethnic cleansing (HRW, 2001, p. 110). The inconvenient reality is that NATO's air campaign seems to have backfired enormously by exposing rather than protecting civilians. According to Carla del Ponte, former prosecutor for the ICTY, and Sudetic, the ethnic cleansing operation of Albanians in Kosovo perpetrated by the Serbian security forces 'began under the cover of NATO airstrikes' (2009, p. 275). In addition, as next chapter will show in detail, NATO was also unable, despite their tens of thousands of soldiers deployed, to prevent 'reverse' ethnic cleansing against Serbs after the Yugoslav's forces withdrawal paving the way to further criticism: 'the inability to stop a new wave of ethnic cleansing in Kosovo ... was a major failure for the international community' (Independent International Commission on Kosovo, p. 7).

Last but not least, the campaign is also controversial due to the numerous cases of so-called collateral damage or unintended killings of civilians[22] (500 according to HRW and the ICTY and 1,200 in the opinion of the Yugoslav authorities). Proponents of the operation have argued that it represented a 'new low in American wartime experience', at least compared to other U.S.-led wars such as Vietnam or Operation Desert Storm in Iraq (Lambeth, 2001, p. 219). Amongst the intervening policy-makers the issue of civilian casualties appears to have been a crucial matter, judging by the insistence on highlighting how few mistakes were made by the transatlantic organisation. U. S. Defense Secretary, William Cohen, explained in September 1999 that

> [O]f the thousands of bombs that were dropped and the missiles that were fired, nearly all of them hit their intended target. Of all those thousands of weapons that were dropped and expended, approximately 20 had unintended consequences[23] or were not on target.
>
> (Cited by HRW, 2000, p. 16)

The 'Committee Established to Review the NATO Bombing Campaign Against the Federal Republic of Yugoslavia', in a report to the ICTY Prosecutor, listed the key incidents involving civilian targets.

Box 2.2: Civilian targets bombed by NATO, according to the ICTY Review Committee

1 the attack on a civilian passenger train at the Grdelica Gorge – 12/4/99 – ten or more civilians killed, 15 or more injured,
2 the attack on the Djakovica Convoy – 14/4/99 – 70–75 civilians killed, 100 or more injured,
3 the attack on Surdulica – 27/4/99 – 11 civilians killed, 100 or more injured,
4 the attack on Cuprija – 8/4/99 – one civilian killed, five injured,
5 the attack on the Cigota Medical Institute – 8/4/99 – three civilians killed,
6 the attack on Hotels Baciste and Putnik – 13/4/99 – one civilian killed,
7 the attacks on the Pancevo Petrochemical Complex and Fertilizer Company – 15/4/99 and 18/4/99 – no reported civilian casualties,
8 the attack on the Nis Tobbaco Factory – 18/4/99 – no reported civilian casualties,
9 the attack on the Djakovica Refugee Camp – 21/4/99 – five civilians killed, 16–19 injured,
10 the attack on a bus at Lu`ane – 1/5/99 – 39 civilians killed,
11 the attack on a bus at Pec – 3/5/99 – 17 civilians killed, 44 injured,
12 the attack at Korisa village – 13/5/99 – 48–87 civilians killed,
13 the attack on the Belgrade TV and Radio Station – 23/4/99 – 16 civilians killed,
14 the attack on the Chinese Embassy in Belgrade – 7/5/99 – three civilians killed, 15 injured,
15. attack on Nis City Centre and Hospital – 7/5/99 – 13 civilians killed, 60 injured,
16 attack on Istok Prison – 21/5/99 – at least 19 civilians killed,
17 attack on Belgrade Hospital – 20/5/99 – three civilians killed, several injured,
18 attack on Surdulica Sanatorium – 30/5/99 – 23 killed, many injured,
19 attack on journalists convoy Prizren-Brezovica Road – 31/5/99 – one civilian killed, three injured
20 attack on Belgrade Heating Plant – 4/4/99 – one killed,
21 attacks on Trade and Industry Targets.

Source: ICTY 2000

The Yugoslav government published a white book where, with the use of graphic evidence, they documented that NATO had attacked a total of 59 residential areas, 36 medical facilities, 44 educational centres, five sport and recreational amenities as well as dozens of economic facilities (Yugoslav Federal Ministry of Foreign Affairs, 1999). Together with the mistaken attack on the Chinese embassy, which caused a serious diplomatic stir with Beijing, one of the most controversial bombings was that on the Serbian TV and Radio Station [RTS] on 23 April 1999, where 16 civilians, workers of the channel, died. It was polemic for many reasons, not least because unlike most of the bombings listed above this one was deliberate and justified *a fortiori*. According to former British PM, Tony Blair, it was 'entirely justified' due to the fact that 'these television stations [RTS] are part of the apparatus of dictatorship and power of Milosevic' (cited by the *Guardian*, 1999). In a similar vein, Colonel Konrad Freytag, NATO's Chief of Public Information, stated the very day of the RTS bombing that the aim was 'to disrupt the national command network and to degrade the Federal Republic of Yugoslavia's propaganda apparatus; our forces struck at the regime leadership's ability to transmit their version of the news' (NATO 1999e).

The statement from Colonel Freytag is problematic in many respects. The fact that the reason given to justify the bombing of the RTS headquarters is to disable the channel from transmitting their 'version of the news' seems to be a direct attack on media pluralism. According to the ICTY Public Prosecutor Report, '[I]f the media is used to incite crimes, as

Figure 2.2 Bombed building of Radio Television Serbia (2017).

Source: Gisela Gorbalán.

in Rwanda, then it is a legitimate target. If it is merely disseminating propaganda to generate support for the war effort, it is not a legitimate target' (ICTY, 2000). NATO did not provide any evidence whatsoever that RTS was inciting hate crimes or calling for genocide, like the infamous Rwandan *Radio Télévision Libre des Mille Collines.* A prominent Serbian journalist confirms that the channel had propagandistic aims but was in no way comparable to the Rwandan case because there was no call for massacres or genocide against ethnic Albanians.[24] This journalist points out that the decision to bomb the RTS headquarters illustrates a turning point in the bombing campaign; whereas it was initially aimed at the Milošević administration, it gradually 'became a war against the entire population'.[25] This argument is also shared by Chomsky, who believes that Operation Allied Force shifted the focus towards targeting civilians because they were also perceived to be as integral part of the problem (1999, p. 93).

A second journalist, who worked for the channel in 1999, contends that the chief reason behind the bombing of RTS was the fact that the Serbian public broadcaster was the main source of images and videos of civilian deaths caused by NATO bombings, and, therefore such a dissenting voice represented a burden which had to be silenced at all costs.[26] In effect, RTS represented an enormous problem in terms of PR for Operation Allied Force because it was challenging the humanitarian discourse of the campaign; those images could be used as a counter narrative to discredit NATO with the argument that the organisation was 'saving civilians' by killing other civilians.

General Clark epitomises such preoccupations when he argues that

> [T]he fact was, the Serbs were on the ground and we weren't. They had an immediate advantage in knowing what happened when the bombs struck and, when the result was embarrassing to NATO, they could assure world media coverage faster than we could investigate it and explain it.... We found that there was usually an element of truth when they shone the spotlight on NATO's failures.... The consequence was an enormous burden on the alliance top leadership.
>
> (2001, p. 443)

The implications of bombing a target because it constitutes an 'enormous burden on the alliance top leadership' are indeed extremely serious. In a very devastating report for Operation Allied Force, Amnesty International concluded that the RTS headquarters could not be considered a legitimate military target and consequently 'the attack on the RTS headquarters violated the prohibition to attack civilian objects contained in Article 52 (I)[27] and therefore constitutes a war crime' (2000, p. 46).

To conclude, 20 years on, NATO's 78-day bombing campaign against Yugoslavia is far from being free of controversies and harsh critiques. In military terms, nevertheless, Operation Allied Force was a clear success as it achieved its major objectives. Perhaps the most important aim was, through the Kumanovo agreement, the withdrawal of the Yugoslav/Serbian security forces from Kosovo. A withdrawal, which on the one hand seems to have a permanent nature, as there is no indication that Kosovo will return to the *status quo ante*. On the other hand, such a troop withdrawal has substantial implications for the main theme of this book. As the next chapter will examine, the fact of the matter is that the Yugoslavian/Serbian government has not exerted control over its former province, losing the de facto sovereignty over the territory, since June 1999, that is, since the end of Operation Allied Force.

Notes

1 OSCE officer, author interview, undisclosed location, 15 August 2017; UNMIK officer, author interview, Pristina, 31 May 2014; UNMIK officer II, author interview, Mitrovica, 1 August 2012.
2 The *Guardian* reported in 2010 that Walker was supporting a Pan-Albanian nationalist party (Self-Determination, Vetëvendosje in Albanian) in Kosovo (Lewis, 2010).
3 See Chapter 1 for further details on the report.
4 OSCE officer, author interview, undisclosed location, 15 August 2017.
5 Ibid.
6 Dragiša Djoković, author interview, Mitrovica, 3 August 2017.
7 Ibid.
8 Earlier massacres of civilians committed by Yugoslavian security forces in areas of intense insurgent activities by the KLA such as Drenica and Gornje Obrinje (both in 1998) did not receive the same attention from the media nor policymakers. Similarly, KLA massacres of Serbian civilians, prior to the NATO intervention, such as Klečka (22 killed) or Lake Radonjić (34 bodies found) were largely ignored by the Western media.
9 The bodies of five additional alleged victims had been removed from the scene by family members, according to the OSCE (1999).
10 This position entails overall command of NATO military forces stationed in Europe.
11 As the article from the Finnish pathologists shows there was a single woman and a single under 15-year-old amongst the victims.
12 An example of this coercion can be found in Albright's response to the claim by British foreign secretary, Robin Cook, that he had encountered problems with British lawyers regarding the legality of waging war against Yugoslavia. Albright response was both laconic and sardonic: 'Get new lawyers' (cited by Glennon, 2002).
13 According to the Bahador study of U.S. TV networks (ABC, NBC, CBS, and CNN) in the Kosovo conflict, 86 per cent of American TV reports regarding Račak displayed a pro-Albanian framing (2007, pp. 88–89).
14 The Contact Group was a non-formalised group of states which met irregularly to discuss conflict developments in the former Yugoslavia. It was made up of six states: the United States, the United Kingdom, France, Germany, Italy and Russia.
15 U.S. Ambassador to Macedonia, Christopher Hill, EU Special Envoy for Kosovo, Wolfgang Petritsch, and Russian Ambassador, Boris Mayorsky.
16 It included Serbs, Albanians, Gora, Bosniaks, Turks, Roma and Ashkali.

17 This position is officially known as the British Minister for Defence Procurement.
18 In the end, the referendum never took place. The Unilateral Declaration of Independence (UDI) of February 2008 was proclaimed by the Kosovo Assembly in the absence of a referendum.
19 Some years earlier, in 1994 and 1995, NATO had engaged in air operations (Deny Flight and Deliberate Force) against the Army of Republika Srpska in Bosnia which were coordinated with and supported by the UN. Therefore, unlike in Kosovo, NATO's bombings in Bosnia did not constitute a unilateral illegal war against a sovereign state.
20 Dragiša Djoković, author interview, Mitrovica, 3 August 2017.
21 It is hard to determine how many fled to escape the conflict and how many fled as a result of a deliberate campaign of ethnic cleansing.
22 NATO's use of depleted uranium bombs and cluster bombs has also been controversial although it has been deemed as not illegal according to International Law because at the time of the bombing there was no treaty or convention prohibiting its use (ICTY, 2000). It has been reported, however, that since the end of the war, in June 1999, 200 people have been killed in Kosovo as a result of cluster bombs (Abrams, 2000).
23 Other sources within the U.S. administration, such as Deputy Secretary of Defense John Hamre, elevate the figure of 'unintended incidents' to 30 (HRW, 2000, p. 16).
24 Serbian journalist, author interview, Belgrade, 20 October 2017.
25 Ibid.
26 RTS journalist, author interview, Belgrade, 21 October 2017. This journalist claims that it was impossible that NATO didn't know that there would be workers in the RTS building because there were people working around the clock with uninterrupted broadcasting. The journalist recalls the dramatic situation of not knowing which colleagues were alive and which had perished.
27 Amnesty International refers to the 'Protocol Additional to the Geneva Conventions of 12 August 1949, and relating to the Protection of Victims of International Armed Conflicts (Protocol I), 8 June 1977'.

Bibliography

Abrams, F. (2000, 7 August). 'Britain "broke law with Kosovo cluster bombs"'. *Independent*. Retrieved from: www.independent.co.uk/news/uk/politics/britain-broke-law-with-kosovo-cluster-bombs-711028.html

B92 (2017, 12 May). 'Racak operation was legitimate, and flawless, commander says'. Retrieved from: www.b92.net/eng/news/politics.php?yyyy=2017&mm=05&dd=12&nav_id=101258

Bahador, B. (2007). *The CNN Effect in Action. How the News Media Pushed the West toward War in Kosovo*. New York: Palgrave Macmillan.

Bancroft, I. (2009, 24 March). 'Serbia's anniversary is a timely reminder'. *Guardian*. Retrieved from: www.theguardian.com/commentisfree/2009/mar/24/serbia-kosovo

Barry, J. (2000, 14 May). 'The Kosovo cover-up'. *Newsweek*. Retrieved from: www.newsweek.com/kosovo-cover-160273

Barthe, S. and David, C. (2007). 'Kosovo 1999: Clinton, Coercive Diplomacy, and the Use of Analogies in Decision Making'. *The Whitehead Journal of Diplomacy and International Relations*, 8(2): 85–102.

BBC (1999a, 16 January). 'Serbs say terrorists killed at Racak'. Retrieved from: http://news.bbc.co.uk/1/hi/world/monitoring/256392.stm

BBC (1999b, 19 January). 'Europe Pathologist: 'No Kosovo massacre'. Retrieved from: http://news.bbc.co.uk/1/hi/world/europe/258529.stm

BBC (2000, 12 March). 'Moral Combat: NATO at war'. Retrieved from: http://news.bbc.co.uk/hi/english/static/events/panorama/transcripts/transcript_12_03_00.txt

Bellamy, A. J. (2000). 'Lessons unlearned: Why coercive diplomacy failed at Rambouillet'. *International Peacekeeping*, 7(2): 95–114.

Bellamy, A. J. (2002). *Kosovo and International Society*. New York: Palgrave Macmillan.

Bellamy, A. J. and Griffin, S. (2002). 'OSCE peacekeeping: Lessons from the Kosovo Verification Mission'. *European Security*, 11(1): 1–26.

Bird, C. and Steele, J. (1999, 20 January). 'Race to get massacre evidence'. *Guardian*. Retrieved from: www.theguardian.com/world/1999/jan/20/jonathansteele

Bouckaert, P. (1999). *Week of Terror in Drenica: Humanitarian Law Violations in Kosovo*. New York: Human Rights Watch.

Bricmont, J. (2006). *Humanitarian Imperialism: Using Human Rights to Sell War*. New York: Monthly Review Press.

Burke, A. (2005). 'Against the new Internationalism'. *Ethics and International Affairs*, 19(2): 73–89.

Carpenter, T. G. (2000) 'Kosovo as an Omen: The Perils of the "New NATO"', in T. G. Carpenter (ed.), *NATO's Empty Victory* (pp. 171–183).

Carr, E. H. (1939/2001). *The twenty years' crisis. An Introduction to the Study of International Relations*. Palgrave: Basingstoke.

Chandler, D. C. (2001) 'The Road to Military Humanitarianism: How the Human Rights NGOs Shaped a New Humanitarian Agenda'. *Human Rights Quarterly*, 23(3): 678–700.

Chatelet, C. (1999, 21 January). 'Les morts de Racak ont-ils vraiment été massacrés froidement ?'. *Le Monde*. Retrieved from:

www.lemonde.fr/archives/article/1999/01/21/les-morts-de-racak-ont-ils-vraiment-ete-massacres-froidement_3533047_1819218.html?xtmc=les_morts_de_racak_ont_ils&xtcr=41

Chomsky, N. (1999). *The New Military Humanism. Lessons from Kosovo*. London: Pluto Press.

Chomsky, N. (2008). 'Humanitarian Imperialism: The New Doctrine of Imperial Right'. *Monthly Review*, 60(4). Retrieved from: https://monthlyreview.org/2008/09/01/humanitarian-imperialism-the-new-doctrine-of-imperial-right/

Clark, W. K. (2001). *Waging Modern War*. New York: Public Affairs.

CNN (1999, 20 June). 'President Clinton talks with "Late Edition"'. Retrieved from: http://edition.cnn.com/ALLPOLITICS/stories/1999/06/20/clinton.transcript/

Cordesman, A. H. (2000). *The Lessons and Non-Lessons of the Air and Missile Campaign in Kosovo*. Westport: Praeger Publishers.

Crawford, T. (2001). 'Pivotal Deterrence and the Kosovo War: Why the Holbrooke Agreement Failed'. *Political Science Quarterly*, 116(4): 499–523.

Daalder, I. H. and O'Hanlon, M. E. (2000). *Winning Ugly. NATO's war to save Kosovo*. Washington: The Brookings Institution.

Del Ponte, C. and C. Sudetic (2009). *Madame Prosecutor. Confrontations with Humanity's Worst Criminals and the Culture of Impunity*. New York: Other Press.

Djoković, D., author interview, Mitrovica, 3 August 2017.

Erlanger, S. (1998, 8 March). 'Albright Warns Serbs on Kosovo Violence'. *New York Times*. Retrieved from: www.nytimes.com/1998/03/08/world/albright-warns-serbs-on-kosovo-violence.html

Evans G. (2009). 'The Responsibility to Protect', in R. H. Cooper and J. V. Kohler (eds) *Responsibility to Protect* (pp. 15–29). New York: Palgrave Macmillan.

Fenrick, W. J. (2001). 'Targeting and Proportionality during the NATO Bombing Campaign against Yugoslavia'. *European Journal of International Law*, 12(3): 489–502.

Gellman, B. (1999, 18 April). 'Slaughter in Racak Changed Kosovo Policy'. *Washington Post*. Retrieved from: www.washingtonpost.com/wp-srv/national/longterm/policy041899.htm

Gibbs, D. (2009). *First Do No Harm: Humanitarian Intervention and the Destruction of Yugoslavia*. Nashville: Vanderbilt University Press.

Gibbs, D. (2015). 'The Principle of "First Do No Harm"', in R. Mac Ginty and J. H. Peterson (eds) *The Routledge Companion to Humanitarian Action* (pp. 109–119). Abingdon: Routledge.

Gilbert, J. (2000). 'Examination of witness (Questions 1080–1092)'. *House of Commons*. Retrieved from: https://publications.parliament.uk/pa/cm199900/–cmselect/cmdfence/347/0062005.htm

Glennon, M. (1999, 21 November). 'How War Left the Law Behind'. *New York Times*. Retrieved from: www.nytimes.com/2002/11/21/opinion/how-war-left-the-law-behind.html

Guardian. (1999, 23 April) '23 April: Nato defends TV attack'. Retrieved from: www.theguardian.com/world/1999/apr/23/balkans17

Habermas, J. (2005). 'Interpreting the fall of a monument', in M. Pensky (ed.) *Globalizing Critical Theory* (pp. 19–26).

Hamzaj, B. (2000). *A Narrative About War and Freedom (Dialog with the Commander Ramush Haradinaj)*. Pristina: Zeri.

Havel, V. (1999). 'Kosovo and the End of the Nation-State'. *The New York Review of Books*, 46(10).

Hehir, A. (2008). *Humanitarian Intervention after Kosovo: Iraq, Darfur and the Record of Global Civil Society*. London: Palgrave Macmillan.

Hehir, A. (2012) *The Responsibility to Protect. Rhetoric, Reality and the Future of Humanitarian Intervention*. London: Palgrave Macmillan.

Herman, E. and Peterson, D. (2000). 'CNN: Selling Nato's War Globally' in P. Hammond and E. Herman (eds) *Degraded Capability: The Media and the Kosovo Crisis* (pp. 111–122). London: Pluto Press.

Hoffman, G. (1999, 12 May). 'Wie Deutschland in den Krieg geriet'. *Die Zeit*. Retrieved from: www.zeit.de/1999/20/199920.krieg_.xml

Human Rights Watch (2000). *Civilian Deaths in the NATO Air Campaign*. New York: Human Rights Watch.

Human Rights Watch (2001). *War Crimes in Kosovo*. New York: Human Rights Watch.

Hyde-Price, A. (2008). 'A "tragic actor"? A realist perspective on "ethical power Europe"'. *International Affairs*, 84(1): 29–44.

ICTY (2000). 'Final Report to the Prosecutor by the Committee Established to Review the nato Bombing Campaign against the Federal Republic of Yugoslavia'. Retrieved from: www.icty.org/en/press/final-report-prosecutor-committee-established-review-nato-bombing-campaign-against-federal

ICTY (2003). 'Case IT-02-54, *Prosecutor* v. *Slobodan Milošević*', pp. 17704–17821.

ICTY (2008). 'Case IT-05-87-T, *Prosecutor* v. *Milan Milutinović et al.*, pp. 21837–21463. Retrieved from: http://icr.icty.org/LegalRef/CMSDocStore/Public/English/Final Brief/NotIndexable/IT-05-87/MSC6654R0000227249.pdf

Independent International Commission on Kosovo (2000). *The Kosovo Report; Conflict, International Response, Lessons Learned.* Oxford: Oxford University Press.

Johnstone, D. (2002). *Fools' Crusade. Yugoslavia, NATO and Western Delusions.* London: Pluto Press.

Judah, T. (1999, 7 February). 'Nato deadline on peace deal in Kosovo'. *Guardian.* Retrieved from: www.theguardian.com/world/1999/feb/07/balkans

Kaiser, R. and McGuire, M. (1999, 23 April). 'Blair unveils bold intervention doctrine'. *Chicago Tribune.* Retrieved from: http://articles.chicagotribune.com/1999-04-23/news/9904230097_1_blair-third-world-debt-cold-war

Keegan, J. (1999, 6 June). 'Please Mister Blair never take such risk again'. *Sunday Telegraph.* Retrieved from: www.airforcemag.com/MagazineArchive/Documents/2009/December%202009/1209keeperfull.pdf

Krieger, H. (2001). *The Kosovo Conflict and International Law: An Analytical Documentation 1974–1999.* Cambridge: Cambridge University Press.

Krstić-Brano, B. (2004). *Kosovo. Facing the Court of History.* New York: Humanity Books.

Lambeth, B.S. (2001). *NATO's Air War for Kosovo. A Strategic and Operational Assessment.* Santa Monica: RAND Corporation.

Layne, C. (2000). 'Miscalculations and Blunders Lead to War' in Carpenter, T. G. (ed.) *NATO's Empty Victory. A Post-mortem on the Balkan War* (pp. 11–20). Washington DC: Cato Institute.

Le Monde Diplomatique (1999). 'Interim Agreement for Peace and Self-Government in Kosovo'. Retrieved from: www.monde-diplomatique.fr/cahier/kosovo/rambouillet-en

Lewis, P. (2010, 12 December.). 'Former US diplomat backs Albanian nationalist in Kosovo elections'. *Guardian.* Retrieved from: www.theguardian.com/world/2010/dec/12/former-diplomat-backs-albanian-nationalist

NATO (1999a, 28 January). 'Statement to the Press by NATO Secretary General, Dr. Javier Solana'. NATO Press Release (99)11. Retrieved from: www.nato.int/docu/pr/1999/p99-011e.htm

NATO (1999b, 30 January). 'Statement by the North Atlantic Council on Kosovo'. Press Release (99)12. Retrieved from: www.nato.int/docu/pr/1999/p99-012e.htm

NATO (1999c, 23 March). 'Press Statement by Dr. Javier Solana, Secretary General of NATO'. Press Release (99)40. Retrieved from: www.nato.int/docu/pr/1999/p99-040e.htm

NATO (1999d, 24 March). 'Statement to the Press by NATO Secretary General, Dr. Javier Solana'. Press Release (99)41. Retrieved from: www.nato.int/docu/pr/1999/p99-041e.htm

NATO (1999e, 23 April). 'Press Conference by NATO Spokesman, Jamie Shea and Colonel Konrad Freytag, SHAPE'. Retrieved from: www.nato.int/kosovo/press/p990423l.htm

New York Times (1999, 20 March) 'Clinton Voices Anger and Compassion at Serbian Intransigence on Kosovo'. Retrieved from: www.nytimes.com/1999/03/20/world/clinton-voices-anger-and-compassion-at-serbian-intransigence-on-kosovo.html

Norton-Taylor, R. (2000, 9 March). 'How the Serb Army escaped NATO'. *Guardian.* Retrieved from: www.theguardian.com/world/2000/mar/09/balkans1

O'Connor, M. (1998, 29 October). 'Despite a Truce, Kosovo Albanians Dig New Graves and Vow Revenge'. *New York Times.* Retrieved from: www.nytimes.com/

1998/10/29/world/despite-a-truce-kosovo-albanians-dig-new-graves-and-vow-revenge.html
Office of the High Representative (1999a, 29 January). 'Chairman's Conclusions'. Retrieved from: www.ohr.int/?ohr_archive=chairmans-conclusions-london-29-january-1999-2
Office of the High Representative (1999b, 23 February). 'Rambouillet Accords: Co-Chairmen's Conclusions'. Retrieved from: www.ohr.int/?ohr_archive=contact-group-statement-rambouillet-23-february-1999
OSCE (Organisation for Security and Co-operation in Europe) (1999). 'Kosovo/Kosova as seen as told: an analysis of the human rights findings of the OSCE Kosovo Verification Mission October 1998 to June 1999'. *OSCE Office for Democratic Institutions and Human Rights*. Retrieved from: www.osce.org/odihr/17772?download=true
OSCE officer, author interview, undisclosed location, 15 August 2017.
Parenti, M. (2000). *To Kill a Nation: The Attack on Yugoslavia*. London: Verso.
Perlez, J. (1999, 24 February). 'Kosovo Albanians, in Reversal, Say They Will Sign Peace Pact'. *New York Times*. Retrieved from: www.nytimes.com/1999/02/24/world/kosovo-albanians-in-reversal-say-they-will-sign-peace-pact.html
Pilger, J. (1999, 17 May). 'Revealed: the amazing NATO plan, tabled at Rambouillet, to occupy Yugoslavia'. *New Statesman*. Retrieved from: www.newstatesman.com/node/149146
Radio Liberty (2000). *Balkan Report*, 4(30). Retrieved from: www.rferl.org/a/1341208.html
Rainio, J., Lalu, K. and Penttilä, A. (2001). 'Independent forensic autopsies in an armed conflict: investigation of the victims from Račak, Kosovo'. *Forensic Science International*, 116: 171–185.
RTS journalist, author interview, Belgrade, 21 October 2017.
Scolino, E. and Bronner, E. (1999, 18 April). 'How a President, Distracted by Scandal, Entered Balkan War'. *New York Times*. Retrieved from: https://partners.nytimes.com/library/world/europe/041899kosovo-recap1.html
Serbian journalist, author interview, Belgrade, 20 October 2017.
Shue, H. (2004). 'Limiting sovereignty', in J. Welsh (ed.) *Humanitarian Intervention and International Relations* (pp. 11–29). Oxford: Oxford University Press.
UNHCR (1999a). 'UNHCR Kosovo Crisis Update – 1 April 1999'. Retrieved from: https://reliefweb.int/report/albania/unhcr-kosovo-crisis-update-1-apr-1999
UNHCR (1999b). 'UNHCR Kosovo Crisis Update – 11 June 1999'. Retrieved from:
United Nations Security Council (1998). 'Resolution 1199: The Situation in Kosovo (FRY)'. Retrieved from: http://unscr.com/en/resolutions/1199
United Nations Security Council (1999a). 'Statement on Kosovo issued by the Minister for Foreign Affairs of the Russian Federation and the Secretary of State of the United States of America in Moscow, on 26 January 1999'. Retrieved from: http://repository.un.org/bitstream/handle/11176/35344/S_1999_77-EN.pdf?sequence=3&isAllowed=y
United Nations Security Council (1999b). 'Statement by the President of the Council' Retrieved from: www.un.org/en/ga/search/view_doc.asp?symbol=S/PRST/1999/5
UNMIK officer, author interview, Pristina, 31 May 2014.
UNMIK officer II, author interview, Mitrovica, 1 August 2012.
U.S. Government Publishing Office (1999, 24 March). 'Address to the Nation on Airstrikes Against Serbian Targets in the Federal Republic of Yugoslavia'.

Retrieved from: www.gpo.gov/fdsys/pkg/WCPD-1999-03-29/pdf/WCPD-1999-03-29-Pg516.pdf

Smith, J. (1999, 17 March). 'Kosovo attack report issued'. *Washington Post*. Retrieved from: www.washingtonpost.com/wp-srv/inatl/daily/march99/racak17.htm

Sperling, J. and Webber, M. (2009). 'From Kosovo to Kabul'. *International Affairs*, 85(3): 491–511.

Walker, W. G. (2000). 'OSCE verification experiences in Kosovo: November 1998–June 1999'. *The International Journal of Human Rights*, 4(3–4): 127–142.

Waltz, K. N. (2000). 'Structural Realism after the cold war'. *International Security*, 25 (1): 8–41

Weller, M. (1999). 'The Rambouillet Conference on Kosovo'. *International Affairs*, 75(2): 211–251.

Wheeler, N. J. (2001). 'Review article Humanitarian intervention after Kosovo: emergent norm, moral duty or the coming anarchy?' *International Affairs*, 77(1): 113–128.

Williamson, C. (2014). 'Statement by the Chief Prosecutor of the Special Investigative Task Force, 29 July 2015'. *Special Investigative Task Force*. Retrieved from: http://sitf.eu/images/Statement/Statement_of_the_Chief_Prosecutor_of_the_SITF_EN.pdf

Wolff, S. (2003). 'The limits of Non-Military International Intervention: A Case Study of the Kosovo Conflict', in F. Bieber and Ž. Daskalovski (eds) *Understanding the War in Kosovo* (pp. 77–98). London: Frank Cass Publishers.

Yugoslav Federal Ministry of Foreign Affairs. (1999). NATO Crimes in Serbia (Yugoslavia): Documentary Evidence. Belgrade: Službeni glasnik.

3 Quasi-independence

The political and territorial impact of humanitarian intervention

Operation Allied Force was a success in the sense that it achieved its major military objective. The key questions faced by victors in Kosovo, arguably like in any other belligerent conflict, were: what to do next, how to handle such military success? As the geopolitical genie had escaped from the bottle, even more daunting matters came forward. How can a *defensive* organisation with barely any experience in post-conflict management deal with such situation? How will international actors interact with local indigenous partners? What kind of territorial solution will be proposed to a territory where a territorially-driven war has literally just ended? With such daunting challenges, it seemed clear that the political architecture was going to be much more problematic and complex than the military victory. This chapter will scrutinise some of these challenges arguing that, indeed, the post-conflict situation in Kosovo has been characterised by bumps on the road. Twenty years on and despite the enormous international efforts, both diplomatic and financial, some of these *enjeux* are still unsettled.

Post intervention idiosyncrasies

Towards a new scenario: Resolution 1244

On 9 June 1999, President Milošević agreed through the Kumanovo Agreement[1] that the Serbian/Yugoslavian security forces would withdraw from Kosovo and that an international security force, that is NATO's mission named as KFOR, would deploy throughout the territory of this Serbian province (NATO, 1999). Arguably, this represented a downright capitulation by the Yugoslavian President. This retreat had been interpreted by former British Defence Minister and former NATO Secretary General, George Robertson, as the acceptance by Milošević that NATO was willing to do 'whatever was necessary to ensure compliance' with the demands of the transatlantic organisation (1999, p. 5). It was, in other words, the ultimate triumph of coercive diplomacy. His compliance, however, could also be explained by factors related to internal political weakness, due to the fact that he had been losing the support of his pundits and allies after over a decade in power. Needless to say, this erosion of power was exacerbated by 78 days of uninterrupted bombing which resulted in the devastation of the Yugoslavian economy and the destruction of its infrastructure, international isolation etc. This political weakness is illustrated by the fact that President Milošević was overthrown in October 2000 by a popular uprising supported with U.S. and European funds,[2] a year after Operation Allied Force terminated.

Interestingly, the conditions laid out in Kumanovo were not as harsh as those proposed during the Rambouillet negotiations some months earlier: Kumanovo called for the deployment of NATO forces through Kosovo, not the entire Yugoslavian territory, like Appendix B from Rambouillet stipulated. In brief, what is particularly striking in this case is that the conditions of a negotiation were far more punitive than those of a capitulation. This is perhaps accounted for by the argument, developed in the previous chapter, that Rambouillet was designed to fail from its very inception.

The most important provisions of the Kumanovo agreement were legalised via the renowned UNSC Resolution 1244, which embodied the 'spirit' of the military accords. This resolution sets up the legal basis for both NATO's presence in Kosovo as well as for the establishment of a UN-led interim administration (UNSC, 1999a). In Weberian terms, it could be argued that Resolution 1244 recognises that 'the monopoly of the legitimate use of physical force' within Kosovo is going to be enjoyed by NATO and the UN Mission in Kosovo (UNMIK).

The consequence of this is two-fold. On the one hand, it denies the Federal Republic of Yugoslavia de facto sovereignty over Kosovo and this is sealed with a UN resolution that can only be terminated with the consent of permanent members of the Security Council. In fact, that means that NATO's foreign military presence will only be finished when the U.S., France and the UK consent to do so because they have the power to veto a hypothetical 'end of the mission' in Kosovo at the Security Council. On the other hand, it also implies that these two international forces, UNMIK and KFOR, were not subordinated to any 'indigenous authorities' led by Kosovo Albanians (Bellamy, 2001, p. 46).

While it is true that the resolution contemplates the creation and 'development of provisional institutions for democratic and autonomous self-government' (UNSC, 1999a), there was little evidence to believe that, at any point, these local institutions would be hierarchically superior to the ones imposed by the 'International Community'. Some authors have stressed that after UNSC 1244, Kosovo had become a UN protectorate, or even more explicitly, a 'UN colony' (Carpenter, 2000; Bellamy, 2001; Yannis, 2004; Perritt, 2010). Yannis, for instance, claims that the powers allocated to UNMIK are more in line with 'extensive mandates of UN trusteeships and international protectorates' than with traditional peacekeeping missions (2004, p. 71).

These power tensions have dominated the political debate in Kosovo over the past two decades. As this chapter will examine, the most crucial turning point in these disputes over who calls the shots in this territory occurred in February 2008 when Kosovo's autonomous assembly declared unilateral independence. A key question is whether the possibility of independence was contemplated by international actors or if it was somehow incorporated in UNSC 1244. This resolution, on the one hand, reproduces the euphemistic and ambiguous language of Rambouillet.[3] It intends to promote 'the establishment, pending a final settlement, of substantial autonomy and self-government in Kosovo' (UNSC, 1999a). This 'final settlement' reference could – with a vivid imagination – be interpreted as a clumsy, distorted substitute for independence. This is, however, at least debatable and at most tremendously unspecific. Instead, the recurrent term in the resolution is 'substantial autonomy' or 'substantial self-government'. More importantly, the resolution insists, up to three times, in the necessity to uphold 'the principles of sovereignty and territorial integrity of the Federal Republic of Yugoslavia' (UNSC, 1999a).

The tentative conclusion is that the Security Council aimed to solve the crisis in Kosovo with the old formula of everything but a state; that is, a generous offer of self-government but without contemplating the option of self-determination or independence. In addition, the resolution also demanded the demilitarisation of the KLA, a group perceived by many ethnic Albanians as heroes and liberators. It appeared as if the wishes of Kosovo's secessionists had not been taken into account by the UN, which had opted to support a solution which imposed an international protectorate regime while maintaining the territorial status quo. As the 'Report of the International Commission on Intervention and State Sovereignty (ICISS)', which is considered the embryonic document behind the principle of the Responsibility to Protect (R2P), puts it: 'Yugoslavia could be said to have temporarily had its sovereignty over Kosovo suspended, though it has not lost it *de jure*' (ICISS, 2001, p. 44). It is important not to forget that Operation Allied Force had been framed as a humanitarian intervention with the ultimate aim of protecting civilians at risk and, consequently, the operation had no territorial or geopolitical goals. At least, not officially. In fact, the ICISS does remind that the objective of operations aimed at protecting civilians 'is not to change constitutional arrangements, but to protect them' and, as such, these types of interventions shall not undermine sovereignty but instead they must 'sustain forms of government compatible with the sovereignty of the state in which the enforcement has occurred' (ICISS, 2001, p. 44). As this chapter will explain, in the Kosovo case, the sovereignty of the state was, in the end, violated and such violation was supported principally by the states which conducted the humanitarian intervention.

In simple terms, Yugoslavia got a carrot and a stick with its capitulation and the subsequent UNSC resolution 1244. The stick was the fact that it would have to accept an international foreign military (KFOR) and civilian (UNMIK) presence for an indeterminate period of time. It also got the carrot that, at least *de jure*, its sovereignty would not be compromised and its territorial integrity would be respected. While the stick turned out to be solid; the carrot, in light of the territorial developments occurred in Kosovo since 2008, proved to be rather contingent.

Power vacuum on the ground and reverse ethnic cleansing

The withdrawal of the Yugoslav/Serbian army and most state institutions from nearly all areas of Kosovo[4] had an immediate consequence: a power *vacuum* in Kosovo. This power void caused situations of chaos that the recently deployed KFOR forces and UNMIK officers were simply unable to control. More specifically, groups of ethnic Albanians, it has been claimed associated with the KLA insurgent group, engaged in a campaign against Serbs, other minorities and Albanians labelled as collaborators, which included robbery, beatings, forced expulsions and murder. According to Perritt, this occurred under the watch of KFOR soldiers (2010, p. 53). Dragiša Djoković, a former Serbian MP from Mitrovica, goes even further and accuses KFOR of being not only bystanders but also assistants of ethnic cleansing: 'they [FKOR] came here to enable Kosovo Albanian revenge, even though their mission claimed otherwise'.[5] Djoković illustrates his point with the example of Svinjare, a Serbian enclave which became a ghost town after being destroyed by Albanian extremists in 2004, where KFOR troops, according to his version, brought tracks and told residents to leave, instead of protecting them.[6]

According to the ICTY Public Prosecutor, Carla del Ponte, in many areas of Kosovo KLA commanders 'were the only law' after the intervention (2009, p. 275). The Humanitarian Law Centre estimates that in the period between KFOR's deployment, on 12 June 1999, and December 2000 593 non-Albanians were abducted in Kosovo – in nearly half of the cases there is evidence that the KLA or some of its members had been involved. This organisation also confirms that allegations that the KLA had developed a prison system, which included detention centres located in public and private buildings as well as in the open, were confirmed by witnesses (Humanitarian Law Center, 2001). Additionally, up to 1,108 people were killed or kidnapped during the 18 months subsequent to the conflict, most of them Serbs (752) and members or non-Albanian ethnic minorities (Humanitarian Law Center, 2012). Del Ponte contends that these actions went beyond 'post-conflict vengeance' (2009, p. 276).

The brutality conducted by either the KLA or gangs of ethnic Albanians in the aftermath of the conflict was unambiguously condemned by former Kosovo MP, editor and influential Kosovo Albanian thinker Veton Surroi who stated that:

> I cannot hide my shame to discover that, for the first time in our history, we, Kosovo Albanians, are also capable of such monstrous acts.... It is the organised and systematic intimidation of all Serbs simply because they are Serbs.... Such attitudes are fascist.
>
> (1999)

It could be argued that with the departure of the Serbian/Yugoslav security forces, Serbs were exposed to violence and reversed ethnic cleansing. For William Ortiz, a UNMIK officer, the aim of Albanian extremists in the anarchic lawless context after Operation Allied Force was very clear: to rid Kosovo of Serbs.[7] The UNHCR estimates that around 230,000 Serbs, Roma and members of other minorities fled Kosovo after June 1999 (2005, p. 29). That figure is especially alarming, taken into consideration that it represents approximately 60 per cent of the pre-war population of Serbs and Roma. The vast majority of these IDP's/refugees[8] have, as of 2018, not returned to Kosovo.

Organisations such as Human Rights Watch have blamed the KLA for the violence against minorities and, similarly to Del Ponte, have suggested that the violence was more than mere revenge since it had political/territorial motives aimed at expelling 'non-ethnic Albanians in order to better justify an independent state' (HRW, 2001). Likewise, Amnesty International has denounced not only the intimidation, attacks and assassinations of people from minorities but also the impunity for the perpetrators which encourages further crimes (2003). Sladjana Miletić, an ethnic Serb and a former internally displaced person, provides a direct account of such crimes committed by people affiliated with the KLA. She was forced to abandon her village in Western Kosovo shortly after the Kumanovo Agreement was signed:

> Between 15–23rd of June [1999] the entire village left. We put everything we had in tractors and cars and left because of insecurity. The whole village was burned down. If we had stayed ... we would not be alive. We knew for a fact that KFOR would not help us after what happened in Priština, Prizren, South Mitrovica.... We were afraid and sad but we had a feeling that we would come back. At the beginning, we thought it would take us a month. We returned in September 2004. We did so because this is our land but we still suffer constant harassment. My husband does not sleep at night in order to protect the house and the village.[9]

It is therefore possible to conclude that the international organisations in charge of the security framework in Kosovo, KFOR and UNMIK, had failed to protect fleeing civilians escaping persecution as a result of their ethnic background. Ironically, this had been the *casus belli* that prompted Operation Allied Force in the first place.

Figure 3.1 Serbian house burned out in Western Kosovo (2017).
Source: Gisela Gorbalán (2017).

The challenges of UNMIK's institutional build-up

In this context, UNMIK had the arduous task of building institutions which were initially designed to be Kosovo's future self-government institutions, in theory within the frame of the Federal Republic of Yugoslavia. This institution-building process had to be initiated from scratch and, similarly to Bosnia, it was eminently top-down and developed by internationals. As explained above, 1244 did not provide many details about the particularities of the UN-led interim administration. Such details began flourishing promptly with, for instance, a report for the Secretary General, published two days after the resolution established that the division of powers between the different international organisations would be divided in four 'pillars':

a Interim civil administration: the United Nations;
b Humanitarian affairs: the Office of the United Nations High Commissioner for Refugees (UNHCR);[10]
c Institution-building: the Organization for Security and Cooperation in Europe (OSCE);
d Reconstruction: the European Union.

(UNSC, 1999b)

This division of responsibilities, which has never been easy to implement in practice due to institutional clashes and overlaps, is not balanced whatsoever. The reason for this is that the 'interim administration', controlled by UNMIK carried much more weight than the other institutions/responsibilities. They did control the International Civilian Police Unit, International Border Police Unit, civilian affairs functions (education, health, budget, etc.) as well as the judicial system (UNSC, 1999b). In other words, UNMIK was in charge of the executive, the legislative and the judiciary in Kosovo and that inevitably created a concentration of power and a potential lack of accountability and checks and balances. Bearing in mind such elements, it is not far-fetched to determine that UNMIK was Kosovo's de facto government. An administration which, apropos, had enjoyed an enormous concentration of power.

Additionally, UNMIK had to develop the provisional institutions of self-government and, at a certain point, transfer power to them. Like in other UN missions, the person in charge of the mission would be the Special Representative of the Secretary-General (SRSG). The powers of the SRSG, at least initially, could only be categorised as absolute due to the fact that it was able to regulate, 'change, repeal or suspend existing laws' as well as 'to appoint any person to perform functions in the interim civil administration in Kosovo, including the judiciary' and, of course, remove that person from office (UNSC, 1999c, p. 9).

At any rate, it is fair to say that the UN was given a prodigious task which entailed enormous and multifaceted challenges. One of the chief problems was the existence of parallel structures of power. Such parallel institutions existed in Albanian dominated areas, where civil leader Ibrahim Rugova and the KLA operated power structures, officially named the Provisional Government of Kosova (PGK), which enjoyed more popular support than UNMIK. In Serbian populated areas, particularly in the north, the newly created UNMIK structures were in competition with Yugoslavian state institutions, which at that time included the judiciary, local political elites, the health service, education and even some sorts of informal security structures.

The SRSG Bernard Kouchner (1999–2001) pointed out that the mission was not taking place in a post-conflict context but instead in a scenario of low-intensity-conflict (UNSC, 2000a, p. 3). Further complications related to Kouchner's assertion include the fact that the mission had to be conducted in a milieu of inter-ethnic tensions and hatred, a recent governmental policy of ethnic cleansing, destruction caused by the war and the legacy of a socialist economy (Pula, 2003, p. 199). It is possible to add to the list additional problems such as the absence of a liberal-democratic political culture, without which, it makes the endeavour of establishing a democratic regime rather difficult.

UNMIK, if it intended to govern with any efficiency, had to inevitably win the hearts and minds of the people (Perritt, 2010, p. 62), or rather the

Figure 3.2 UNMIK map.

Source: UN Geospatial Information Section.

elites. According to Pula, UNMIK pursued a wide range of strategies to ensure the success of the mission, namely; 'co-option of local elites; economic co-option of the local population ... strategically limited use of coercion' (2003, p. 204). In particular, the co-option of elites presented yet a supplementary challenge. Not least, because not few members of those elites had blood – fresh blood to be precise – on their hands. Carla del Ponte is particularly critical in that regard claiming that UNMIK was being self-deceitful for 'believing that they could rely upon former KLA leaders with dubious backgrounds to help develop functioning institutions and the rule of law' (2009, p. 280).

Notwithstanding del Ponte's legitimate point, the key question is: what was the alternative? An international protectorate which would completely ignore relevant local actors? In that regard, Finn Reske-Nielsen a Danish diplomat with 36 years of experience working for the UN, including several peacekeeping missions in Africa and Asia, asserts that 'without the cooperation and buy-in of the relevant national actors, UN peace operations cannot succeed as there must be a minimum of national ownership for the interventions of the international community to be sustainable'.[11] Co-operation with local actors involves dilemmas which are, in effect, hard to resolve for intervening international organisations.

Two OSCE senior officers working in Kosovo, interviewed on the condition of anonymity, have highlighted the challenges for international organisations in the particular case of Kosovo. The first officer has justified the co-operation with former members of the KLA on the basis of the impossibility of acting differently bearing in mind 'the local idiosyncrasies' and arguing that they had the potential of 'destabilising the whole project' if they were antagonised excessively, pointing out that 'the hard liners [of the KLA] were Kosovo's biggest threat'.[12] The second officer, taking a more critical stand, complains about these ties, labelling them as a mistake, which literally forced the international community to 'turn a blind eye' on the fact that 'we were collaborating with individuals or with an organisation which had been involved in all sorts of criminal activities'.[13]

In the case of UNMIK, there have been periods where the collaboration with former KLA militants was very intense, including the forging of personal ties. One of the evidences of these strong links comes from an official statement of the former head of the UN mission (2004–2006), Søren Jessen-Petersen. Jessen-Petersen stated following the arrest of KLA commander and Kosovo's PM (2004–2005 and 2017–) Ramush Haradinaj that

> I cannot hide the fact that his departure will leave a big gap. Thanks to Ramush Haradinaj's dynamic leadership, strong commitment and vision, Kosovo is today closer than ever before to achieving its aspirations in settling its future status. Personally, I am saddened to no longer be working with a close partner and friend.
>
> (UNMIK, 2005)

Del Ponte deemed outrageous that the head of a UN mission was taking sides with someone accused of war crimes in a case being brought to the International Court of Justice, a UN tribunal, and indignantly asks: '[H]ow can the rule of law be upheld when senior UNMIK officials give such open support and succor to someone indicted for the most serious crimes under international law?'[14] (2009, pp. 300–301). It would be inaccurate, however, to present the relationship between UNMIK and local Albanian actors as ideal or free of trouble. In fact, on many occasions the collaboration between UNMIK and local actors was marred by difficulties and controversy. To express this simply, for secessionists what UNMIK was proposing was generally seen as 'too little too late'. In contrast, for Serbian authorities and most Kosovo Serbs 'it went too far'.

Last, the mission was not immune to geopolitical rifts. One of the common accusations, in particular by Russian diplomats and policymakers, is that the leaders of the mission were biased, were deviating from UNSC Resolution 1244[15] and had a territorial agenda, namely supporting Kosovo's independence. As early as September 2000, Sergey Lavrov, at that time Russian Ambassador to the UN, directly accused Kouchner of preaching his own views and calling for Kosovo's independence (UNSC, 2000a, p. 9). Similar concerns were shared by Chinese diplomats who warned that '[A]ny course of action designed to steer Kosovo towards independence is dangerous and illegal' (UNSC, 2000a, p. 13). In response to these accusations, former UNMIK SRSG Søren Jessen-Petersen, categorically denied that the mission had a political agenda.[16] UNMIK's neutrality, or at least the neutrality of its cadre, remains debatable to say the least, particularly given the fact that Jessen-Petersen contended that 'independence was the only way out if you wanted peace and stability in Kosovo and Europe' and discloses that 'our [UNMIK] actions were status neutral, our hopes were not'.[17]

Despite all the critiques and formidable challenges, the mission in Kosovo has been described as the 'best managed of the U.S. post-Cold War ventures in nation-building' (Dobbins *et al.*, 2003, p. 126). Ironically, it could be asked whether this fact tells us more about Kosovo's success or about the profound failure of other 'ventures'. If anything, UNMIK avoided a return to war, built a relatively functioning legal-institutional framework and managed to gradually decrease the number of killings in Kosovo (Lemay-Hébert, 2013, p. 92).

The Provisional Institutions of Self-Government

It could be argued that the first institution developed by UNMIK, out of scratch and out of necessity, was the Kosovo Police Force (KPF), shortly after its deployment. Such institution had different origins from the rest and it was, at least until 2008, 'under the authority of the SRSG and under the supervision of UNMIK Police' (UNMIK, 2001).

The first somehow successful attempt to establish bridges between UNMIK and the local community in order to engage the latter in the governance process was the Interim Administrative Council (IAC). The logic was based on a *quid pro quo*: local leaders would dissolve the parallel institutions – 'all other Kosovo structures of an executive, legislative or judicial nature shall cease to exist' (UNMIK, 2000a) – and, in exchange, they would be included in the UN-supported structures governing Kosovo. The protagonists from the ethnic Albanian side were all familiar faces: Rugova, Qosja and Thaçi.[18] They were not only the leaders from the main political parties in Kosovo, they were also the men who had represented the Kosovo Albanian delegation at Rambouillet. The presence of Kosovo Serbs, who had a reserved seat, was intermittent as they viewed this new institution with hesitancy and even hostility (Brand, 2003, p. 16).

From the very beginning, territorial issues, labelled as 'cantonisation', were present in the discussions. The concept, which was roughly inspired by previous plans of 'cantonisation' of Serbian municipalities in Bosnia, was based on the idea of recognising a high degree of autonomy for Serb-dominated municipalities. Whereas for Serbs it was some sort of precondition for further dialogue and collaboration, for ethnic Albanians it constituted a 'red line' that they were not willing to accept. For UNMIK it was a burden which had the potential of making the conflict and, in turn, governance intractable. As a result, and perhaps for the sake of stability, the 'cantonisation' project was ruled out by UNMIK.

The IAC went a bit further than similar structures[19] but at the end of the day it was purely a consultative organ. Its powers were limited to making recommendations to the SRSG and to 'propose policy guidelines' (UNMIK, 2000a). Together with other structures, the IAC was under the umbrella of the Joint Interim Administrative Structure, which integrated all institutions which had been perceived by UNMIK as 'parallel structures'. All this institutional assemblage was short-lived. Sixteen months after these institutions had officially entered into force, they were replaced with a new framework: the Provisional Institutions of Self-Government (PISG).

The transfer of power to local institutions had several *raisons d'être*, as it were. For starters, such transfer was a provision in resolution 1244 (UNSC, 1999a) and consequently it ought to be done. Second, it was in accordance to the wishes of the overwhelming majority of Kosovo Albanians. Third, it allowed UNMIK to address the problem and recurrent critique of power concentration. After tense and uneasy negotiations and compromises between different international and local actors, the newly appointed SRSG, Hans Haekkerup, signed the regulation '[O]n a Constitutional Framework for provisional self-government in Kosovo' (UNMIK, 2001).

The first striking aspect of this 'Constitutional Framework' is the fact that it is semantically paradoxical: despite the name of the document, it did not include any provision for a Kosovo Constitution. This was a highly contested matter which provoked that, key figures such as Thaçi, refused to support it. It did include, however, the development of fundamental institutions, the most important of which are the following: Assembly; President of Kosovo; Government; Courts (UNMIK, 2001). The framework led to the first post-intervention elections in Kosovo, under the UNMIK framework and circumventing Belgrade. The crux of the elections was to allow

UNMIK to gradually transfer power to these newly created PISG (UNSC, 2002, p. 3).

It should be noted that those institutions were not independent in any way or form from UNMIK; in fact, they were subordinated to it. Such dependence or curtailed sovereignty is epitomised even at the symbolic level: '[T]he Provisional Institutions of Self-Government shall use only such symbols as are or as may be set forth in UNMIK legislation' (UNMIK, 2001). Nonetheless, what is remarkable about such institutions is that they were independent from Belgrade; the Federal Republic of Yugoslavia (and later Serbia) had no influence whatsoever over them. In addition, unlike Resolution 1244, the document does not include any reference to the FRY and this is not a minor detail, at least in terms of territorial effects. Instead, the Constitutional Framework did suggest, in a very subtle fashion, the possibility of European integration when it pledged to adapt the Kosovo legislation to facilitate 'closer economic, social and other ties between the people of Kosovo and other Europeans' (UNMIK, 2001). It could be argued that the PISG were autonomous vis-à-vis UNMIK, not Yugoslavia, and by the same token a hypothetical independence would de facto be from UNMIK rather than from Yugoslavia. It was becoming clear that the FRY had not just lost its ability to militarily control the territory but it was also entirely side-lined with regard to the legal jurisdiction (or even the discussions around it) over the territory (Sahin, 2015, p. 70).

All things considered, it is not too far-fetched to claim that the Constitutional Framework planted the seeds of Kosovo's independence. It cannot be neglected that, as Summers argues, the unilateral declaration of independence (UDI) of 2008 was the product of two locally controlled (by pro-secession policymakers) yet UN-made institutions, the Kosovo Assembly and the Presidency (2011, p. 28). The critique from those who oppose Kosovo's secession is that the role of UNMIK was not to groom a territory so that it became a state but to create autonomous institutions which would later be transferred to the FRY/Serbia, that is, to the *status quo ante*, prior to the 1989 revocation of the autonomy. Considering the developments in Kosovo in the noughties and the role of international organisations, however, it seems that this scenario was not seriously contemplated.

Bumps on the road of self-governance: the 2004 sectarian riots

The consolidation of the self-government institutions in Kosovo was far from ideal and can hardly be used as a successful textbook example of internationally engineered institution-building. Instead, the process was marred with difficulties. One of the most serious complications occurred in March 2004, as a result of a violent episode driven by sectarianism. In December 2003, UNMIK issued a report – 'Standards for Kosovo' – which was aimed at consolidating good governing practices and respect and equal rights for minorities. The spirit of the document is summarised by this paragraph:

'[A] Kosovo where all – regardless of ethnic background, race or religion – are free to live, work and travel without fear, hostility or danger and where there is tolerance, justice and peace for everyone' (UNMIK/PISG, 2003). The noble intentions of the report clashed with the prosaic reality on the ground.

The death, on 16 March 2004, of three Kosovo Albanian teenagers who drowned in the Ibar river sparked the inaccurate rumour that the tragedy had been caused by Serbs (HRW, 2004; UNSC, 2004a). This incident was followed by what the former UN Secretary General, Kofi Annan, labelled as an 'organized, widespread, and targeted campaign' and as an 'onslaught led by Kosovo Albanian extremists against the Serb, Roma and Ashkali communities of Kosovo' (UNSC, 2004a, p. 1). The balance of the three-day widespread riots which occurred throughout Kosovo was not minor: 19 people dead, nearly 1,000 injured,[20] 730 homes from Serbs and other minorities as well as 36 Orthodox monasteries and churches destroyed and over 4,000 Serbs and members of ethnic minorities forced to flee their homes (HRW, 2004; UNSC, 2004a; Woehrel, 2006). This effectively meant that Serbs had been expelled from several cities, towns and villages, including the capital Pristina (HRW, 2004).

One of the main debates around these events was whether it was a spontaneous act of violence or a deliberate campaign orchestrated by extremist Kosovo Albanian secessionists with the intent of consolidating the expulsion of Serbs from Kosovo. The vast majority of internationals, including

Figure 3.3 Destroyed Orthodox Church in Western Kosovo (2017).

Source: Gisela Gorbalán.

the UN Secretary-General, concur that all the evidence pointed towards a well-planned action. William Ortíz, an UNMIK officer, deployed in Kosovo at the time, asserts with a palpable critical spirit that 'it was not a natural uprising, it was well prepared between the KLA and the Kosovo Police [Kosovo Police Service] with the connivance of KFOR forces. The goal was to expel Serbs from cities'.[21] For Serbs, particularly those living in enclaves south of the Ibar,[22] it meant that staying in Kosovo was a direct threat to their lives and property.

Beyond the immediate consequences, it is essential to focus on the political implications of the March riots.[23] They had a repertoire of multi-layered consequences for the different actors involved. For UNMIK, it undermined its rule, probably like no other event, and it exposed serious flaws in terms of basic governance and the guarantee of law and order in Kosovo. In a rare exercise of political humbleness, the UN fully acknowledged its mistakes: '[T]he international community [in March 2004], with the United Nations Interim Administration Mission in Kosovo (UNMIK) in the lead, gave an impression of being in disarray, without direction and internal cohesion' (UNSC, 2004b, p. 3).

Likewise, for KFOR, a force initially deployed on behalf of vulnerable civilians, it was a shattering failure in terms of protecting civilians. Such failure is illustrated by the fact that tens of thousands of Albanian extremists (the figure of rioters is estimated to be around 50,000) were able to successfully challenge the international security structures led by UNMIK and KFOR (HRW, 2004). The latter, in particular, has been accused of cowardice by local residents[24] but also and more damagingly by a leaked German Police report and by UNMIK itself[25] (HRW, 2004; Peterson, 2004). An extraordinarily critical article in *Der Spiegel* concluded that: '[T]he German [KFOR] soldiers ran away and hid like frightened rabbits in their barracks. They only reappeared in armoured vehicles after the Albanian mob had wreaked its havoc and left a trail of destruction' (Flottau *et al.*, 2004). Finally, the March riots put into question the artificially-engineered narrative of Kosovo as a multi-ethnic territory and arguably the level of commitment of Kosovo's self-government structures to pursue that goal. Particularly, given the reluctance of Kosovo Albanian leaders to condemn the violence, with some members of the PISG even justifying and condoning it (UNSC, 2004a, p. 3).

There is, however, a crucial point, in terms of political ramifications, where there is no consensus. Some have claimed that the March events forced UNMIK to prioritise 'standards', particularly those related to security and protection of minorities, over 'status' (Gardner, 2011, p. 64). The alternative and contradictory interpretation, which interestingly is held by both opponents and supporters of Kosovo's independence, is that the riots worked as a catalyst for change, as a wakeup call for international organisations that after the March riots had realised that they could no longer postpone the final status discussion (Perritt, 2010, p. 80). Similarly,

Father Sava, the Abbot of Dečani (Western Kosovo), one of the most important monasteries from the Serbian Orthodox Church, believes that:

> It became very clear soon that the riots were a major step in replacing the 'standards before status' policy with a completely opposite policy which requested first the definition of status and only then working on standards. Apparently the March riots were in function of this major policy change which makes it much easier to understand why despite all intelligence neither KFOR nor UN managed to prevent it. Immediately after the [international organisations'] condemnation of the crimes committed during the riots there was a common consensus among the world powers to leave the standards for later and define Kosovo status as soon as possible.[26]

The Abbot's view is largely shared by the former UN Special Representative, Søren Jessen-Petersen, who believes that, after March 2004, it had become clear that 'we [UNMIK] could not continue with lack of definition' because this international ambiguity was stirring tensions with locals',[27] with Kosovo Albanian secessionists, that is. As will be shown, the role of Jessen-Petersen, who took office in August 2004, shortly after the riots, would be a determinant in clarifying the role of the UN mission, steering Kosovo's course towards the purposely ambiguous destiny of 'final status'.

It could be argued that this notion of the riots as a galvaniser borrows from Milton Friedman's idea that '[O]nly a crisis – actual or perceived – produces real change' (2002, p. xiv). In turn, that change, Friedman adds, will depend on 'the ideas that are lying around' (ibid.). As the following section will scrutinise, the ideas 'lying around', at least those from the most relevant international stakeholders, with regards to Kosovo pointed overwhelmingly towards Kosovo statehood.

Heading towards final status

Negotiating Kosovo's 'final status'

Shortly after the March violence, on 30 April, Kai Eide, the Norwegian Ambassador to NATO, was asked by Secretary General Annan to evaluate, or rather re-evaluate, the state of things in Kosovo. Eide's report, published a few months later, was eminently vocal in terms of its critique towards UN policies and governance in general, highlighting the discontent from locals and advocating for the abolishment of the 'standards before status' policy, because it was 'untenable' and lacked credibility (UNSC, 2004b). Instead, the document proposed to address the 'hot potato' of Kosovo's final status without any further delay to avoid aggravating the situation and because this was deemed to be 'probably inevitable' (UNSC, 2004b, p. 4).

Once again, nonetheless, the term 'independence' was conspicuous by its absence. By disconnecting 'standards' from 'policy', the previous approach was technically defunct. That does not mean that conditionality had disappeared but that the standards were going to be developed in parallel, rather than in advance, to the status part of the equation. Despite the fact that the report claims that the development of a new strategy did 'not mean that violence is rewarded' (UNSC, 2004b, p. 11), in a rather open reference to the March events, it is hard not to establish a connection between such policy shift and the fear (potential or real) of uncontainable instability. Such instability, from UNMIK's perspective, was the worst-case scenario as it could lead to the failure and eventual collapse of the mission. Perhaps with the aim of avoiding such catastrophic picture, Eide's recommendations became UNMIK's new policy.

The appointment of a new SRSG, Jessen-Petersen, in October 2004 fundamentally contributed to consolidating the new scope. As he himself admits 'my term in office was determinant in terms of final status. I wanted to accelerate transfer in order to accelerate status'.[28] This marks a clear turning point vis-à-vis his predecessors, who had opted for a more restrained strategy, by, for instance postponing the controversial issue of status. Instead, for Jessen-Petersen addressing the 'hot potato' was a *sine qua non* condition:

> when I was approached by the [UN] Secretary General [Kofi Annan], I said yes on the condition that I would be able to develop a strategy to start the process that would lead to status determination. I told Kofi [Annan], I am prepared to do it [take the job offer] on the clear understanding that I can set up a strategy to get on the road. I got green light, my predecessors had said it was too early. I had a different opinion.[29]

Jessen-Petersen's ambitious approach did produce concrete results. Evidence of this is the fact that, in May 2005, Eide, the Norwegian diplomat was appointed as Annan's Special Envoy (UNOSEK) in Kosovo 'to carry out a comprehensive review of Kosovo' (UN, 2005). Eide's report to the Security Council, in early October 2005, emphasised that the final status, a concept used up to 57 times, was gaining 'momentum' (UNSC, 2005a). The thorny aspect, as per usual, was that this 'final status' idea suffered from a chronic lack of definition or even concretion.[30] Tentatively, this semantic camouflage is explained by the fact that the word 'independence', or the 'i' word as international officers referred to it, would appear as too ambitious for some and downright unpalatable for others and thus could potentially lead to sabotage. Independence was, at any rate, the elephant in the room that very few diplomats dared to use and that was euphemistically disguised under the 'final status' formula. The consequences in terms of bordering effects, up until that point, were being kept incognito.

At the end of October, Eide's (and Annan's) initiative was sanctioned by the Security Council, which articulated its support to launching 'a political process to determine Kosovo's future status', effectively providing the framework for the negotiations (UNSC, 2005b, p. 2). Developments were taking place at an unusual speed and only a few days later, the Contact Group,[31] which had literally disappeared from the scene since the Rambouillet (dis)accords, laid out a decalogue of so-called guiding principles that the parties had to adhere to. Beyond the classic calls for a democratic and multi-ethnic Kosovo, the Contact Group's conditions included crucial red lines that are worth highlighting, namely: Kosovo could not return to the *statu quo ante* (pre-June 1999), the partition of Kosovo was out of the menu and the territory could not (re)unite with any other state[32] (UNSC, 2005c, p. 3).

The elephant in the room – independence – was not explicitly mentioned as a potential outcome but what is significant is that unlike most alternative scenarios it was neither considered a red line. In parallel, a new UNOSEK, the diplomat and former Finnish President, Marti Ahtisaari had been appointed by the UN Secretary General. This choice was not uncontroversial since Ahtisaari had been Chairman (2000–2004) and Chairman Emeritus (2004–) of the International Crisis Group (ICG), a non-profit organisation, or political lobby, which had perseveringly and unambiguously advocated for Kosovo statehood (ICG, 2004, 2006a, 2006b, 2007). Ahtisaari won the Nobel Peace Prize in 2008, the same year Kosovo unilaterally declared its independence.

The negotiations, which had the daunting challenge of resolving the sovereignty quagmire in Kosovo, began in February 2006, in Vienna. The ideal outcome of these negotiations was the final endorsement by the Security Council (Knoll, 2015, p. 75), which taking into account the fact that the UN was deeply involved in its architecture did not sound, a priori, too far-fetched. As Weller points out, even though the negotiations were initially steered by the Contact Group, they were, at least formally speaking, a UN-led project (2008, p. 664). Indeed, the main figure behind the negotiations was the UN Special Envoy, Martti Ahtisaari, whereas his deputy, Albert Rohan, was in charge of the technical details of the talks. The rest of the protagonists were the usual suspects: the Serbian government and the Kosovo representatives from the PISG.

It is important to note that while the negotiations were taking place, Montenegro seceded, peacefully and by mutual accord, from Serbia and Montenegro, in June 2006. The New Serbian Constitution, which came into force that year, considers Kosovo a province (with the same status as the northern province of Vojvodina) and Article 8 in an apparently contradictory statement proclaims that '[T]he border of the Republic of Serbia is inviolable and may be altered in a procedure applied to amend the Constitution' (Serbian Constitution, 2006). In other words, it limits the Serbian government's negotiating room for manoeuvre, as accepting

Kosovo's independence would be inexorably unconstitutional and would require the unpopular move of amending it to give up its sovereignty on Kosovo. This is indeed crucial with regards to Serbia's strategies in Vienna and afterwards.

One of the members of the Serbian delegation, Dušan Bataković, claims that Serbia offered a generous autonomy frame 'more than autonomy, less than independence', which would resemble the Hong-Kong model (2012, pp. 217–218). In practice, this model would have meant self-governance with ample autonomy, albeit without a 'Kosovo army' or a UN seat. Needless to say, Serbia's main priority was to 'preserve' its territorial integrity and sovereignty over Kosovo. Belgrade, which once again had a weak position at the negotiation table, was willing to go a step further than what it offered some years ago in Rambouillet. The Serbian strategy also included a proposal to provide autonomy within the autonomy for Serb-inhabited municipalities.

The Kosovo delegation position was also crystal clear and, one may argue, as uncompromising and obstinate as its Serbian interlocutors. The main aim was no other than 'outright independence' (Weller, 2008a, p. 669). The difference with the Serbian delegation was that for Pristina the wind was, as it were, blowing in its favour. First, due to the fact that the majority of members of the Contact Group (five out of six) were either enthusiastic or at least supportive of the idea of independence. Similarly, as seen above and as his March 2007 report showed, the chief mediator, Ahtisaari was also seen as sympathetic to that alternative. Last but not least, there was a general will by the (intervening) international community to sort out the 'Kosovo problem' definitively, and independence appeared as the least troublesome solution in terms of regional peace and stability. As the events in March 2004 had exposed, Kosovo Albanian secessionists had the coercive trump card of sabotaging such peace and stability. The coercive capacity of the Serbian minority in the north was much more 'containable', because the potential saboteurs were quantitatively less significant. The ICG, an organisation which actively lobbied for Kosovo's independence, was also playing that *ad baculum* card, warning that failure to reach a solution in the form of statehood for Kosovo could lead to the bolstering of 'a pan-Albanian ideology corrosive of existing borders and possibly even enriching the soil for radical Islam' (ICG, 2006b, p. 1).

The Ahtisaari Report: unveiling the mystery of 'final status'

Similarly to Rambouillet, and freely paraphrasing Colombian novelist Gabriel García Márquez, the Vienna negotiations seemed to be the chronicle of a failure foretold.[33] In February 2007, after 15 rounds of negotiations and over a year of manifestly unsuccessful talks, Ahtisaari presented his proposals to the two parties and finally forwarded them to the Security Council on 26 March (Summers, 2011, pp. 38–39). Despite the controversy surrounding it, the plan received full support from the UN Secretary General at the time, Ban Ki Moon, (UNSC, 2007a). Ahtisaari proposed a blueprint for independence under international supervision, a *leap forward* justified according to Ahtisaari by, among other things, the failure in the negotiations (UNSC, 2007a, p. 2). The Finnish diplomat admitted, resignedly, that the negotiations had failed abruptly due to the 'irreconcilable position of the parties', despondently adding that '[N]o amount of additional talks, whatever the format, will overcome this impasse' (UNSC, 2007a, p. 2).

This report is of paramount importance for a wide range of reasons. For starters, for the first time the term 'independence' appears without any rhetorical camouflage. At last, after countless reports referring to an ill-defined 'final status', an official document was calling a spade a spade. The concept not only appears but it is also deemed, by Ahtisaari, to be 'the only viable option for Kosovo' (UNSC, 2007a, p. 2). Several reasons are given to justify such a bold statement. One of the main arguments is that any alternative solution to independence would generate internal as well as regional instability. Additionally, the argument of responsibility is also used: '[O]nly in an independent Kosovo will its democratic institutions be fully responsible and accountable for their actions' (UNSC, 2007a, p. 4). Interestingly, Ahtisaari himself is not very certain about whether Kosovo will live up to such responsibilities as he himself proposed not full independence but a supervised form of it for an undetermined period of time. The formula of 'supervised independence', which includes the presence of civilian as well as military international actors, necessarily compromises Kosovo's sovereignty, offering at most a tainted version of it. In practice, it would mean that Kosovo institutions would only be able to legislate if such legislation did not contradict the interests of the international 'supervising' parties.

One of the problems with the 'only viable option' argument is that, as Ker-Lindsay contends, it is disingenuous for if independence is 'the only possible outcome ... it is because it was allowed to become so' (2010, p. 107). Ker-Lindsey's argument resembles the old constructivist argument in International Relations, epitomised by Wendt, according to which concepts such as anarchy cannot be taken for granted since they are social constructs: 'anarchy is what states make of it' (1992, p. 395). Such concepts/systems subsequently become reified with social practices to the extent that they become an apparently inescapable reality. By the same token, if we find ourselves in a Kosovo independence scenario it is because practices and policies have made it that way. Pushing in such a direction was *a* solution not *the* (only) solution. The bottom line is that in any territorially-driven conflict, secessionists and host states have irremediably opposite standpoints. This is hardly a novelty; the originality of the Kosovo case derives from the fact that the solution, far from stemming from compromise, was satisfactory to one of the parties (the secessionist) while fully alienating the other.

The most fundamental part of the Ahtisaari Plan, at least for the argument of this book, is that it linked the fact that independence was the only viable option to the 1999 intervention and the subsequent institutional build-up by the UN. According to the report,

> [F]or the past eight years, Kosovo and Serbia have been governed in complete separation. The establishment of the United Nations Mission in Kosovo (UNMIK) pursuant to resolution 1244 (1999), and its assumption of all legislative, executive and judicial authority throughout Kosovo, has created a situation in which Serbia as not exercised any governing authority over Kosovo. This is a reality one cannot deny; it is irreversible.
>
> (UNSC, 2007a, p. 3)

In other words, the irreversibility of Kosovo's independence is due to the legal architecture which was established by the UN and NATO after the humanitarian intervention was conducted. These exogenous post-intervention dynamics had made any other alternative untenable. This conclusion has tremendous implications for the debate concerning the link between humanitarian intervention and border transformations. The Ahtisaari report suggests that there is a straight, direct and somehow inevitable link between both.

This raises major questions for the concepts of humanitarian intervention and R2P. As seen above, the core document regarding the latter, a report drafted by the International Commission on Intervention and State Sovereignty, explicitly specifies that the sovereignty of the affected state shall not be undermined (ICISS, 2001, p. 44). The push for independence in Kosovo is also in stark contrast with the countless declarations of Western leaders prior to the intervention (but also after it), where they assured that the sole purpose of it was humanitarian and had no connection with (Kosovo) statehood (Ker-Lindsay, 2010, p. 102). In eight years, the discourse and the aims had radically changed. The idea that a humanitarian intervention could be surgically conducted without any impact regarding territoriality had also been challenged. Kosovo and the policies implemented in the post-intervention period were shaping the very notion of humanitarian intervention. In addition, under the veil of 'irreversibility' and 'uniqueness of the case', a precedent, concerning the territorial consequences of humanitarian intervention, was being enacted.

Four scenarios regarding sovereignty

One of the key questions at this stage is whether the Ahtisaari assertion that independence was the only possible option holds water. One of the problems with this assumption of lack of alternatives is that it obscures the fact that there were indeed other options. In Kosovo and elsewhere, supporting a political outcome inevitably constitutes a political statement, a policy recommendation which can hardly be seen as value-free. That being said, none of the alternatives, including the one eventually adopted by Ahtisaari, are exempted from difficulties or controversy. It is worth to succinctly describe them in order to have a wider overview of the *problématique*. The possibilities for Kosovo's future, after NATO's intervention and before the Kosovo Assembly's UDI in 2008, could be reduced to four.

On one end of the spectrum, there is the *transfer option*, that is, the return of the province back to the Federal Republic of Yugoslavia (Republic of Serbia since 2006) by the UNMIK authorities. As explained above, this option would consist of a return to the *status quo ante* albeit with two crucial variations: first, Kosovo would have recuperated its autonomous institutions. Kosovo's self-government, this time, would be supported by UNSC resolutions and more than likely sheltered by the presence of international peacekeeping forces in the territory. The second difference is that after the ousting and downfall of Milošević in 2000, the Serbian government could no longer be considered an irredentist authoritarian regime and therefore the minority rights of Albanians were arguably no longer under threat by Belgrade. Needless to say, this has been the preferred option of successive Serbian governments, at least at a rhetorical level. Perhaps the main argument for this option is that it is the only one that respects the sovereignty and territorial integrity of the host state, a principle which is omnipresent in UNSC resolutions regarding Kosovo. The challenges with this alternative are not hard to ascertain. On the one hand, it would generate a great deal of hostility amongst the Kosovo Albanian population, which accounts for approximately 90 per cent of Kosovo, and could with a high degree of certainty reignite a bloody return to violence and conflict.

Despite that fact that this is rarely recognised by Belgrade, the 'return of Kosovo' with around two million people hostile to its rule would act as a potential destabiliser for Serbia proper. Additionally, the idea of returning the territory to Serbia was not amongst the plans of the Western states and organisations which had enthusiastically supported the intervention in Kosovo in 1999. Before the UDI, the future of Kosovo was uncertain but for U.S. policymakers one thing was clear '[T]he United States and the Contact Group have ruled out a return of Kosovo to full Serbian control' (Woehrel, 2006, p. 3). More worryingly for Belgrade, this idea was not shared by the UNMIK administration either. Evidence of this is the Kosovo Standards Implementation Plan, commonly known as 'standards before status' policy, launched by UNMIK in the spring of 2004. As explained above, this plan subordinates the 'consideration of the future status of Kosovo' to the fulfilment of several good governance criteria (UNSC, 2004a, p. 16). This type of territorial carrot has prompted some scholars to label this UNMIK conditional policy as 'earned sovereignty' (Knoll, 2005; Sahin, 2015). The bottom line is that if Kosovo delivered, statehood would, or at least could, be granted as some sort of award. The status carrot therefore illustrates that there was little appetite by the UNMIK administration to return to the *status quo ante*, even before the Ahtisaari report.

The second potential scenario requires little explanation as it consists of perpetuating the status quo, where UNMIK, with the support of Western powers and NATO, would rule Kosovo while offering some sort of local autonomy. Simply put, this hypothesis would have made a provisional plan permanent. In theory, this scenario would not alienate any of the parties and would allow UNMIK to remain status-neutral. In practice, however, such exercise of political immobilism was generating a growing discontent amongst Kosovo Albanian secessionists, prior to the 2008 UDI. Such political disgruntlement could have degenerated in a serious conflict between local secessionists and the mission itself, as the riots of 2007, where UNMIK riot police fired rubber bullets and tear gas at a demonstration against the UN mission organised by Vetëvendosje,[34] illustrate. An additional problem associated with this scenario is the fact that it requires a *sine die* commitment, financial and political, by the UN and the intervening parties. This is particularly complex in times of austerity and in a context where Kosovo has disappeared from the media and the geopolitical focus. Last but not least, such a scenario could have triggered the 'UN colony' narrative, thus hampering the UN legitimacy in Kosovo and its reputation elsewhere.

The third case consists of a partly independent Kosovo, the Republic of Kosovo, under international tutelage. This scenario is the one presented by Ahtisaari as the only viable option and the one where Kosovo found itself formally until September 2012. Under this scenario, international institutions, namely the UN, NATO, the EU and also the U.S. would be able to curtail and limit Kosovo's sovereignty. The rationale behind this is, in Ahtisaari's view, that the country is unable to address a multiplicity of issues such as 'minority protection, democratic development, economic recovery and social reconciliation' and consequently international supervision to 'assist' Kosovo is indispensable (UNSC, 2007a, p. 4).

It must be noted that this formula of international tutelage was the one finally chosen. The formula of international tutelage in Kosovo was similar to that applied in Bosnia, which some scholars have heavily criticised for usurping the sovereignty of the state (O'Leary, 2016, p. 72), transforming Bosnia into a European Raj (Knaus and Martin, 2004, p. 70). Thus, for instance, the figure of the International Civilian Representative (ICR), proposed in the Ahtisaari Plan, and which enjoyed 'corrective powers' (UNSC, 2007a, p. 8) very much resembled the role of the Office of the High Representative (OHR) in Bosnia which ensures that local policy-makers do not jeopardise the fragile institutional assemblage in place (Sahin, 2015; O'Leary, 2016). The ICR was dismantled in 2012 but other forms of tutelage remain operational in Kosovo, over a decade after the UDI. Further details about this scenario will be examined in the Chapter 4 of the book.

The forth scenario goes a step further than this: independence without tutelage. In this scenario, Kosovo would be fully sovereign in the sense that it would not be subordinated, or at least not essentially, to international institutions. It would not follow what is perceived by Kosovo Albanian nationalists as *diktats* and foreign interference. Instead, Kosovo would be able to develop its judicial system, without foreign judges and advisors, without Courts such as the Kosovo Specialist Chambers and Specialist Prosecutor's Office, which are perceived to be above the state, and of course it would be able to develop its own army. As argued previously and despite the formal termination of 'supervised independence' many structures of the international regime (EULEX, KFOR, UNMIK, the recently created Kosovo Specialist Chambers) have not yet been dismantled.

In the eyes of some international officers, Kosovo is not ready for taking the full independence step and, as a result, international presence (and interference) is necessary in order to ensure that the democratisation process continues and that Kosovo does not take steps which could antagonise Serbia or other neighbours, prompting a return to conflict in the region.[35] It could be argued that the fears of international officers seem to suffer from a certain patronising vision at best and colonial at worst. The fact is that the scenario of lifting international tutelage does not appear to be on the table in the short run.

Interestingly scenario 3 and even scenario 4 are affected by a situation where 'independence' is not complete not because of the role of international organisations but because Kosovo is unable to get full international recognition in the form of UN membership. Even in the best-case scenario, from the secessionist point of view, that independence is incomplete because the de facto control of the territory does not translate into becoming a fully legitimate member of the international community. The consequence of this is quasi-independence; in other words, Kosovo has become a new member of the parastate[36] club. Chapter 4 will examine the challenges and difficulties derived from being a paratstate.

The proverbial hits the fan: Kosovo's Unilateral Declaration of Independence

It was precisely in order to avoid that parastate scenario that the U.S. and key European states attempted, until the very last minute, to find a compromise with partners in the international community – basically Russia and China – which were not as keen on Kosovo's secession. A member of the influential U.S. think tank Council of Foreign Relations, Henry Perritt, claims that the mood amongst Western diplomats in the summer of 2007 was 'decidedly grim', some of them even advocating for a UDI in order to overcome the deadlock (2010, p. 179). In a desperate attempt to prevent both, a deadlock and a UDI, the recently retired UNSG Kofi Annan, set up a Troika in August 2007 with three officials representing the United States, the European Union and Russia (Ker-Lindsay, 2012, p. 47).

The main goal of the Troika was to achieve a 'mutually acceptable outcome' (UNSC, 2007b, p. 2), which seemed unreachable to say the least. The Troika negotiations were dominated, once again, by 'fruitless discussions' (Weller, 2008b) and yet again gloomy results. In December 2007, three months after its inception, the Troika concluded that: '[A]fter 120 days of intensive negotiations … the parties were unable to reach an agreement on Kosovo's status. Neither side was willing to yield on the basic question of sovereignty' (UNSC, 2007b, p. 4). Once again, international diplomats were bumping into the zero sum game that characterises sovereignty disputes.

The stress, and even fright, was coming from the Western diplomats and policymakers and this is perhaps unsurprising as the stakes were very high. Their aim was to persuade Russia to embrace the Ahtisaari Plan and persuade it to agree, or at least not to be an obstacle, to Kosovo's (supervised) independence. This undertaking was a bit of an impossible mission as Russia had few incentives to grant such a hugely significant concession to its Western counterparts. The West needed a way out of the Kosovo imbroglio, a quagmire that they themselves had contributed to creating, and Russia had more to gain by defecting and letting the issue stay in a legal limbo. Such an uncooperative move would not only highlight the contradictions of the West but it would also create a perpetual deadlock which only Russia had the key to solve.

Similarly to what occurred with the NATO intervention in 1999 or with Rambouillet, some key U.S. diplomats disagreed with the belligerent/unilateral policy followed by the U.S. administration. John Bolton, former U.S. ambassador to the United Nations, together with other senior American diplomats, stated in late January 2008 that the attempts 'to impose a settlement on Serbia would be a direct challenge to the Russian Federation' and thus advocated for an urgent re-examination of U.S. policy that would 'discourage Kosovo's Albanians from taking that [UDI] step' (Bolton *et al.*, 2008).

That restrained policy was not shared by of one of the key figures of U.S. foreign policy in Kosovo at the time, Frank G. Wisner. He was 'the U.S. representative to the Kosovo status talks' and unlike Bolton, Wisner fully embraced the unilateral option, even if it came with a price. A few days before the UDI, Wisner lamentably admitted that the Western states had failed in their persuasive mission: '[T]hey [the Russian government] have made it clear that they aren't going to accept Kosovo independence or any agreement that Belgrade didn't agree to' (cited by Gwertzman, 2008). Wisner was one of those common figures in international politics who operate mostly behind the scenes and, despite lacking a celebrity status, play a vital role in decisive moments. In the weeks prior to the UDI, for instance, he provided the Kosovo leadership with all sorts of useful advice, from keeping silent after the Troika fiasco to lobbying the secessionist cause worldwide to suggesting an ideal timing for the UDI (Perritt, 2010, p. 208). More significantly, Wisner's recommendations also included matters related to the content and substance of that declaration such as linking it to the Ahtisaari Plan and issuing an explicit invitation to a military and civilian foreign presence (Perritt, 2010, p. 208), that is, acknowledging that Kosovo's independence would be supervised.

When the Kosovo assembly eventually made the final step, on 17 February 2008, and unilaterally declared the territory's independence by stating that '[W]e, the democratically elected leaders of our people, hereby declare Kosovo to be an independent and sovereign state' (cited by BBC, 2008), it appeared clear that Wisner's pieces of advice had been seriously considered. Article 5 of the declaration welcomed the presence of the international community and the Ahtisaari Plan was explicitly mentioned in six different articles as well as in the preamble (BBC, 2008).

The mystery over the meaning of 'final status' had been unveiled and as it was not born out of compromise, it was inevitably going to create winners and losers. The declaration was received with great enthusiasm by the vast majority of Kosovo Albanians and arguably by many internationals working for foreign organisations[37] in Kosovo. The massive demonstrations that took place in many cities around Kosovo welcoming the declaration where met with huge gatherings of Kosovo Serbs opposing independence in Northern Kosovo as well as in Belgrade, where hundreds of thousands took to the streets on 21 February to show their disapproval with Kosovo's UDI. If one conclusion could be drawn from the UDI it is that the conflict over Kosovo's sovereignty had been decisively transformed and had even entered a new phase. The conflict and the challenges associated with it, however, were far from disappearing. For many, Kosovo's independence represented the closure of a chapter in the former Yugoslavia, a development which would lead to the 'end of conflict'. As the following chapters will discuss, this *Fukuyamaesque* perspective may, nonetheless, correspond more to wishful thinking than to the complex reality/realities on the ground.

Notes

1 It is popularly known as the Kumanovo Agreement because it was signed in this Macedonian city. The proper name of the agreement, however, is: 'Military Technical Agreement between the International Security Force ("KFOR") and the Governments of the Federal Republic of Yugoslavia and the Republic of Serbia'.

2 An official from the National Endowment for Democracy (NED), a non-profit entity which nevertheless receives most of its funding from U.S. governmental agencies, admitted to the New York Times that 'from August 1999 the dollars started to flow to Otpor [the main organisation behind the anti-Milošević revolution] pretty significantly' (Cohen, 2000). Similarly, senior members of Otpor have also acknowledged that they received substantial financial support from governmental and non-governmental Western agencies (Cohen, 2000).

3 See the previous chapter for further details on the language used in Rambouillet related to self-determination.
4 As Chapter 5 will show, Serbian institutions have retained a more prominent role in the Serb-dominated northern municipalities.
5 Dragiša Djoković, author interview, Mitrovica, 3 August 2017.
6 See previous footnote.
7 William Ortiz, author interview, Pristina, 2 August 2012
8 If one considers Kosovo a state they are refugees, otherwise they must be considered IDP's.
9 Sladjana Miletić, author interview, Peć, 31 July 2012.
10 As the Humanitarian situation was gradually improving, this Pillar was removed in July 2000 (UNSC, 2000b, p. 10).
11 Finn Reske-Nielsen, author interview, Copenhagen, 11 December 2017.
12 OSCE officer I, author interview, undisclosed location, 10 July 2012.
13 OSCE officer II, author interview, undisclosed location, 15 August 2017.
14 Søren Jessen-Petersen responds to these accusations by arguing that Haradinaj had been indicted not sentenced, and therefore he was innocent until found guilty. In addition, the SRSG believes that 'when Haradinaj was acquitted [in 2012], I was vindicated'. Søren Jessen-Petersen, author interview, Copenhagen, 9 March 2018.
15 Kouchner had argued that the resolution was ambiguous when it came to the definition of concepts such as substantial autonomy and self-government (UNSC, 2000, p. 5)
16 Søren Jessen-Petersen, author interview, Copenhagen, 9 March 2018.
17 See previous footnote.
18 Rugova was the leader of the LDK, Qosja the head of the United Democratic Movement and Thaçi was the main figure of Democratic Party of Kosovo (PDK) as well as the former political head of the KLA.
19 Such as the Kosovo Transitional Council formed in July 1999.
20 Amongst them 65 international police officers, 58 members of the Kosovo Police Force and 61 soldiers from KFOR.
21 William Ortiz, author interview, Pristina, 31 May 2014.
22 As Chapter 5 will explain, north of the Ibar Serbs constitute a majority. Self-organised defence committees like the 'Bridge Watch' in Mitrovica prevented similar destruction in Serb-dominated municipalities in Northern Kosovo.
23 Serbian scholars often refer to this episode as the 'March pogrom'. See, for instance, Bataković (2012).
24 Local resident expelled from Kosovo Polje in March 2004, author interview, 9 July 2012.
25 The HRW report 'Failure to Protect' accuses KFOR of leaving (Serbian) civilians at the mercy of rioters, failing to offer protection even to villages, which were a few hundred meters away from KFOR military bases, and which were eventually burned down (HRW, 2004).
26 Father Sava Janjić, author interview, Dečani, 29 July 2012.
27 Søren Jessen-Petersen, author interview, Copenhagen, 9 March 2018.
28 See previous footnote
29 See footnote 27.
30 According to the SRSG Jessen-Petersen, everyone knew that 'final status' meant independence. However, no one dared to say it: 'Publicly and privately I was very careful never to pronounce the term independence, the 'I' word''. Søren Jessen-Petersen, author interview, Copenhagen, 9 March 2018.
31 The United States, the United Kingdom, France, Germany, Italy, and Russia.
32 This was an implicit reference to a potential unification with Albania.
33 The exact title of the 1981 novel from García Márquez is 'Chronicle of a Death Foretold'.

34 Vetëvendosje is a political movement, and since 2010 a political party, which opposes UNMIK rule and presence and which advocates for Kosovo's full sovereignty; that is, without foreign interference. More controversially, it also aims to reunify with Albania.
35 OSCE officer II, author interview, undisclosed location, 15 August 2017.
36 A parastate is an entity which has formally declared independence from a host state, it controls territory and therefore it de facto enjoys sovereignty over that territory. It lacks, however, legal international recognition to achieve full sovereign independence and that hampers its ability to enter normal diplomatic relations with other states or to sign international agreements.
37 An OSCE officer who was present at one of the organisation's headquarters in Kosovo has complained that many of his colleagues went out to celebrate to the streets with locals. This, in view of this officer, seriously compromised the OSCE policy of neutrality with regards to Kosovo's status. OSCE officer II, author interview, undisclosed location, 15 August 2017.

Bibliography

Amnesty International (2003). 'Kosovo: Minorities are prisoners in their own homes'. Retrieved from: www.amnesty.org.uk/press-releases/kosovo-minorities-are-prisoners-their-own-homes

Bataković, D. (2012). *Serbia's Kosovo Drama*. Belgrade: Cigoja.

BBC (2008, 17 February). 'Full text: Kosovo declaration'. Retrieved from: http://news.bbc.co.uk/2/hi/europe/7249677.stm

Bellamy, A. (2001). 'Reconsidering Rambouillet'. *Contemporary Security Policy*, 22(1): 31–56.

Bolton, J. *et al.* (2008, 31 January). 'Warning Light on Kosovo'. *Brookings Institution*. Retrieved from: www.brookings.edu/opinions/warning-light-on-kosovo/

Brand, M. (2003). *The Development of Kosovo Institutions and the Transition of Authority from UNMIK to Local Self-Government*. Geneva: CASIN report.

Carpenter, T. G. (2000) 'Kosovo as an Omen: The Perils of the "New NATO"', in T. G. Carpenter (ed.), *NATO's Empty Victory* (pp. 171–183).

Cohen, R. (2000, 26 November). 'Who really brought down Milosevic'. *New York Times*. Retrieved from: www.nytimes.com/library/magazine/home/20001126mag-serbia.html

Del Ponte, C. and C. Sudetic (2009). *Madame Prosecutor. Confrontations with Humanity's Worst Criminals and the Culture of Impunity*. New York: Other Press.

Djoković, D., author interview, Mitrovica, 3 August 2017.

Dobbins, J., J. McGinn, K. Crane, S. Jones, R. Lal, A. Rathmell, R. Swanger, and A. Timilsina (2003). 'America's role in nation-building: from Germany to Iraq'. Santa Monica: RAND.

Flottau, R., O. Ihlau, A. Szandar and A. Ulrich (2004, 3 May). 'Die Hasen vom Amselfeld'. *Der Spiegel*. Retrieved from: www.spiegel.de/spiegel/print/d-30748386.html

Friedman, M. (2002). *Capitalism and Freedom*. Chicago: University of Chicago Press.

Gardner, A. M. (2011). *Democratic Governance and Non-State Actors*. New York: Palgrave Macmillan.

Gwertzman, B. (2008). 'Wisner: Russian Opposition to Kosovo Independence 'Unbelievably Regrettable'. *Council on Foreign Relations*. Retrieved from: www.cfr.

org/interview/wisner-russian-opposition-kosovo-independence-unbelievably-regrettable

Humanitarian Law Center (2001). 'Abductions and disappearances of Non-Albanians in Kosovo'. Retrieved from: www.hlc-rdc.org/wp-content/uploads/2013/02/KO-Abductions-and-disappearances-of-non-Albanians-in-Kosovo-1.pdf

Humanitarian Law Center (2012). www.hlc-rdc.org/?p=19413&lang=de

HRW (2001). *Under Orders. War Crimes in Kosovo*. New York: Human Rights Watch.

HRW (2004). *Failure to Protect: Anti-Minority Violence in Kosovo, March 2004*. New York: Human Rights Watch.

International Commission on Intervention and State Sovereignty (ICISS) (2001). *The Responsibility to Protect. Report of the International Commission on Intervention and State Sovereignty*. Ottawa: International Development Research Centre.

ICG (2004). 'Collapse in Kosovo'. *ICG Europe Report 155*. Retrieved from: www.crisisgroup.org/europe-central-asia/balkans/kosovo/collapse-kosovo

ICG (2006a). 'The Challenge of Transition'. *ICG Europe Report 170*. Retrieved from: www.crisisgroup.org/europe-central-asia/balkans/kosovo/kosovo-challenge-transition

ICG (2006b). 'Kosovo's Status: Difficult Months Ahead'. *Europe Briefing 45*. Retrieved from: https://reliefweb.int/report/serbia/kosovos-status-difficult-months-ahead

ICG (2007). 'Kosovo: No Good Alternatives to the Ahtisaari Plan'. *ICG Europe Report 182*. Retrieved from: www.crisisgroup.org/europe-central-asia/balkans/kosovo/kosovo-no-good-alternatives-ahtisaari-plan

Janjić, S., author interview, Dečani, 29 July 2012.

Jessen-Petersen, S., author interview, Copenhagen, 9 March 2018.

Ker-Lindsay, J. (2010). *Kosovo. The Path to Contested Statehood in the Balkans*. London: I.B. Tauris.

Ker-Lindsay, J. (2012). *The Foreign Policy of Counter Secession: Preventing the Recognition of Contested States*. Oxford: Oxford University Press.

Knaus, G. and F. Martin (2003) 'Lessons from Bosnia and Herzegovina: Travails of the European Raj'. *Journal of Democracy*, 14(3): 60–74.

Knoll, B. (2005). 'From Benchmarking to Final Status? Kosovo and The Problem of an International Administration's Open-Ended Mandate'. *The European Journal of International Law*, 16(4): 637–660.

Knoll, B. (2015). 'The Settling of a Self-Determination Conflict? Kosovo's Status Process and the 2010 Advisory Opinion of the ICJ', in M. Milanovic and M. Wood (eds) *The Law and Politics of the Kosovo Advisory Opinion* (pp. 73–95). Oxford: Oxford University Press.

Lemay-Hébert, N. (2013). 'Everyday Legitimacy and International Administration: Global Governance and Local Legitimacy in Kosovo'. *Journal of Intervention and Statebuilding*, 7(1): 87–104.

Miletić, S. author interview, Peć, 31 July 2012.

NATO (1999). 'Military Technical Agreement between the International Security Force ("KFOR") and the Governments of the Federal Republic of Yugoslavia and the Republic of Serbia'. Retrieved from: www.nato.int/kosovo/docu/a990609a.htm

O'Leary, B. (2016). 'Traitors within bridges across Derry and Mostar: an exploratory comparison', in E. O Ciardha and G. Vojvoda (eds), *Politics of Identity in Post-Conflict States* (pp. 59–78). Abingdon: Routledge.

Ortiz, W., author interview, Pristina, 12 August 2012; 31 May 2014.

OSCE officer I, author interview, undisclosed location, 10 July 2012.

OSCE officer II, author interview, undisclosed location, 15 August 2017.

Perritt, H. H. (2010). *The Road to Independence for Kosovo. A Chronicle of the Ahtisaari Plan*. Cambridge: Cambridge University Press.

Peterson, T. (2004, 9 May). 'German troops "hid like rabbits" in Kosovo riots'. *Telegraph*. Retrieved from: www.telegraph.co.uk/news/1461366/German-troops-hid-like-rabbits-in-Kosovo-riots.html

Pula, B. (2003). 'The UN in Kosova: Administering Democratization?', in F. Bieber and Ž. Daskalovski (eds) *Understanding the War in Kosovo* (pp. 199–216). London: Frank Cass Publishers.

Reske-Nielsen, F., author interview, Copenhagen, 11 December 2017.

Robertson, G. (1999). 'Some preliminary lessons'. *The RUSI Journal*, 144(4): 1–6.

Sahin, S. (2015). *International Intervention and State-Making. How the Exception Became the Norm*. Abingdon: Routledge.

Serbian Constitution (2006). Retrieved from: www.constituteproject.org/constitution/Serbia_2006.pdf?lang=en

Summers, J. (2011). 'Kosovo: From Yugoslav Province to Disputed Independence', in J. Summers (ed.) *Kosovo – A Precedent?: The Declaration of Independence, the Advisory Opinion and Implications for Statehood, Self-Determination and Minority Rights* (3–52). Leiden: Martinus Nijhoff publishers.

Surroi, V. (1999) 'The Bells of Shame'. *Koha Ditore*. Retrieved from: http://news.bbc.co.uk/2/hi/world/monitoring/428400.stm

UN (2005). 'Secretary-General Appoints Ambassador Kai Eide of Norway as His Special Envoy to Undertake Comprehensive Review of Kosovo'. SG/A/927. Retrieved from: www.un.org/press/en/2005/sga927.doc.htm

UNHCR (2005). 'The Balkans after the war was over'. *Refugees*, 3(140): 1–32.

UNMIK (2000a). 'On the Kosovo Joint Interim Administrative Structure'. UNMIK/REG/2000/1. Retrieved from: www.unmikonline.org/regulations/2000/re2000_01.htm

UNMIK (2001). 'On a Constitutional Framework for provisional self-government in Kosovo'. UNMIK/REG/2001/9. Retrieved from: www.unmikonline.org/regulations/2001/reg09-01.htm

UNMIK/PISG (2003). 'Standards for Kosovo'. Retrieved from: www.securitycouncilreport.org/atf/cf/%7B65BFCF9B-6D27-4E9C-8CD3-CF6E4FF96FF9%7D/Kos%20Standards.pdf

UNMIK (2005). 'SRSG's statement on the Prime Minister's resignation' Press Release UNMIK/PR/1325.

UNSC (1999a). 'Resolution 1244 Adopted by the Security Council at its 4011th meeting, on 10 June 1999'. Retrieved from: https://documents-dds-ny.un.org/doc/UNDOC/GEN/N99/172/89/PDF/N9917289.pdf?OpenElement

UNSC (1999b). 'Report of the Secretary-General Pursuant to Paragraph 10 of Security Council Resolution 1244'. S/1999/672. Retrieved from: www.phdn.org/archives/www.ess.uwe.ac.uk/Kosovo/Kosovo-Closure4.htm

UNSC (1999c). 'Report of the Secretary-General of the United Nations Interim Administration Mission in Kosovo'. S/1999/779. Retrieved from: www.securitycouncilreport.org/atf/cf/%7B65BFCF9B-6D27-4E9C-8CD3-CF6E4FF96FF9%7D/Kos%20S1999%20779.pdf

UNSC (2000a). '4200th meeting'. S/PV.4200. Retrieved from: www.securitycouncilreport.org/atf/cf/%7B65BFCF9B-6D27-4E9C-8CD3-CF6E4FF96FF9%7D/kos%20SPV4200.pdf

UNSC (2000b). S2000/878. Retrieved from: www.securitycouncilreport.org/atf/cf/%7B65BFCF9B-6D27-4E9C-8CD3-CF6E4FF96FF9%7D/kos%20S2000%20878.pdf

UNSC (2002). S2002/62. Retrieved from: www.securitycouncilreport.org/atf/cf/%7B65BFCF9B-6D27-4E9C-8CD3-CF6E4FF96FF9%7D/kos%20S2002%2062.pdf

UNSC (2004a). S/2004/348. Retrieved from: https://unmik.unmissions.org/sites/default/files/old_dnn/S-2004-348.pdf

UNSC (2004b). S/2004/932. Retrieved from: www.securitycouncilreport.org/atf/cf/%7B65BFCF9B-6D27-4E9C-8CD3-CF6E4FF96FF9%7D/kos%20S2004%20932.pdf

UNSC (2005a). S/2005/635. Retrieved from: www.securitycouncilreport.org/atf/cf/%7B65BFCF9B-6D27-4E9C-8CD3-CF6E4FF96FF9%7D/Kos%20S2005%20635.pdf

UNSC (2005b). S/PV.5290. Retrieved from: www.securitycouncilreport.org/atf/cf/%7B65BFCF9B-6D27-4E9C-8CD3-CF6E4FF96FF9%7D/kos%20SPV5290.pdf

UNSC (2005c). S/2005/709. Retrieved from: www.un.org/en/ga/search/view_doc.asp?symbol=S/2005/709

UNSC (2007a). 'Report of the Special Envoy of the Secretary-General on Kosovo's future status'. S2007/168.

UNSC (2007b). 'Report of the European Union/United States/Russian Federation Troika on Kosovo'. S2007/723. Retrieved from: www.securitycouncilreport.org/atf/cf/%7B65BFCF9B-6D27-4E9C-8CD3-CF6E4FF96FF9%7D/Kosovo%20S2007%20723.pdf

Weller, M. (2008a). 'The Vienna negotiations on the final status for Kosovo'. *International Affairs*, 84(4): 659–681.

Weller, M. (2008b). 'Kosovo's final status'. *International Affairs*, 84(6): 1223–1243.

Wendt, A. (1992) 'Anarchy is what states make of it: The social construction of power politics'. *International Organization*, 46(2): 391–425.

Woehrel, S. (2006). 'Kosovo's Future Status and U.S. Policy'. *Congressional Research Service Report for Congress* RS21721: 1–6.

Yannis, A. (2004). 'The UN as Government in Kosovo'. *Global Governance*, 10(1): 67–91.

4 Curtailed sovereignty

The complexities of consolidating the territorial transformation

Mark Weller insightfully calls Kosovo's independence process a 'saga' (2011, p. 146). Such unfinished saga contains several episodes and the declaration of independence is one of the most significantly thrilling ones. As Chapter 3 anticipated, the UDI did not 'end' the dispute over sovereignty in Kosovo but it did situate it at a different level. A level, which was made up of contradictions; on the one hand Kosovo was *de facto* a state where the host state (Serbia) no longer called the shots. Better yet, this state had been promptly recognised by prominent great powers, who had pledged to politically and diplomatically support Kosovo. This seemingly ideal picture was however ruined by the fact that Kosovo's international support was not overwhelming as many actors considered the unilateral move controversial. The ultimate danger of such contradictions was that Kosovo ran the risk of ending up in a legal limbo, in a trap where escaping is practically an impossible mission.

This trap has been conceptualised in different terms such as 'unrecognised state', 'quasi state', 'de facto state', 'pseudo-state' and 'parastate' (Kolstø, 2006, p. 723). While this is not the worst-case scenario for a secessionist region, neither is it the ideal one. This chapter will argue that, since 2008, Kosovo has transformed into a parastate which, similarly to all parastates, aims to surmount such reality. Despite its industrious diplomatic efforts and some important victories, such as the International Court of Justice (ICJ) advisory opinion of 2010 which ruled that Kosovo's UDI was not against international law, Kosovo has so far been unsuccessful in becoming a universally recognised state.

Sovereignty with a foreign touch

The international flavour of the Independence Declaration

The 17 February declaration was overwhelmingly supported by members of the Kosovo Assembly; 109 MPs out of 120 voted in favour of secession. The declaration was wholeheartedly celebrated by the Albanian community in Kosovo. Marigone Drevinja, former president of Vetëvendosje, and currently a member of Kosovo's Social Democratic party believes that the declaration was the right move to end nine years of political impasse in Kosovo.[1] The choice, in view of this pro-secession political activist, was either independence or 'going back'. Such enthusiasm for independence, however, was not shared by the representatives from the Serbian and the Gorani[2] communities, who absented themselves from the Kosovo Assembly on the day of the voting (UNSC, 2008a, p. 2) with the aim of visualising their opposition to the declaration. In a more explicit display of discontent, a demonstration of Kosovo Serbs in Northern Kosovo ended up with border posts operated by the Kosovo Police Service (KPS) and UNMIK being burned down (BBC, 2008b).

Similarly, a large peaceful demonstration in Belgrade, a few days later, was followed by a night of riots where a mob set ablaze the U.S. embassy in the Serbian capital (BBC, 2008c). On the diplomatic front, Serbia temporarily withdrew its ambassador from Washington and the Serbian President at the time, Boris Tadić, expressed his profound disapproval of Kosovo's independence at the UNSC, where he stated that the declaration was a 'flagrant violation' of UNSC Resolution 1244 and that it annulled international law and consecrated injustice (UNSC, 2008b, p. 4). Tadić also warned of the danger of setting a precedent for there were 'dozens of other Kosovos in the world' and denounced the idea that the ethnic cleansing of Serbs in Kosovo[3] would be rewarded if states recognised Kosovo's independence (UNSC, 2008b, p. 4).

As for the content of the declaration, it cannot be considered in any other fashion than impeccable. It covers every single angle and relevant aspect. It mentions up to eight times the Ahtisaari Plan, claiming that the newly born state will comply with its principles and obligations (see BBC, 2008a). In effect, it seems to be written to please not simply states in the international community but in particular those states directly engaged in Kosovo.

It is imperative to bear in mind that the UDI and the Constitution which came into force subsequently, in June 2008, signify the end of UNMIK rule, albeit not the end of UNMIK presence. The dramatic downgrade of UNMIK can be easily and visually quantified: whereas in the 2007/2008 period it had a budget of $198M with 4,749 personnel working for the mission, a year later, in 2008/2009 the budget had been reduced four-fold to $47M and the number of staff 90 per cent[4] to 479 (UNGA, 2008b, 2008c). These figures were coupled by words from the Secretary General Ban Ki Moon who explicitly expressed his intention 'to adjust', 'recalibrate' and 'reconfigure the international civil presence in Kosovo' (UNSC, 2008c, pp. 4–5). In plain language, that meant UNMIK was going to become irrelevant, keeping merely a testimonial presence, relinquishing its operational capabilities such as the provision of rule of law (Eckhard and Dijkstra, 2017, p. 106), UNMIK's flagship, transferring them to the EU (see below for further details). In that regard, the words of the former head of the UNMIK mission, Søren Jessen-Petersen, speak volumes:

> I feel sorry for UNMIK and for the people in that situation. After the UDI, they are in a trap that can go on forever: they cannot leave because Russia would not approve this at the UNSC, and they cannot play a role. They are out of touch with the [Kosovo] government and no one listens to them today in Kosovo. They [UNMIK] have to play a game, they are pretending to do something because they have to justify their 8 hours a day, but they are irrelevant. It is an enormous waste of resources.[5]

The poetic element of this is that the very institutions (Provisional Institutions of Self-Government or PISG) created by UNMIK are the ones that disempowered the mission, dispossessing it from any real governmental power and de facto terminating it. On the other hand, the declaration welcomes international civilian and military presence in Kosovo (Article 5), that is supervised independence, as requested by the Ahtisaari Plan. This supervised independence was monitored by the International Steering Group for Kosovo (ISG) an entity, formed by European states that had recognised Kosovo plus the U.S., which had the mandate of appointing the International Civilian Representative for Kosovo (ICR). The mandate of the ICR and therefore the supervised independence period, terminated in September 2012 (European Commission, 2012, p. 4), at least formally speaking.

In addition, the UDI commits Kosovo to respect the European Convention on Human Rights (Article 4) and pledges to collaborate with the International Criminal Tribunal for the Former Yugoslavia (Article 9). An example of the outstanding quality of the declaration can be found in Article 8:

> With independence comes the duty of responsible membership in the international community. We accept fully this duty and shall abide by the principles of the United Nations Charter, the Helsinki Final Act, other acts of the Organization on Security and Cooperation in Europe, and the international legal obligations and principles of international comity that mark the relations among states. Kosovo shall have its international borders as set forth in Annex VIII of the Ahtisaari Plan, and shall fully respect the sovereignty and territorial integrity of all our neighbours. Kosovo shall also refrain from the threat or use of force in any manner inconsistent with the purposes of the United Nations.
>
> (cited by BBC, 2008a)

This article epitomises Kosovo's commitment towards relevant international treaties, including the UN Charter, and obligations. The newly declared state appears as a trustworthy and responsible actor, aware of its duties as a (potential) member of the international community. Significantly, it explicitly abandons one of the core aims of Albanian nationalism (reunification with Albania) by promising to respect the sovereignty and territorial integrity of its neighbours. In other words, the declaration covers all the necessary angles to present Kosovo as an international law-abiding responsible actor. The wording and the framing is so immaculate that suspicions may arise with regards to the authorship of the document. Such speculations were clarified by the International Crisis Group (ICG), a powerful non-profit organisation which had consistently lobbied for Kosovo's independence since the 1999 intervention. According to this group, local leadership did not enjoy a major role in the drafting of the declaration; on the contrary: '[T]he independence declaration read out by Prime Minister Thaçi was largely written by the U.S. State Department' (ICG, 2008, p. 4). This foreign-driven top-down approach is not restricted to the declaration. Kosovo's Constitution, for instance, which entered into force some months after the declaration, in June 2008, is crucially influenced by the Ahtisaari Plan and therefore also subject to foreign interference (Papadimitriou and Petrov, 2012, p. 749).

Foreign-developed state elements

This lack of local agency is also epitomised by the example of the flag. National flags are not value-free artefacts, they carry an enormous symbolic power, they are, according to Billig, banal reminders of nationhood (1995, p. 41). The case of the Kosovo flag is particularly interesting for it illustrates how anomalous the Kosovo statehood process is. The bottom line is that up until the declaration Kosovo did not have a flag. In fact, it could be argued that it did not have an identity. This is at least what Kosovo's President and former PM, Hashim Thaçi, stated in 2007: '[A] Kosovo identity does not exist' (cited by Bilefsky, 2007). The reason for this is straightforward: Kosovo Albanians,[6] who represent 90 per cent of the population, share the same national identity (and common language and culture), as Albanians residing in Albania proper, Macedonia or Montenegro (Jano, 2013, pp. 32–33). As a result, a Kosovo encompassing identity as well as a Kosovo flag or an anthem had to be created out of the blue. The underlying and perhaps inconvenient question is why could not Kosovo use the Albanian symbols which were (and are) overwhelmingly accepted by the vast majority of the local population?

Gellner's renowned quote stating that '[N]ationalism … invents nations where they do not exist' (1964, p. 169) is particularly relevant in this conundrum. The crucial specificity of Kosovo, however, is that this invention of the 'Kosovar nation' was not carried out by indigenous nationalists, as is typically the case, but was the result of foreign-driven initiatives. For starters, the project to create a new flag was set up by the UN Special Envoy, Marti Ahtisaari, as part of the 'Comprehensive Proposal for the Kosovo Status Settlement', popularly known as the Ahtsaari Plan, in 2007. The conditions, laid out by Ahtisaari, were that the flag and the other future symbols of the state had to reflect 'the multi-ethnic character' of Kosovo

Figure 4.1 Kosovo and Albanian flags adorning a financial bank's façade in Pristina (2017).

Source: Gisela Gorbalán.

(UNSC, 2007). As bizarre as it may sound, an international competition was launched, with a €10,000 reward for the winner, to create the new flag for the newly born state. In addition to representing the multi-ethnic character of Kosovo, the new flag could not resemble any existing flag, have any allegiance to any particular ethnic group and ought to 'reflect the aspirations of the people of Kosovo for integration into European and Euro-Atlantic institutions' (*Express*, 2007). In other words, the out of scratch process to *invent* a flag could not be linked to history or the past but had to be oriented to the future. Taking all these elements into account, it is possible to argue that Kosovo's process of nation-construction can be categorised as eccentric, unprecedented and internationally-driven.

This foreign flavour was further consolidated by the fact that there was a strong U.S. involvement from behind the scenes: '[T]he issue of the flag ... was resolved behind closed doors between the U.S. Liaison Office and the prime minister's office' (ICG, 2008, p. 4). The final version of the flag (see Figure 4.1), which is the official one since February 2008, contains six white stars representing Kosovo's six communities (Albanians, Serbs, Turks, Gorani, Roma and Bosniaks), the territorial map of Kosovo in gold and a blue background (Cosentino, 2015, p. 610). The overall design and choice of colours (those of the European Union and NATO flags) is not coincidental but deliberate so that, as stated above, it captures the wish of the people of Kosovo to join the European and Euro-Atlantic clubs. The inclusion of the map is significant because it illustrates Kosovo's insecurities in relation to its territorial integrity, due to a well-grounded fear of a potential secession of Serb-dominated areas, particularly in the north of the country. In a symbolic manner, the inclusion of the map is a message that Kosovo is there to stay, in its present form, that is, without being partitioned by Serbs nor integrated into Albania, as some pan-Albanian nationalists would aim for. This presence of the map on its flag makes the Kosovo case even more uniquely peculiar as there is no other state, with the exception of Cyprus, which depicts its territory on its national flag.

The newly created flag has not been overwhelmingly welcomed by local actors. Albin Kurti, a prominent figure in Kosovo politics and current leader of the party/movement Vetëvendosje, complained shortly after the unveiling of the new flag that '[A] flag should have a history. I don't think people will identify with these ad-hoc flags' (cited by Borger, 2008). Similarly to the flag, Kosovo's anthem also has some specificities: it is called 'Europa' and is purely instrumental. The lack of lyrics is arguably explained by the fact that it could not possibly please all of Kosovo's communities simultaneously. To avoid a negative reaction by Serbs and other minorities and to be fully inclusive in the name of 'multi-ethnicity', the formula chosen was to completely de-emphasise ethnicity and identity elements. It is, therefore, hardly surprising that the anthem, like the flag, has been criticised by local organisations for erasing the Albanian identity and for being empty of substance, history and meaning (Vetëvendosje, 2008). According to Annita McKinna, by attempting to artificially construct a new identity void of ethnicity elements in Kosovo 'the international presence in Kosovo has succeeded both in entrenching ethnic division even further, as well as ensuring that Kosovo's people feel little connection to the new symbols' (McKinna, 2012, p. 18).

This lack of connection with the artificially created symbols can be empirically verified when visiting Kosovo: the recently created official state flag is flown at public and private institutions (see Figure 4.1). On the other hand, ethnic flags are preponderant in streets and private buildings: the Albanian flag in Albanian-dominated areas, the Serbian flag in Serbian municipalities. It remains to be seen whether this internationally-led project to symbolically erase identity symbols will be able to permeate deeper into Kosovo in the foreseeable future. It is fair to conclude that so far, not much. The flags outside the Mitrovica (see Figure 4.2) municipality epitomise both Kosovo's complex identity as well as the foreign prominence of Kosovo's independence and institutions. In addition to the recently-designed Kosovo flag, many official institutions in Kosovo wave the Albanian flag, technically the flag of a foreign country, as well as the flag of a supranational organisation (the EU) and a defence organisation (NATO)

Figure 4.2 Flags outside the Mitrovica municipality (2017).
Source: Gisela Gorbalán.

that Kosovo is not a member of. Last but not least, the flag of another foreign state, the United States, is common in private and public buildings. This can be explained as a sign of appreciation for the unwavering support Washington has provided for Kosovo's statehood.

In retrospect, when one analyses the Ahtisaari Plan, the first realisation is that one of the two sides of the conflict, the Kosovo Albanians, has been granted its essential aim: statehood. The price to pay by ethnic Albanians for such a victory is two-fold: the continued international presence, thus curtailing the new entity's sovereignty, and a pledge to multi-ethnicity. The international actors have succeeded in imposing such multi-ethnicity at legal (for instance, at the declaration of independence and constitution) and symbolic levels. The question is whether this multi-ethnicity narrative is materially sustainable in a territory where over 90 per cent of the population belongs to one particular group – ethnic Albanians – whereas the second largest group, Serbs, have since independence followed a policy of (self) alienation from Pristina's structures of power. This tendency seemed to have been partly redressed in September 2017, when the main Serbian party in Kosovo (Srpska Lista) entered a coalition government, led by former KLA commander Ramush Haradinaj, where Serbs held three ministries and a post of deputy PM (*Gazeta Express*, 2017). This cooperation was, however, short-lived. In March 2018, as a result of an incident where a Serbian official was arrested by Kosovo security forces in Northern Kosovo, Srpska

Lista abandoned the coalition government. Chapter 5 will explain this incident in greater detail and will address the issue of internal ethnic and territorial divisions in Kosovo.

The problem-ridden quest for recognition and UN membership

The struggle for recognitions

Once independence had been declared and its symbols had been created, the subsequent priority for Kosovo was to seek international recognition as promptly as possible. In that regard, good news did not take long to arrive. On the same day of the declaration, Kosovo was recognised by Costa Rica and the next day prominent states such as Turkey, the UK, the U.S., Australia and France had done so too (Kosovo's Ministry of Foreign Affairs, 2018). Given the fact that, as explained above, the independence declaration was largely written by the U.S. State department it is hardly a surprise that Secretary of State Condoleezza Rice reacted with unusual promptness recognising the new (para)state (U.S. Department of State, 2008). According to a European diplomatic source in Belgrade, 'the role of the US is crucial. They are the main driving force behind the Kosovo independence'.[7] The fact that significant players such as the United States, the United Kingdom and France among others recognised Kosovo's independence only a day after the declaration is indicative that it was not entirely unilateral but that the move had been coordinated with Western powers. A Kosovo senior political advisor, Bashmir Xhemaj, confirms that the independence declaration was conducted 'in coordination with our allies'.[8] It could therefore be argued that the declaration is unilateral vis-à-vis the host state, Serbia, but not with regards to relevant members of the international community which were backing secession.

Within a month, the newly established 'Republic of Kosovo' had been formally recognised by 26 states, most of them European. The initial enthusiasm has, nevertheless, soon faced stagnation in the number of recognitions. According to Kosovo's Ministry of Foreign Affairs (KMFA), 114 UN states[9] have formally recognised Kosovo, as of September 2018 (2018). The problem is that in the period 2013–2018, Kosovo has only managed to obtain ten recognitions. As Kosovo official Bashmir Xhemaj admits, the struggle for recognitions is far from easy: '[W]e have to fight every day to get recognitions of our independence one by one'.[10] Serbia's Foreign Minister, Ivica Dačić, disputes the numbers given by Kosovo's diplomacy alleging that some of the recognitions are fake, lacking formal confirmation from the respective states (B92, 2017c). The fact that KMFA has recently removed Uganda and Nigeria from the list of recognitions seems to partly confirm these allegations.

Belgrade's policy has not been fully consistent with regards to its reaction to states that recognised Kosovo. Whilst it had initially threatened to recall its ambassadors from any country which recognised Kosovo (Ker-Lindsay, 2012, p. 84), this policy has been abandoned probably due to its inefficacy and instead the strategy currently is to target states that have already recognised Kosovo. Belgrade has begun to play with the strategy of de-recognition, bringing up the ghost of Taiwan, which has suffered a multiplicity of de-recognitions as a result of an active policy based on pressure pursued by the Chinese diplomatic body. The result of this is that in parallel to the EU-led negotiations between Belgrade and Pristina, aimed at the 'normalisation' of relations between both actors, there is an open diplomatic war to win the hearts and minds of world states. The first de-recognition, a worrying development for Kosovo, arrived in September 2017, when according to Serbian diplomacy, São Tomé and Príncipe revoked its recognition of Kosovo's independence (Ministry of Foreign Affairs of the Republic of Serbia, 2017). This trend would continue in October 2017, when the Republic of Suriname confirmed via a letter that this South American state was withdrawing their recognition of Kosovo's (B92, 2017a), confirmed only a year earlier.

An additional case, Guinea Bissau, presents further complications and a contradictory 'war of claims'. During a visit to Belgrade, the current PM, Umaro Sissoco Embalo, explained that, contrary to the Pristina claims,[11] this West African country had never recognised Kosovo's secession: 'If one of you has some paper, you should show it to me, I have searched everywhere and found nothing' (cited by B92, 2017b). Some months later, however, the chief of Kosovo's diplomacy Behgjet Pacolli affirmed that Guinea Bissau had reconfirmed its recognition (*Gazeta Express*, 2018). Burundi is yet another state whose recognition is disputed and which is affected by the 'war of claims' between Belgrade and Pristina. The latter claims that the Republic of Serbia offers Burundi and other potential states such as Mali shipments of weapons in exchange for de-recognitions (B92, 2018). Beyond the confusion and contradictions, what seems crystal clear is that both governments are actively engaged on the diplomatic front to achieve, prevent and revoke recognitions.

Kosovo has certainly obtained some significant victories in terms of membership of inter-governmental organisations. Its achievements in that regard are fairly remarkable, compared to other parastates. For instance, since 2009, Kosovo is a member of the International Monetary Fund (IMF, 2009) and the World Bank (WB, 2009). Since 2016, Kosovo is also a member of the most important football associations in Europe and globally: the Union of European Football Associations (UEFA) and the International Federation of Football Association (FIFA) respectively. FIFA's admittance represented a robust diplomatic victory, not least because FIFA's Congress voted manifestly in favour of its membership: 141 delegations supported its bid and 23 opposed it (FIFA, 2016). Similarly, Kosovo belongs to the International Olympic Committee (IOC) and dozens of international sports federations and associations. In practice, that means that Kosovo's national teams can compete in the most significant international sports competitions.

Kosovo's success in joining a multiplicity of international organisations has been, nevertheless, obscured by its failure to join the United Nations Educational, Scientific and Cultural Organization (UNESCO). Kosovo's bid to join the UN cultural agency became frustrated by a very narrow margin in November 2015. Its bid had to obtain a two-thirds majority (95 affirmative votes) at UNESCO's General Conference and instead it secured 'only' 64.7 per cent, that is 92 votes in favour, while 50 states voted against it and 29 abstained (Brunwasser, 2015). UNESCO's membership vote, which could be interpreted as a victory for Serbia, was the result of a mutual lobbying effort by both Pristina and Belgrade in the preceding months and years. UNESCO's membership was, however, not the final station but a stepping stone towards a greater goal: UN membership.

Serbia's own goal: The ICJ opinion

Interestingly, the most comprehensive legal endorsement for Kosovo's independence can be qualified as Serbia's own goal. A few months after the UDI, in August 2008, at a time when Kosovo had been recognised by 45 UN members (KMFA, 2018), the Serbian government filed a request to the UNGA to seek an opinion from the International Court of Justice (ICJ) to establish whether or not Kosovo's independence was legal. Eventually, in October 2008, the General Assembly adopted a resolution requesting an advisory opinion from the ICJ on the matter. Seventy-seven states voted in favour of the resolution, 74 states abstained and only six, including the United States, voted against it (UNGA, 2008a). The specific question that the ICJ judges had to determine was: 'Is the unilateral declaration of independence by the Provisional Institutions of Self-Government of Kosovo in accordance with international law?' (UNGA, 2008a).

Needless to say, this request to the ICJ has to be understood in the context of Belgrade's policy of counter-recognitions whose main aim was to halt or at least prevent further recognitions. More ambitiously, the ultimate aim for the Serbian government was to derail and definitively sabotage Kosovo's independence bid. The opinion of the Court was not legally binding but it did carry an enormous symbolic significance. Indeed, a clearly negative conclusion from the ICJ would have put the *recognisers* in a very awkward spot because they would be flagrantly supporting an act which violated international law. The hype connected to the ICJ opinion contributed to reviving debates not just on Kosovo but also on the relationship between this case and the legitimacy of secession, with scores of academic articles focusing on the topic being published at the time (Borgen, 2010; Bothe, 2010; Burri, 2010; Dietrich, 2010; Jamar and Vigness, 2010; Weller, 2011; Wilde, 2011).

Eventually, in July 2010, the International Court of Justice issued its much-expected opinion. The ICJ opinion has two central vectors. First, it acknowledges the limits and lack of competence of International Law in the matter: '[I]nternational law does not regulate the act of making a declaration of independence, which should be regarded as a political act' (ICJ, 2010a, p. 27). Second, with regards to Kosovo, it concludes that 'the adoption of that declaration did not violate any applicable rule of international law' (ICJ, 2010a, p. 53). Summers points out that the question that the Court had to address was narrow but its interpretation of it was even narrower and, consequently, the ICJ focused 'on the legality of declaring independence, but not on the wider process of obtaining it' (2011, p. 43).

At any rate, this conclusion represented an enormous blow to Serbia's counter-recognition strategy and interests. It has been claimed that the opinion neither endorsed nor condemned Kosovo's secession (Vrbetić, 2013, p. 321). However, even though the ICJ fell short of explicitly ratifying Kosovo's secession, by negatively claiming that the declaration was not illegal, it ruined Belgrade's plans to sabotage Kosovo's secession, at least from the international law front. As previously discussed, the Serbian government has used alternative methods – such as using (bilateral) diplomatic leverage to persuade states to de-recognise Kosovo – to fight against the secession of its former province.

The Court's decision was not unanimous but it obtained a solid majority of ten votes in favour to four votes against it (ICJ, 2010a, p. 53). Despite this majority, the conclusions of the Court's *advisory opinion* have been criticised from several angles. It has been argued, for instance, that that the Court did not address some fundamental issues (Bothe, 2010; Burri, 2010). Burri contends that 'the Court evaded the main question' (Burri, 2010, p. 882), namely whether Kosovo had the right to secede from Serbia and used an over simplistic logic by inferring 'permission from the absence of explicit prohibition' (2010, p. 889). Similarly, Wilde has argued that the conclusions from the Court were 'minimalist' and 'said little about Kosovo' (Wilde, 2011, p. 303).

Further to this, an in-depth reading of the *advisory opinion* presents us with two issues which are particularly contentious and notably problematic. The first one is the fact that territorial integrity, according to the *advisory opinion*, is confined to inter-state relations and therefore does not apply to internal challenges coming, for instance, from non-state actors: 'the scope of the principle of territorial integrity is confined to the sphere of relations between States' (ICJ, 2010a, p. 38). Needless to say, the implications for other secessionist-driven conflicts of this statement are enormous. Unwillingly, the ghost of a potential precedent for other similar cases worldwide was revived. The impact of Kosovo in general for other secessionist conflicts, and the ICJ *advisory opinion* in particular, will be comprehensively examined in Chapter 6.

The second problem is related to agency, more specifically to who was responsible for the declaration of independence on 17 February 2008. The key issue is that if it was the Kosovo Assembly, that is, an institution created by the UN[12] under the frame of UNSC 1244 as a 'Provisional Institution of Self-Government' (PISG), this would represent a serious issue. According to one of the judges who voted against the *advisory opinion*, ICJ Vice-President Judge Peter Tomka, the declaration was indeed proclaimed by the Kosovo Assembly (ICJ, 2010b, p. 66). The majority of judges from the ICJ, however, disagreed with Tomka and argued that the

> authors of the declaration of independence ... did not act as one of the Provisional Institutions of Self-Government within the Constitutional Framework, but rather as persons who acted together in their capacity as representatives of the people of Kosovo outside the framework of the interim administration.
>
> (ICJ, 2010a, pp. 48–49)

This rather confusing wording leaves a pertinent question unaddressed: if these 'authors' did not act as PISG representatives, where did their legitimacy emanate from, how did they gain their ability to represent the people of Kosovo? It seems clear that such legitimacy emanated from the legislative elections at the Kosovo Assembly, *ergo*, from an institution created under the PISG frame by UNMIK.

The crux is that if 'the authors' were indeed declaring independence as PISG representatives that would be extremely problematic as the UDI effectively terminated the international regime for Kosovo established by the UNSC. Critics, such as dissenting ICJ Judge Bennouna, contend that one of the disputing parties is not entitled to do so as the UNSC is the only institution with the authority to alter Kosovo's status: 'no unilateral declaration affecting Kosovo's future status ... has any legal validity until it has been endorsed by the Security Council' (ICJ, 2010, p. 112). Bennouna raises a further critique by claiming that it is irrelevant whether 'the authors' were members of the Kosovo Assembly or not as 'all those living in Kosovo are subject' to UNMIK authority, as stipulated by UNSC Resolution 1244 (ICJ, 2010c, p. 115). In short, (allegedly) not being part of the PISG did not exempt 'the authors' from complying with the 'legal order' established by the UNSC.

Both Tomka and Bennouna show their perplexity at the fact that several laws in the past affecting Kosovo's external relations,[13] including a potential independence declaration in 2005, were annulled due to being in violation of UNSC 1244 Resolution but the same criteria was not applied to the UDI in 2008 (ICJ, 2010b; ICJ, 2010c). These double standards are even more puzzling given the fact that the competences of the Kosovo Assembly had not been altered (ICJ, 2010b, pp. 66–67). The counterargument to this is that those who had the ultimate word and ability to invalidate the laws and decisions emanating from the Kosovo Assembly, the UN Special Representative, remained silent thus providing a de facto consent to the UDI.

The diplomatic victory obtained by Pristina at the ICJ Courts, however, did not translate into UN membership or even into an easier path towards it. In fact, such an aspiration seems to be as unfeasible as ever, at least without major dramatic changes in the geopolitical arena.

UN membership: an unfeasible aspiration?

Kosovo's aspiration to join the UN is unequivocally clear. Bashmir Xhemaj, a Kosovo government official, optimistically points out that '[W]e see ourselves as part of the UN family. It won't be easy but it is the only way forward. Unlike other cases, we have democratic powerful states supporting us'.[14] Thus far the substantial support of these powerful states has not been sufficient for Kosovo to achieve its goal.

The eagerness to obtain UN membership by Kosovo, or indeed by any seceded entity or parastate, is self-evident and hardly surprising. UN membership provides a state with the ultimate validation, with legitimacy and legitimation. It is the Rubicon from which there is no way back, the *to be or not to be*, the element that safeguards and perpetuates sovereign statehood. Several authors have emphasised the utter importance of joining the UN (Franck, 1988; Keating, 2008; Griffiths, 2017). According to Franck, UN membership delivers a 'symbolic conferral of status' which entails validation, legitimacy, entitlements and obligations for the state (1988, p. 736). Likewise, Joshua Keating points out that UN membership 'has become a gold standard of international legitimacy', that is, a stamp that certifies that an entity is a legitimate member of the international community (2008). For Griffiths, a seat at the UNGA is 'the defining feature of joining the sovereignty club' which provides entities with a legal identity which has positive implications in terms of diplomacy and economics (2017, p. 180). In other words, UN membership is the recognition by other states that the former aspiring member is a sovereign equal, that is, *one of them*. Given the fact that thus far Kosovo has failed to achieve UN membership, it could be argued that Kosovo's independence process is ongoing and is far from being completed.

On the other hand, for the host state, it represents the final defeat, the evidence that the former region/province will not return. What prior to UN membership would have been an operation against insurgent secessionists would now constitute a war of aggression against a UN member and thus a violation of Article 2 of the UN Charter.[15] It is therefore not surprising that host states attempt to prevent recognitions, using all the means at their disposal such as legal arguments, appeals to solidarity, enticements or even threats (Ker-Lindsay, 2012, p. 81). As explained above, in those cases where some recognitions have already occurred, the host state may still engage in diplomatic efforts to push for de-recognition.

The membership application process for aspiring states is fairly simple, at least at first glance. The document 'Rules of Procedure of the General

Assembly' specifies the conditions that potential UN members must follow in order to gain membership of this universal intergovernmental organisation. The first step is to submit an application to the Secretary-General where the territory accepts the obligations derived from the UN Charter and, subsequently, the Security Council must 'recommend' such member to the General Assembly which 'shall consider whether the applicant is a peace-loving State' (UNGA, 2016, p. 38). The candidate must secure two-thirds of the votes in both UN bodies. The fiddly part is that, in the case of the Security Council, there is an addendum which is of paramount importance: the Permanent Five (the United States, the United Kingdom, the Russian Federation, France and China) have the power to veto an aspiring member and therefore it is not sufficient to obtain two-thirds of support. As a result, a potential member also needs all Permanent Five to vote in favour or at most to abstain in order to reach the General Assembly phase. This confers the veto-wielding powers with the authoritative role of gate-keeper.

At the current level of recognitions (114 as of September 2018, according to the disputed numbers offered by Pristina), Kosovo would have some chance of succeeding in the UNGA, depending on the number of abstentions. Prior to reaching that step, however, Pristina must overcome an obstacle which appears insurmountable: the Chinese and, particularly, the Russian veto. At this stage, Russia does not seem to have any incentive to lift its veto. On the contrary, the veto over Kosovo empowers Russia in a multifaceted fashion. As Chapter 6 will examine, Kosovo provides Moscow with a precedent which has already been used several times by the Kremlin as a pretext for its own territorial adventurism. Further, it allows Russia to be obstructive to the geopolitical redesign of the former Yugoslavia championed by the U.S. and its European counterparts over the past decades. In terms of discourse, it permits Russia to use a powerful narrative by positioning itself as a legalist, as a defender of territorial integrity and sovereignty[16] (Allison, 2013; Averre and Davies, 2015).

It also positions Moscow as a loyal supporter of its 'historical ally', Serbia, thus exerting decisive influence over an EU candidate member. As Bečka point out, however, Russia's position has less to do with Russia's historical friendship with Serbia and more with its own national interest (2017, p. 215). At first glance, this opens the door for a future solution based on *quid pro quo* concessions. Those concessions, however, would have to be substantial to satisfy Russia. The crux is that if the West would like to finally conclude Kosovo's independence successfully, they will have to pay a price (to Russia and probably China), a heavy price more than likely, for it. It seems therefore evident that, as Vrbetić asserts, 'Kosovo has entered a grey area of international legitimacy' (2013, p. 326), a trap which requires the consent of China and Russia to get into the UN club.

Bearing all these elements in mind, it is possible to conclude that the West's policies in Kosovo have resulted in a blowback, which has empowered Russia by providing it with a golden key, that of permanent non-recognition/veto at the Security Council. The bottom line is that given that Russia seems to have no appetite to recognise Kosovo, it appears obvious that Kosovo's independence is far from being complete. The recent growing geopolitical tensions between Russia and the U.S. over Syria and Ukraine complicate even further an agreement over Kosovo. In the view of the former UNMIK Special Representative, Søren Jessen-Petersen, 'given the current climate, it [Kosovo's aspiration to get a UN seat] will not move forward. It is linked to so many other developments. Kosovo has become a pawn in the tit-for-tat geopolitical confrontation'.[17] Kosovo, consequently, seems to be trapped in a wider geopolitical conflict which has, as a matter of fact, very little connection with this South-Eastern European territory. To put it poetically, initially Kosovo's statehood benefited from geopolitical clashes[18] but the tables have turned and those very clashes currently represent the main burden for Kosovo's UN membership.

The roles of the EU and the U.S.

Deep divisions at the UN level regarding Kosovo are to a certain extent understandable, given the geopolitical dimension of the *problématique*. What is perhaps more shocking are the profound discrepancies within the European Union, particularly when we bear in mind that the EU is deeply invested in Kosovo and that European powers such as the UK, France and Germany have been key supporters of Kosovo's secession. With such diplomatic endorsement accompanied by the institutional support on the ground, it is not too far-fetched to argue that 'the birth of Kosovo as a (para)state is partly due to the legitimizing actions carried out by [prominent] EU member states' (Castan Pinos, 2018, p. 247). Additionally, this territory is part of the EU's near abroad and it is even a potential candidate for EU membership. These divisions are even more inexplicable when considering that the EU and Kosovo, in 2015, signed a Stabilisation and Association Agreement[19] (European Commission, 2015), a covenant which has often been the stepping stone towards EU membership for aspiring states.

The core problem for the EU with regards to Kosovo is that it does not speak with a single coherent voice. Five EU states (Spain, Romania, Greece, Slovakia and Cyprus) representing nearly 20 per cent of the member states, have hitherto refused to recognise Kosovo despite the pressures they have received from their European partners. As Chapter 6 will explain at great length, all these five states have internal issues related to secessionist or minority conflicts[20] (Castan Pinos, 2015, p. 231). The most relevant out of these five states, Spain, responded clearly and promptly to Kosovo's UDI. Spain's Foreign Minister at the time, Miguel Ángel Moratinos, stated, a day after the declaration, that: 'The government of Spain will not recognise the unilateral act proclaimed yesterday by the assembly of Kosovo, it … does not respect international law' (cited by Reuters, 2008). Spain's position remains unchanged as of 2018.

The problem for the EU is that the persistent opposition of five of its members to Kosovo's secession has the potential to jeopardise the entire EU policy with regards to Kosovo. One of the vital ingredients of this policy is the carrot of membership, but this incentive cannot materialise with five states potentially sabotaging it. The seemingly irreconcilable differences over Kosovo, a territory in Europe's backyard, put into question the very adjective 'common' which the EU so adamantly uses when referring to its foreign policy. In the case of Kosovo, in particular, there seems to be a preponderance of the member states' national interest over EU collective objectives. The former head of the UN Mission in Kosovo, Søren Jessen-Petersen, believes that this impasse – that is, Kosovo's inability to obtain UN membership – will only change if the EU agrees internally: 'as long as there are five countries in the EU refusing to recognise, it will be very hard. The EU disagreement reinforces Russia's arguments'.[21]

Despite the acute discrepancies over Kosovo's status, the EU has been able to develop two major political initiatives in Kosovo: the European Union Rule of Law Mission in Kosovo (EULEX) and the EU-led Brussels agreement, between the Belgrade and Pristina governments. The following paragraphs will shed light over the nature and the debates surrounding the former. The latter will be analysed in the following chapter, in connection with EU plans to solve the *problem of the north* [of Kosovo].

EULEX, an unwelcome initiative?

EULEX has been often lauded, at least initially, as the most significant and ambitious civilian of the EU common foreign policy (Wet, 2009; Chivvis, 2010; Spernbauer, 2010). It has been argued that with the United States endorsing unilateral independence, the EU was left between a rock and a hard place having to choose between little or no international supervision (as explained previously, UNMIK became devoid of power after the UDI) or hastily developing a mission without internal consensus over status (Ker-Lindsay and Economides, 2012, p. 90). As the result of a spirit of political pragmatism, the lack of agreement among member states over Kosovo's independence did not represent an impediment to launching the EULEX mission. The fact that EULEX is, at least nominally, status-neutral[22] has allowed the EU to accommodate the internal dissonant voices, which have even participated in the mission. This accommodation, however, has been far from unproblematic. A leaked cable from the U.S. embassy in Pristina reveals that EULEX's policy chief Dominique Orsini was distraught about the fact that 'Madrid and the other four non-recognizing [EU] capitals complain to Brussels each time a routine report even suggests that EULEX is venturing beyond the bounds of status-neutrality' (cited by Wikileaks, 2009). Disagreements over Kosovo's status, therefore, have seemingly acted as a systematic burden to the mission.

The legitimacy and legality of the mission operate in mysterious and controversial ways. The mission is EU-led but has been supported by

Washington through funding and personnel[23] (Chivvis, 2010, p. 31). One of its sources of legitimacy is Kosovo's UDI, whose Article 5 invites and welcomes a 'European Union-led rule of law mission' (BBC, 2008). Such legitimacy, however, is at least tricky and at most tautological since, as previously explained, the UDI was largely drafted by the U.S. Department of State.

More disturbingly, the original sin of EULEX is that it is an EU initiative which, as laudatory as it may be, lacks the authorisation of a UNSC Resolution. Initially, its main endorsement is the fact that the UN Secretary General at the time, Ban Ki Moon, acknowledged having received a letter from Javier Solana, the European Union's High Representative for the Common Foreign and Security Policy, where the latter informed the Secretary General about the deployment of EULEX (UN, 2008). The fact that the Secretary General or the UNSC did not de-authorise the mission may be considered as an implicit authorisation. This idea, however, is contested by Wet, who believes that far from being an implicit authorisation, Moon was simply acknowledging 'a fait accompli brought about by the European Union and the United States' (2009, p. 88). Secretary General Moon, however, issued a more explicit endorsement shortly before the Kosovo Constitution came into force by asserting that 'the objectives of the United Nations would be best obtained through an enhanced operational role for the European Union in the area of the rule of law' (UNSC, 2008c, p. 4).

Beyond the debates about its legality and legitimacy, EULEX was met with two challenges upon its arrival in Kosovo; overlaps and discrepancies with UNMIK and hostility from the local population(s). William Ortiz, a former UNMIK officer, complains that the arrival of EULEX represented an illegal institutional takeover, replacing UNMIK surreptitiously:

> EULEX is an international shame, they have no international mandate. Their mission was to kick UNMIK out so that Europeans would be in charge. The EU had a bigger aim, to use EULEX as a stepping stone to replace UN civilian and police missions all over the world.[24]

As the statement shows, cooperation between the multiple international organisations operating in Kosovo has been far from smooth. Some have warned about the operational problems derived from potential overlaps between UNMIK and EULEX (Greiçevci, 2011, p. 296). In practice however, since UNMIK fell from grace in 2008, becoming a symbolic actor at best and an irrelevant one at worst, the potential overlaps do not represent a major encumbrance. In terms of local hostility, EULEX has been able to antagonise both Kosovo Serbs and Kosovo Albanians for very similar reasons. To the former, it is perceived as a non-neutral actor whose main goal is to consolidate and enhance Kosovo's independence thus jeopardising any possibility to the return of Serbian rule.[25] To the latter, it is

Figure 4.3 Graffiti critical of EULEX in North Mitrovica (2012).
Source: author.

perceived as an organisation which systematically interferes in Kosovo's internal affairs thus vitally compromising Kosovo's sovereignty.[26]

One of the problems of EULEX[27] is ontological, namely its difficulty or even inability to fulfil the main purpose of its own mission, that is, to establish a rule of law regime. Critiques of EULEX have come from a wide range of actors, including from internal sources. In 2012, the European Court of Auditors, an EU institution concluded that '[d]espite some modest successes ... EU assistance to the police audited by the Court did not lead to significant improvements' (2012, p. 16). It should be noted that this is a difficulty inherited from UNMIK, which was also notably unsuccessful in establishing an effective rule of law regime. The former head of UNMIK, Søren Jessen-Petersen, highlights that his biggest regret from his term in office was his failure in terms of rule of law and consequently his inability to tackle organised crime and corruption.[28] A EULEX officer operating in Northern Kosovo maintained that 'all criminal cases against powerful Kosovo Albanians end up in nothing because they are the too powerful. The cases are *forgotten* [emphasis added by author] in order to keep good relations with the government'.[29] The rationale for this is straightforward: the main concern of EULEX, the EU and its member states is to ensure stability and to avoid situations that may jeopardise the international supervision regime. The fear is that if an influential political figure is indicted that stability could be seriously compromised and an outbreak of violence may erupt. In practice, that means that EULEX, similarly to its predecessor (UNMIK), is hostage and unable to conclude many of the criminal investigations they initiate. Needless to say, the consequence for this is downright impunity, including cases involving the most serious crimes.

The Specialist Chambers: a solution to a problem through further foreign interference?

In order to address this inconvenient problem and perhaps to respond to critics, the EU pushed for the establishment of the Specialist Chambers of Kosovo (SC) and the Specialist Prosecutor's Office (SPO). The process leading to the inception of these Courts is, like many other developments in Kosovo, *sui generis*. According to Williams, the establishment of these institutions was the result of 'an exchange of letters between the EU High Representative and the President of Kosovo in April 2014'[30] (2016, p. 29). This exchange of correspondence subsequently became part of the national legislation when Kosovo added a new article to its Constitution (Article 162) and its assembly adopted a law in August 2015 (Law No. 05/L-053) establishing the mandate of the SC and the SPO (Kosovo Assembly, 2015). Some details of these Courts may appear as peculiar and abnormal to many readers. For one, the Courts, despite being a Kosovo institution, are based at The Hague and all its judges are international and appointed by the EU through the head of EULEX (SCSPO, 2018b). In turn, the EU, together with the U.S., Canada and Turkey among other states, is responsible for financing this unprecedented judicial institution (SCSPO, 2018a). Intuitively, the reason for this is to guarantee their independence and to protect witnesses.

The challenge of the SC/SPO is that by tackling criminal impunity, particularly when it comes to confronting the crimes committed by Kosovo Liberation Army (KLA) members,[31] discontent and alienation from local actors towards internationally-made institutions may develop. This has, in fact, already been the case. As the Courts were preparing the first indictments, opposition from Kosovo Albanians began to materialise. According to Nait Hasani, an MP from the ruling Democratic Party of Kosovo (PDK), '[T]he special court [SC] has been and will be unacceptable to Kosovo' because 'it is a political court and wants to punish only Kosovo Liberation Army soldiers for alleged war crimes' (cited by Hopkins, 2018). The important aspect of this puzzle is, once again, sovereignty, which lies at the very centre of this debate. Mahr has argued that by addressing the issue of the rule of law the EU engages with very sensitive and fundamental political matters: 'EU's rule of law activities are also intrinsically political in that they touch upon what Kosovar locals perceive as core attributes of their sovereignty' (Mahr, 2018, p. 76). In a similar vein, an activist from Kosovo's Social Democratic Party, Marigone Drevinja, has claimed that EULEX, and in particular the SC/SPO, compromise Kosovo's sovereignty because these courts are 'above the sovereignty of the [Kosovo] state'.[32]

The counter-argument to this is that, as seen at the beginning of this chapter, Kosovo accepted the deal, namely to obtain independence in exchange that it would be supervised by international institutions such as the EU. As explained at the beginning of this chapter, formally speaking, supervised independence ended in September 2012 with the termination of the ICR mandate (European Commission, 2012, p. 4). Visoka has pointed out that this premature culmination of international supervision is due to 'local demands for full sovereignty and non-interference in Kosovo' (2017, pp. 15–16). The end of the ICR mandate, however, did not result in the end of interference in Kosovo. As these last paragraphs have illustrated, international actors have used a multiplicity of instruments of interference, supervision and explicit intervention in Kosovo. The interference is so obvious that it is possible to argue that, de facto, Kosovo's independence is still supervised.

Washington calls the shots

The EU is not alone when it comes to critiques related to foreign interference compromising Kosovo's ability to manage its internal affairs. The United States has also played a prominent role in terms of curtailing Kosovo's sovereignty. This has been denounced by local non-governmental organisations in Kosovo who complain about the 'widespread omnipotence' of U.S. ambassadors in contrast to the 'powerlessness of local elites' (Zogiani and Bajrami, 2014, pp. 17–18). More importantly, this unconstrained power of the U.S. embassy has also been highlighted by an internal audit carried out by the U.S. Department of State. In a document titled 'Report of Inspection', the Department of State asserts that the U.S. embassy in Pristina 'exerts a wide and unusual influence over the Kosovo Government's policies and actions. Both the cause and effect of this influence is the embassy's access to all levels of government by all members of its operating elements' (2010, p. 7). The consequence of this, the report claims, is that Kosovo government officials consult with the embassy 'on a daily basis on actions, large and small' (U.S. Department of State, 2010, p. 8).

Taking into account the conclusions from this official report, political activist Marigone Drevinja's claim that 'when we [Kosovo institutions] have important decisions, we have to ask permission to the U.S. Embassy'[33] does not appear to be exaggerated. The outstanding influence of the U.S. embassy has a direct and vital impact on Kosovo's politics. In 2011, for instance, amidst a political crisis, U.S. ambassador at the time, Christopher Dell, acted as a self-appointed broker to reach a deal between the government and the opposition (Janssens, 2015, p. 334) to elect a new President. The fact that Dell himself appeared on television to announce an agreement between the different parties and the name of the new President, a relatively unknown figure (Atifete Jahjaga) until then, contributed to his reputation and image as a kingmaker in Kosovo (Brunwasser, 2015). A political rival, Kosovo's current Minister of Foreign Affairs, Behgjet Pacolli went as far as to claim that Dell had put forward 'the name of the newly elected president, Atifete Jahjaga', in a sealed envelope (cited by Marzouk, 2011). An anonymous journalist in Pristina confirms this claim by adding that 'Dell was caught red handed sending messages to [Kosovo Assembly] MP's to pressure them so that they would choose a particular President'.[34]

An analogous episode occurred in 2014. As in 2011, Kosovo's political leaders could not reach a decision to elect a key figure, in this case the Prime Minister. The disagreements between the two main political parties in Kosovo at the time, the Democratic Party of Kosovo (PDK) and Democratic League of Kosovo (LDK), were so significant that Kosovo had been without a government for several months. While this is not uncommon in parliamentary democracies, in Kosovo this could prompt the risk of instability, or at least that was the perception of the U.S. embassy. The new U.S. ambassador, Tracey Ann Jacobson, like her predecessor, acted as a broker. In what it appeared to be an ultimatum for the Kosovo ruling elites, she stated in a TV interview that: '[M]y message to the politicians has been clear, I can even say it in Albanian, Mos e dhi punen (Don't screw up)' (cited by Bytyci, 2014). Those pressures had immediate effects and shortly afterwards the political impasse had been solved and a new PM, Isa Mustafi, had been appointed. Unsurprisingly, this has been perceived by some in

Pristina[35] as unacceptable meddling by a foreign power in Kosovo's internal affairs. These episodes confirm that, as reported by the audit from the U.S. state department, the work of the U.S. embassy in Pristina 'goes well beyond traditional advocacy' (U.S. Department of State, 2010, p. 8). Indeed, the fact that the U.S. embassy has played a very influential role in the election of a President and a Prime Minister has a very strong connotation of symbolic (and tangible) power.

Arguably, Washington's influence has not only manifested itself in local politics but also affected international organisations operating in Kosovo. William Ortiz, a former UNMIK civilian officer has condemned the interference that these organisations experienced from the very first day of their deployment in June 1999:

> The US state department has manipulated International Organizations [in Kosovo]. The vast majority of internationals [working in Kosovo] understood the process and they feel frustrated, manipulated and misused to achieve some geopolitical goals. The [independence] process is not fair or negotiated- it is imposed by the Pentagon through its tentacles, that is, through us.[36]

Privatisation, a policy which according to Belloni and Strazzari 'has helped to create vast opportunities for manipulation and abuse' in Kosovo (2015, p. 864), illustrates the potentially perverse consequences of Washington's influence. In 2010, against the recommendations of the World Bank, the IMF, the EU and its own legal advisors, the Kosovo government signed a deal with a U.S. corporation – Beltech – to build a motorway from Kosovo to Albania (Lewis, 2014; Brunwasser, 2015). In the view of Peiter Feith, former European Union Special Representative in Kosovo, U.S. ambassador Dell[37] actively lobbied for the deal with Bechtel, concealed information about the details of the contract and eventually pushed through it, leaving the newly created state of Kosovo heavily indebted[38] (Collaku *et al.*, 2014; Lewis, 2014).

The U.S. influence also has a more geopolitical tangible feature: Camp Bondsteel. This 400-hectares military base, which was built immediately after the deployment of the KFOR mission, is located in Southern Kosovo, close to the Macedonian border. It has 52 helipads and can host up to 7,000 troops, making it the largest U.S. base in the region.[39] Despite the numerous rumours that alleged that the base would be closed down, Camp Bondsteel has managed to survive, becoming a controversial landmark of post-intervention Kosovo.[40] A report from a U.S. think tank closely linked to NATO, the Atlantic Council, has advocated for Camp Bondsteel to become 'the United States' first permanent military base in Southeastern Europe' (Marusic *et al.*, 2017, p. 17). Interestingly, one of the report's justifications for such move is intimately connected to borders, more specifically, the permanent base would act as a deterrent to 'reckless revisionism of existing borders – something that Russian adventurism has encouraged' (Marusic *et al.*, 2017, p. 17). The irony of that argument is that Camp Bondsteel would not exist without the West *revisionism of existing borders* and its military *adventurism* in Kosovo.

This enormous geopolitical leverage which is visible in local and international institutions is hardly surprising when considering the wider picture. It is worth remembering that, as Chapter 2 explained, *Operation Allied Force* was a U.S.-led operation which could not have taken place without Washington's decisive push. The U.S. has therefore been deeply invested in Kosovo from 1999 and therefore it is one of the actors that has a bigger interest in ensuring that the situation does not get out of hand. The U.S.'s active role must be understood not only in terms of power but also in relation to reputation. Simply put, if Kosovo fails, the U.S. strategy in the region over the past 20 years fails. In other words, there is too much at stake for the U.S. not to care, or more precisely, not to interfere. The paradox is that by protecting Kosovo from internal and external threats through interference, the U.S. has decisively contributed to curtailing Kosovo's sovereignty. As next chapter will show, the U.S. (as well as the EU) leverage is also determinant when it comes to dealing with *the problem of the north.*

Notes

1 Marigone Drevinja, author interview, Pristina, 4 August 2017.
2 Small Slavic-speaking Muslim community in Southern Kosovo. During the conflict between the KLA and the Yugoslavian security forces in the late 1990s, Gorani sided with the latter.
3 See Chapter 3 for further details.
4 The figures for the period 2018/2019 are similar to that of 2008/2009: the budget is $37M and the total number of personnel is 349 (UNGA, 2008d).
5 Søren Jessen-Petersen, author interview, Copenhagen, 9 March 2018.
6 Likewise, Serbs, Kosovo's second largest community, have a Serbian identity, not a 'Kosovar' one.
7 European diplomat, author interview, Belgrade, 30 June 2014.
8 Bashmir Xhemaj, author interview, Skype, 28 May 2018.
9 The list includes a total of 116 recognitions; however, two of them (Cook Islands and Niue) are not UN members states.
10 Bashmir Xhemaj, author interview, Skype, 28 May 2018.
11 According to the KMFA, Guinea Bissau recognised Kosovo in 2011.
12 See Chapter 3 for further details on this.
13 An exclusive competence of the UN Special Representative in Kosovo.
14 Bashmir Xhemaj, author interview, Skype, 28 May 2018.
15 Article 2.4 of the UN Charter, for instance, stipulates that '[A]ll Members shall refrain in their international relations from the threat or use of force against the territorial integrity or political independence of any state' (UN, 1945).
16 Such narrative has partly been compromised by Russia's own actions in Georgia (2008) and Crimea (2014).
17 Søren Jessen-Petersen, author interview, Copenhagen, 9 March 2018.
18 As Chapters 2 and 3 have discussed, there was a crucial geopolitical element behind NATO's 'Operation Allied Force'. As President Clinton admitted,

Kosovo was for NATO an opportunity to demonstrate the transatlantic organisation's seriousness and credibility (U.S. Government Publishing Office, 1999). It could also be argued that by weakening a key Russian ally, NATO's intervention did also contribute to alter the balance of power between Russia and the U.S. in favour of the latter.

19 Every time Kosovo appears in an official document, an asterisk is added stating that: '[T]his designation is without prejudice to positions on status, and is in line with UNSCR 1244/1999 and the ICJ Opinion on the Kosovo declaration of independence' (European Commission, 2015, p. 1).

20 The Greek position is arguably connected to the Turkish-occupied Northern Cyprus case.

21 Søren Jessen-Petersen, author interview, Copenhagen, 9 March 2018.

22 A EULEX officer has admitted that, in practice, the status-neutral formula does not apply for the very reason that EULEX aims to assist Kosovo with institutions so that it can consolidate its independence. EULEX officer, author interview, Mitrovica, 3 June 2014.

23 According to Chivvis, 70 U.S. staff were operating under EULEX, when the mission was launched (2010, p. 31).

24 William Ortiz, author interview, Skype, 8 March 2018.

25 Dragiša Djoković, author interview, Mitrovica, 3 August 2017; Nemanja Jaksić, author interview, Mitrovica, 2 June 2014.

26 Marigone Drevinja, author interview, Pristina, 4 August 2017.

27 EULEX mission is, according to the EU Council to

> assist the Kosovo institutions, judicial authorities and law enforcement agencies in their progress towards sustainability and accountability and in further developing and strengthening an independent and multi-ethnic justice system and a multi-ethnic police and customs service, ensuring that these institutions are free from political interference and adhering to internationally recognised standards and European best practices.
>
> (Official Journal of the European Union, 2008, p. 93)

28 Søren Jessen-Petersen, author interview, Copenhagen, 9 March 2018. Jessen-Petersen illustrates his inefficiency in terms of rule of law with a very specific case which failed as a result of pressures 'from above':

> In June 2005, we had one major case. We had done all our work. We had prepared to start a persecution on a very senior politician. We had prepared everything. We were ready to enter his building to confiscate potentially incriminating documents because we had a very strong case. We had planned the operation for days. We had asked KFOR to be behind when we went to that building. There was a risk of violence. We worked together with the KFOR commander on the plan, they were fully on board. Everything was under control but the evening before the operation, I got a telephone call from the Secretary General of NATO [Jaap de Hoop Scheffer] and he told me that 'KFOR cannot participate, the operation is too dangerous, it risks provoking a lot of violence and stability would be at risk in Kosovo'. NATO was worried that this would endanger the status process. Without NATO's support we had to call off the operation. We failed.

29 EULEX officer, author interview, Mitrovica, 3 June 2014.

30 Far from being a rumour or a conspiracy theory, the fact that the Courts originated from an exchange of letters is confirmed by the SCO webpage itself (SCSPO, 2018a).

31 Those alleged crimes are well documented. See Chapter 1 and Marty (2011) for further details.

32 Marigone Drevinja, author interview, Pristina, 4 August 2017.
33 Marigone Drevinja, author interview, Pristina, 4 August 2017.
34 Kosovo Journalist, author interview, Pristina, 2 August 2017.
35 Marigone Drevinja, author interview, Pristina, 4 August 2017; Kosovo Journalist, author interview, Pristina, 2 August 2017.
36 William Ortiz, author interview, Skype, 8 March 2018.
37 Dell's efforts paid off well for him personally. A year after finishing his term in Pristina, Dell joined Bechtel, the firm he had lobbied for while he was the U.S. ambassador in Kosovo (Collaku, 2014).
38 According to Brunwasser, the project represented 20 per cent of Kosovo's GDP in 2010 (2015).
39 For further details see: https://militarybases.com/overseas/kosovo/camp-bondsteel/
40 The base has been marred with controversy. In addition to its dubious legal status – it was originally built without the permission of the state where it is located (Yugoslavia and later Serbia) – the base was used as an illegal prison camp, holding suspects of Salafist terrorism. According to Álvaro Gil Robles, Human Rights Commissioner for the Council of Europe, the conditions of the prisoners, imprisoned without trial, were similar to those of Guantánamo (cited by *Der Spiegel*, 2005).

Bibliography

Allison, R. (2013) *Russia, the West, and military intervention*. Oxford: Oxford University Press.

Averre, D. and Davies, L. (2015) 'Russia, humanitarian intervention and the Responsibility to Protect: the case of Syria' *International Affairs*, 91 (4): 813–834.

B92 (2017a, 31 October). 'South American country revokes recognition of Kosovo – FM'. Retrieved from: www.b92.net/eng/news/politics.php?yyyy=2017&mm=10&dd=31&nav_id=102684

B92 (2017b, 17 November). 'African country denies it ever recognized Kosovo'. Retrieved from: www.b92.net/eng/news/politics.php?yyyy=2017&mm=11&dd=17&nav_id=102832

B92 (2017c, 27 November). 'Pristina has "at least 7 or 8 bogus recognitions" – Dacic'. Retrieved from: www.b92.net/eng/news/politics.php?yyyy=2017&mm=11&dd=27&nav_id=102890

B92 (2018, 27 February). '"FM offered arms in exchange for revoking Kosovo recognition"' Retrieved from: www.b92.net/eng/news/politics.php?yyyy=2018&mm=02&dd=27&nav_id=103586

BBC (2008a, 17 February). 'Full text: Kosovo declaration'. Retrieved from: http://news.bbc.co.uk/2/hi/europe/7249677.stm

BBC (2008b, 19 February). 'Russia warns US over Kosovo move'. Retrieved from: http://news.bbc.co.uk/2/hi/europe/7252512.stm

BBC (2008c, 22 February). 'US embassy in Belgrade attacked'. Retrieved from: http://news.bbc.co.uk/2/hi/europe/7256158.stm

Bečka, J. (2017). 'Long Way to Recognition: Challenges Facing the European "Newborn" from the 2015 Perspective', in M. Riegl and B. Doboš (eds), *Unrecognized States and Secession in the 21st Century*, (pp. 205–221). Cham: Springer.

Belloni, R. and Strazzari, F. (2014). 'Corruption in post-conflict Bosnia-Herzegovina and Kosovo: a deal among friends', *Third World Quarterly*, 35(5): 855–871.

Bilefsky, D. (2007, 9 December). 'A difficult question for Kosovars: Who are we?'. *New York Times*. Retrieved from: www.nytimes.com/2007/12/09/world/europe/09iht-kosovo.4.8660025.html

Billig, M. (1995). *Banal Nationalism*. London: Sage Publications Ltd.

Borger, J. (2008, 18 February). 'A country in search of an identity'. *Guardian*. Retrieved from: www.theguardian.com/world/2008/feb/18/kosovo.balkans1

Borgen, C. J. (2010). 'From Kosovo to Catalonia: Separatism and Integration in Europe'. *Goettingen Journal of International Law*, 2(3): 997–1033.

Bothe, (2010). 'Kosovo – So What – The Holding of the International Court of Justice is Not the Last Word on Kosovo's Independence'. *German Law Journal*, 11: 837–840.

Brunwasser, M. (2015, 30 January). 'Steamrolled. A special investigation into the diplomacy of doing business abroad'. *Foreign Policy*. Retrieved from: http://foreignpolicy.com/2015/01/30/steamrolled-investigation-bechtel-highway-business-kosovo/

Brunwasser, M. (2015, 9 November). 'Unesco Rejects Kosovo Membership in a Victory for Serbia'. *New York Times*. Retrieved from: www.nytimes.com/2015/11/10/world/europe/unesco-rejects-kosovo-membership-in-a-victory-for-serbia.html

Burri, T. (2010) 'The Kosovo Opinion and Secession: The Sounds of Silence and Missing Links'. *German Law Journal*, 11: 881–890.

Bytyci (2014, 6 November). '"Don't screw up": U.S. envoy losing patience with Kosovo political impasse'. *Reuters*. Retrieved from: www.reuters.com/article/us-kosovo-usa-impasse/dont-screw-up-u-s-envoy-losing-patience-with-kosovo-political-impasse-idUSKBN0IQ1RU20141106

Castan Pinos, J. (2015). 'The Challenge to Territorial Integrity, Kosovo and beyond', in C. Gaitanides (eds), *Diversity in Europe* (pp. 220–236). Baden-Baden: Nomos Verlagsgesellschaft.

Castan Pinos, J. (2018). 'Conflicts over Sovereignty in Europe in the so-called Post-Sovereignty Era', in B. Wassenberg (ed.), *Castle-talks on Cross-Border Cooperation. Fear of Integration? The Pertinence of the Border* (239–252). Stuttgart: Franz Steiner Verlag.

Chivvis, C. (2010). *EU Civilian Crisis Management: The Record So Far*. Santa Monica: RAND Corporation.

Collaku, P. *et al*. (2014, 23 April). 'Albania-Kosovo Highway Costs Soar To 2 Billion Euros'. *Balkan Insight*. Retrieved from: www.balkaninsight.com/en/article/albania-kosovo-highway-costs-soar-to-2-billion-euro

Cosentino, D. (2015) 'Designing the Identity of a New State: Kosovo Flag'. *The Design Journal*, 18(4): 607–612.

Der Spiegel (2005, 5 December). 'Clandestine Camps in Europe "Everyone Knew What Was Going On in Bondsteel"'. Retrieved from: www.spiegel.de/international/clandestine-camps-in-europe-everyone-knew-what-was-going-on-in-bondsteel-a-388556.html

Dietrich, F. (2010). 'The Status of Kosovo – Reflections on the Legitimacy of Secession'. *Ethics and Global Politics*, 3(2): 123–142.

Djoković, D., author interview, Mitrovica, 3 August 2017.

Drevinja, M., author interview, Pristina, 4 August 2017.

Eckhard, S. and Dijkstra, H. (2017). 'Contested Implementation: The Unilateral Influence of Member States on Peacebuilding Policy in Kosovo'. *Global Policy*, 8(5): 102–112.

EULEX officer, author interview, Mitrovica, 3 June 2014.

European Commission (2012). 'Communication on a Feasibility Study for a Stabilisation and Association Agreement between the European Union and Kosovo*'. COM(2012) 602 final. Retrieved from: http://eur-lex.europa.eu/legal-content/EN/TXT/PDF/?uri=CELEX:52012DC0602&from=en

European Commission (2015). 'Stabilisation and association agreement between the European Union of the one part, and Kosovo*, of the other part'. Retrieved from: https://ec.europa.eu/neighbourhood-enlargement/sites/near/files/news_corner/news/news-files/20150430_saa.pdf

European Court of Auditors. (2012). *European Union Assistance to Kosovo Related to the Rule of Law*. Brussels: European Court of Auditors.

European diplomat, author interview, Belgrade, 30 June 2014.

Express (2007, 13 June). 'Kosovo Unity Team announces the Competition for the Flag and emblem of Kosovo'. Retrieved from: https://web.archive.org/web/20071021074123/www.kajtazi.info/flag-emblem-kosovo.pdf

FIFA (2016). 'FIFA Congress drives football forward, first female secretary general appointed'. Retrieved from: www.fifa.com/about-fifa/news/y=2016/m=5/news=fifa-congress-drives-football-forward-first-female-secretary-general-a-2790957.html

Franck, T. (1988). 'Legitimacy in the International System'. *The American Journal of International Law*, 82(4): 705–759.

Gazeta Express (2017, 9 September). 'Ramush Haradinaj elected new prime minister of Kosovo'. Retrieved from: www.gazetaexpress.com/en/news/ramush-haradinaj-elected-new-prime-minister-of-kosovo-172958/

Gazeta Express (2018, 30 January). 'Guinea Bissau reconfirms recognition of Kosovo's Independence'. Retrieved from: www.gazetaexpress.com/en/news/guinea-bissau-reconfirms-recognition-of-kosovo-s-independence-173532/

Gellner, E. (1964). *Thought and Change*. London: Weidenfeld and Nicolson.

Greiçevci, L. (2011). 'EU Actorness in International Affairs: The Case of EULEX Mission in Kosovo'. *Perspectives on European Politics and Society*, 12(3), 283–303.

Griffiths, R. (2017) 'Admission to the sovereignty club: the past, present, and future of the international recognition regime'. *Territory, Politics, Governance*, 5(2), 177–189.

Hopkins, V. (2018, 5 January). 'Kosovo politicians in 'panic attack' over war crimes court'. *Politico*. Retrieved from: www.politico.eu/article/ramush-haradinaj-hashim-thaci-kosovo-politicians-in-panic-attack-over-war-crimes-court/

ICG (2008). 'Kosovo's First Month'. *Europe Briefing no. 47*. Retrieved from: https://d2071andvip0wj.cloudfront.net/b47-kosovo-s-first-month.pdf

ICJ (2010a). 'Accordance with International Law of the Unilateral Declaration of Independence in Respect of Kosovo, Advisory Opinion, I.C.J. Reports 2010'. Retrieved from: www.icj-cij.org/files/case-related/141/141-20100722-ADV-01-00-EN.pdf

ICJ (2010b). 'Accordance with International Law of the Unilateral Declaration of Independence in Respect of Kosovo: declaration of [ICJ] Vice President Tomka'. Retrieved from: www.icj-cij.org/files/case-related/141/141-20100722-ADV-01-01-EN.pdf

ICJ (2010c). 'Accordance with International Law of the Unilateral Declaration of Independence in Respect of Kosovo: dissenting opinion of Judge Bennouna'. Retrieved from: www.icj-cij.org/files/case-related/141/141-20100722-ADV-01-06-EN.pdf

IMF (2009). 'Press Release: Kosovo Becomes the International Monetary Fund's 186th Member'. Retrieved from: www.imf.org/en/News/Articles/2015/09/14/01/49/pr09240

Jaksić, N., author interview, Mitrovica, 2 June 2014.

Jamar, H. and Vigness, M. (2010) 'Applying Kosovo: Looking to Russia, China, Spain and beyond after the International Court of Justice Opinion on Unilateral Declarations of Independence'. *German Law Journal*, 11, 913–928.

Jano, D. (2013). 'Kosovar Multi-Layer Identity: What is the Same, Different and in Common with Albanian Identity'. *Journal of European and International Affairs*, 1(1): 27–40.

Janssens, J. (2015). *State-Building in Kosovo. A Plural Policing Perspective*. Antwerp: Maklu.

Jessen-Petersen, S., author interview, Copenhagen, 9 March 2018.

Keating, J. (2008). 'How to Start Your Own Country in Four Easy Steps'. Retrieved from: http://foreignpolicy.com/2008/02/26/how-to-start-your-own-country-in-four-easy-steps/

Ker-Lindsay, J. (2012). *The Foreign Policy of Counter Secession: Preventing the Recognition of Contested States*. Oxford: Oxford University Press.

Ker-Lindsay, J. and Economides, S. (2012). 'Standards before Status before Accession: Kosovo's EU Perspective'. *Journal of Balkan and Near Eastern Studies*, 14(1), 77–92.

Kosovo Assembly (2015). 'Law No. 05/L-053 On Specialist Chambers and Specialist Prosecutor's Office'. Retrieved from: www.kuvendikosoves.org/common/docs/ligjet/05-L-053%20a.pdf

Kosovo journalist, author interview, Pristina, 2 August 2017.

Kosovo's Ministry of Foreign Affairs (2018). 'Lista e njohjeve'. Retrieved from: www.mfa-ks.net/?page=1,259

Kolstø, P. (2006). 'The Sustainability and Future of Unrecognized Quasi-States'. *Journal of Peace Research*, 43(6): 723–740.

Lewis, P. (2014, 14 April). 'US ambassador to Kosovo hired by construction firm he lobbied for'. *Guardian*. Retrieved from: www.theguardian.com/world/2014/apr/14/us-ambassador-kosovo-construction-contract-firm-highway

Mahr, E. (2018). 'Local contestation against the European Union Rule of Law Mission in Kosovo'. *Contemporary Security Policy*, 39(1), 72–94.

Marty, D. (2011). 'Inhuman treatment of people and illicit trafficking in human organs in Kosovo'. *Council of Europe*, Doc. 12462. Retrieved from: www.sitf.eu/images/110107CoEReport.pdf

Marusic, D. *et al*. (2017). 'Balkans Forward. A new US Strategy for the Region'. *Atlantic Council*. Retrieved from: www.atlanticcouncil.org/images/Balkans_Forward_web_1128.pdf

Marzouk, L. (2011, 25 April). 'State Department Cleans Dell's Wiki Log of Controversial Material'. *Balkan Insight*. Retrieved from: www.balkaninsight.com/en/article/state-department-cleans-dell-s-wiki-log-of-controversial-material

McKinna, A. (2012). 'Kosovo: The International Community's European Project'. *European Review*, 20 (1): 10–22.

Military Bases (2018). 'Camp Bondsteel Army Base in Ferizaj, Kosovo'. Retrieved from: https://militarybases.com/overseas/kosovo/camp-bondsteel/

Ministry of Foreign Affairs of the Republic of Serbia (2017). 'Principled position of Sao Tome and Principe concerning the respect of international law and non-recognition of Kosovo'. Retrieved from: www.mfa.gov.rs/en/press-service/statements/16946-principled-position-of-sao-tome-and-principe-concerning-the-respect-of-international-law-and-non-recognition-of-kosovo

Official Journal of the European Union (2008). 'European Council Joint Action 2008/124/CFSP, 4 February 2008, on the European Union Rule of Law Mission in Kosovo, OJ L 42/92'. Retrieved from: https://eur-lex.europa.eu/legal-content/EN/TXT/PDF/?uri=CELEX:32008E0124&from=EN

Ortiz, W., author interview, Skype, 8 March 2018.

Papadimitriou, D. and Petrov, P. (2012). 'Whose Rule, Whose Law? Contested Statehood, External Leverage and the European Union's Rule of Law Mission in Kosovo'. *Journal of Common Market Studies*, 50(5): 746–763.

Reuters (2008). 'Spain says won't recognise Kosovo independence'. Retrieved from: www.reuters.com/article/idUSL18645227

SCSPO (2018a). 'Background'. Retrieved from: www.scp-ks.org/en/background

SCSPO (2018b). 'Chambers'. Retrieved from: www.scp-ks.org/en/specialist-chambers/chambers

Spernbauer, M. (2010). 'EULEX Kosovo: The Difficult Deployment and Challenging Implementation of the Most Comprehensive Civilian EU Operation to Date'. *German Law Journal*, 11: 769–802.

Summers, J. (2011). 'Kosovo: From Yugoslav Province to Disputed Independence', in J. Summers (ed.) *Kosovo – A Precedent?: The Declaration of Independence, the Advisory Opinion and Implications for Statehood, Self-Determination and Minority Rights* (3–52). Leiden: Martinus Nijhoff publishers.

UN (1945). 'Charter of the United Nations'. Retrieved from: https://treaties.un.org/doc/publication/ctc/uncharter.pdf

UN (2008). 'Secretary-General in Security Council Statement Says UN Aim in Kosovo Stable Political, Security Situation, Protection of Population, Minorities'. UN Press Release SG/SM/1 1426-SC/9253. Retrieved from: www.un.org/press/en/2008/sgsm11426.doc.htm

UNGA (2008a). 'Request for an advisory opinion of the International Court of Justice on whether the unilateral declaration of independence of Kosovo is in accordance with international law'. A/RES/63/3. Retrieved from: http://repository.un.org/bitstream/handle/11176/171736/A_RES_63_3EN.pdf?sequence=1&isAllowed=y

UNGA (2008b). 'Budget for the United Nations Interim Administration Mission in Kosovo for the period from 1 July 2008 to 30 June 2009'. A/62/687. Retrieved from: www.un.org/ga/search/view_doc.asp?symbol=A/62/687

UNGA (2008c). 'Budget for the United Nations Interim Administration Mission in Kosovo for the period from 1 July 2009 to 30 June 2010'. A/63/803. Retrieved from: www.un.org/ga/search/view_doc.asp?symbol=A/63/803

UNGA (2008d). 'Budget for the United Nations Interim Administration Mission in Kosovo for the period from 1 July 2018 to 30 June 2019'. A/72/718. Retrieved from: https://digitallibrary.un.org/record/1472949/files/A_72_718-EN.pdf

UNGA (2016). 'Rules of Procedure of the General Assembly'. Retrieved from: http://undocs.org/en/A/520/rev.18

UNSC (2007). 'Report of the Special Envoy of the Secretary-General on Kosovo's future status'. S2007/168.

UNSC (2008a). S/2008/211. Retrieved from: www.securitycouncilreport.org/atf/cf/%7B65BFCF9B-6D27-4E9C-8CD3-CF6E4FF96FF9%7D/Kos%20S%202008%20211.pdf

UNSC (2008b). S/PV/5839. Retrieved from: www.securitycouncilreport.org/atf/cf/%7B65BFCF9B-6D27-4E9C-8CD3-CF6E4FF96FF9%7D/Kos%20S%20PV%205839.pdf

UNSC (2008c). S/2008/354. Retrieved from: www.securitycouncilreport.org/atf/cf/%7B65BFCF9B-6D27-4E9C-8CD3-CF6E4FF96FF9%7D/Kos%20S%20 2008%20354.pdf

U.S. Department of State (2008). 'U.S. Recognizes Kosovo as Independent State'. Retrieved from: https://2001-2009.state.gov/secretary/rm/2008/02/100973.htm

U.S. Department of State (2010). 'Report of Inspection Embassy Pristina, Kosovo Report Number ISP-I-10–38A, March 2010'. Retrieved from: https://oig.state.gov/system/files/141666.pdf

U.S. Government Publishing Office (1999, 24 March). 'Address to the Nation on Airstrikes Against Serbian Targets in the Federal Republic of Yugoslavia'. Retrieved from: www.gpo.gov/fdsys/pkg/WCPD-1999-03-29/pdf/WCPD-1999-03-29-Pg516.pdf

Vetëvendosje (2008, 10 March). 'The next step in erasing Albanian identity'. Newsletter no. 85. Retrieved from: http://arkiva.vetevendosje.org/wp-content/uploads/2013/09/newsletter_85.pdf

Visoka, G. (2017). *Shaping Peace in Kosovo: The Politics of Peacebuilding and Statehood*. Cham: Palgrave Macmillan.

Vrbetić, M. (2013). 'Afraid of a 'Kosovo Scenario': A Disquieting Precedent for International Conflict Management'. *Journal of Intervention and Statebuilding*, 7(3): 308–334.

Weller, M. (2011). 'Modesty Can Be a Virtue: Judicial Economy in the ICJ Kosovo Opinion?'. *Leiden Journal of International Law*, 24(1), 127–147.

Wet, E. (2009). 'The Governance of Kosovo: Security Council Resolution 1244 and the Establishment and Functioning of EULEX'. *American Journal of International Law*, *103*(1), 83–96.

Wikileaks (2009). 'KOSOVO/EULEX: At Full Operational Capability, but Not without Problems'. US Embassy in Pristina, 8 April 2009. Retrieved from: https://wikileaks.org/plusd/cables/09PRISTINA148_a.html

Wilde, R. (2011). 'Accordance with International Law of the Unilateral Declaration of Independence in Respect of Kosovo'. *The American Journal of International Law*, 105(2): pp. 301–307.

Williams, S. (2016). 'The Specialist Chambers of Kosovo. The Limits of Internationalization?'. *Journal of International Criminal Justice*, 14(1). 25–51.

World Bank (2009). 'Kosovo Joins World Bank Group Institutions'. Retrieved from: http://web.worldbank.org/WBSITE/EXTERNAL/NEWS/0,,contentMDK:22230081~pagePK:34370~piPK:34424~theSitePK:4607,00.html

Xhemaj, B., author interview, Skype, 28 May 2018.

Zogiani, A. and Bajrami, L. (2014). 'Culture of Impunity in Kosovo'. *Forum 2015*. Retrieved from: http://kfos.org/wp-content/uploads/2014/04/Culture-of-Impunity-in-Kosovo-ENG.pdf

5 The problem of the north and the potential for further border transformations in Kosovo

Chapter 4 assessed the difficulties of consolidating Kosovo's independence externally. The present one will invert the telescope and will focus instead on the other legitimacy problem faced by Kosovo: internal challenges. There is little doubt that the chief difficulty for Kosovo to consolidate its authority internally stems from the hostility of the Serbian-majority municipalities of Northern Kosovo. In that regard, Pristina's struggle to exert its authority over the north of Kosovo has Weberian connotations; while the Kosovo Republic is overwhelmingly supported by ethnic Albanians, the case is fundamentally divergent when it comes to Serbs. The chapter will argue that Kosovo's deadlock in relation to its international legal recognition opens the door to potential further territorial transformations.

The 'problem' of the north

In effect, since its inception in 2008, the Kosovo state has struggled to gain legitimacy from the Serbian community in Kosovo. The contestation against Kosovo statehood has been particularly prominent north of the Ibar river, where Serbs constitute a solid majority. The 75,000 Serbs south of the Ibar, on the other hand, are much more vulnerable[1] and arguably due to this minority position they have been considerably less hostile to Pristina's rule. In order to address the lack of legitimacy of the Kosovo state, several strategies – both coercive and co-optative – have been put in place by Pristina and its international backers. Among the co-optative ones, the most relevant has probably been the emphasis on Kosovo being a multi-ethnic state, a principle which is included in several articles of the Kosovo Constitution, adopted in 2008. According to Landau, this emphasis on multiethnicity, or on being a 'state of communities', had a two-fold objective: on the one hand, it is aimed at gaining international legitimacy and, on the other, at persuading the Serbian community to buy-in the idea of the Kosovo state (2017, p. 443). Over a decade after declaring its independence, Kosovo does not seem to have fully achieved either of these two goals. As the last chapter discussed, the multi-ethnicity card is not simply instrumental but it was also a mandatory requirement from the Ahtisaari Plan.

Kosovo Serbs have been a fundamental actor in the Kosovo conflict. It is worth noting that, as argued in Chapter 1, Kosovo Serbs were *instrumentalised* by Slobodan Milošević in the mid and late eighties to consolidate his political career, strategically exploiting their grievances. After NATO's intervention, 226,418 Serbs (and Roma) fled Kosovo, according to figures from Kosovo's Ministry for Community and Return (2018), and as of 2018 most of them have not returned. In addition, Kosovo Serbs have been 'the target of continual harassment and discrimination in post-war Kosovo' (Jenne, 2009, p. 283) which culminated in the anti-Serb riots of March 2004.

It is therefore not too far-fetched to say that Kosovo Serbs have been on the losing end of the Kosovo conflict, both in terms of demographics but also in political terms; the state they identified with was forced to withdraw from Kosovo in June 1999 and international institutions they did not trust filled the power vacuum (1999–2008). To make matters worse, those international institutions paved the way for a new state which they perceived as antagonistic to their interests, to the extent that many members of the Serbian community view it as the final nail in the coffin for the presence of Serbs in Kosovo.[2] Nemanja Jaksić,[3] an activist for the rights of Serbs in Kosovo, claims that many Serbs in this territory feel they are in a situation of statelessness.

According to data from the OSCE, in 2013 there were approximately 145,000 Serbs in Kosovo, around 70,000 of them living in Northern Kosovo, representing nearly 90 per cent of the population in the municipalities of Leposavić, Zvečan, Zubin Potok and North Mitrovica (ECMI, 2013). In these municipalities, which are territorially contiguous and adjacent to the Serbian border, institutions controlled by Belgrade such as schools that follow the Serbian curriculum and hospitals have been able to survive, causing Pristina's outrage. Kosovo Albanian political activist, Marigone Drevinja, denounces the existence of parallel governmental institutions and finds it ludicrous that the Kosovo state is unable to fully control 10 per cent of its territory[4] (in reference to Northern Kosovo). The term 'parallel', which has connotations of illegality, sparks a semantic dispute. For Serbs, the 'parallel structures' are those established by Pristina, not the ones from Belgrade.

At any rate, successive Kosovo governments have demanded EULEX and KFOR intervention in Northern Kosovo 'to establish the authority of Kosovo institutions there' (Visoka, 2017, p. 15). Attempts to intervene by international organisations to enforce Pristina's rule have used force, including the deployment of NATO armed vehicles in civilian areas, and, in turn, have been confronted by force by local Serbs. This has, on several occasions, created a spiral of violence which has threatened to jeopardise stability in Kosovo.

In 2011, for instance, police and customs officers from Pristina were deployed in Northern Kosovo, a move which was highly controversial for the Kosovo-Serb community. Prior to this, the visibility of the Kosovo state

Figure 5.1 Barricades at the Mitrovica bridge (2014).
Source: author.

had been conspicuous by its absence in the north. Serb residents in the north responded to what they perceived as an occupation with, blockades and barricades to prevent the presence of Kosovo border officers (Castan Pinos, 2013, p. 57). In addition, border posts were burned down, both in 2008 and 2011, and shots were fired at KFOR troops (*Al Jazeera*, 2011). For three years (2011–2014), many of these barricades were part of the landscape in Northern Kosovo. The barricades were eventually removed by the North Mitrovica (Serb-dominated) municipality, as tensions were being eased in the context of the Brussels agreement which will be analysed in this chapter.

In addition to demonstrating and erecting barricades, Kosovo Serbs have also showed their opposition to Pristina-led institutions through a referendum, deemed as invalid by the Kosovo and the Serbian governments, in February 2012. An overwhelming majority (99.74 per cent) of those who participated in the referendum (which had a 75 per cent turnout) held in the Serb-dominated northern municipalities, voted against accepting the Kosovo institutions (*Al Jazeera*, 2012). It seems therefore clear that Kosovo Serbs in the north were the last internal obstacle for fully consolidating Kosovo statehood.

William Ortiz, a former UNMIK officer, claims that Western powers and some international organisations have systematically attempted to subjugate Kosovo Serbs, forcing them to either accept Pristina's institutions or leave Kosovo.[5] Despite the fact that the violence and contestation have diminished in Northern Kosovo over the past few years, the observation conducted by the author over the period of five years (2012–2017) in Kosovo confirms Maloku *et al.* findings that the Serbian and Albanian communities live 'highly segregated, with very little interaction … and little willingness to establish contact' (2016, p. 255).

As the next paragraphs will argue, the current political deadlock with regards to the status of Kosovo, the lack of consensus over an autonomy regime for Serbian municipalities in Kosovo and the lack of progress in terms of 'normalisation of relations' between Belgrade and Pristina, significantly contribute to entrench and perpetuate the problem of the north.

Double partition

Partition is a tempting solution. As a matter of fact, this policy was the chosen option by Western powers to resolve, or at least to attempt to resolve, the Kosovo problem. At an academic level, scholars have been divided over the desirability of partition. Its advocates argue that by creating separate territorial entities and thus distinct spaces of power for the different ethnic groups, partition reduces the chances for further ethnic conflict (Kaufmann, 1996; Downes, 2001; Johnson, 2008). Critics, on the other hand, contend that partition cannot be considered as a magic universal solution for solving ethnic conflicts because this 'remedy' can have pervasive results such as the perpetuation of the conflict or ethnic cleansing and population displacement in the name of peace (Horowitz and Weisiger, 2009; Jenne, 2009, 2012).

In the Kosovo case, such perpetuation of the conflict after partition, which became legally formalised with the proclamation of the UDI, did not take long to develop. The new boundary redrawing effected by the UDI did not end the conflict in Kosovo, it simply changed the location of the border fault lines. The influential think-tank International Crisis Group (ICG) warned a month after Kosovo's secession that partition (a new partition) had become a real risk in the Serb-dominated north of Kosovo (ICG, 2008, p. 1). The fear was of a *de jure* partition because, as Jenne points out, de facto Northern Kosovo was already partitioned (2009, p. 282).

Bearing in mind this particular context, it is understandable that partition has appeared as one of the possible solutions to solve the conflict over lack of legitimacy of the Kosovo state in the northern Serb-inhabited municipalities. The bottom line behind this idea is straightforward. The Kosovo conflict was solved using the old formula of Western powers-backed partition, that is, settling an ethno-territorial dispute by separating the disgruntled area from the hostile host state and effectively conducting a border redrawing. By the same token, a similar solution could be applied to the territorially contested north of Kosovo. One of the chief differences between both cases is that the north of Kosovo instead of constituting itself into an independent polity would be reintegrated into Serbia. Provided that de facto the territory is in many ways already institutionally integrated to Serbia, this would not pose excessive institutional challenges.

Shortly after NATO's bombing campaign and its subsequent deployment of troops, this idea was openly advocated by IR scholar John Mearsheimer, who argued in favour of a 'grand bargain' where Serbia would concede most of the territory to Kosovo Albanians and in return it would be able to keep the 'slice' that is mostly inhabited by Serbs (2000, p. 133). In Mearsheimer's opinion that imperfect solution would provide Kosovo Albanians with a homeland, would allow refugees to return, and most importantly, it would allow the U.S. to withdraw its troops 'out of that Potemkin state', avoiding a permanent American occupation scenario (2000, p. 136). The main problem with that last resort solution is that, at least officially, it has been rejected by all parties, albeit for different motives (Rossi, 2014, p. 871).

Western diplomats and policymakers have been particularly vocal in their opposition to the double partition idea. Their declarations invariably point in the same direction: partition must be rejected. A 2010 cable released by Wikileaks from an officer from the U.S. Department of State stresses the importance of coordination between Western states to fight against de facto and *de jure* partition in Kosovo:

> [A]ny strategy must include a coordinated statement from Washington and European capitals at the highest levels that Kosovo's partition is not an option and that continued de facto partition through Serbian interference will also put Serbia's EU membership on hold.
>
> (Cited by the *Guardian*, 2010)

Hillary Clinton, the former U.S. Secretary of State, for instance, stressed that '[W]e oppose any discussion of territorial changes.... The boundaries of an independent, sovereign Kosovo are clear and set' (cited by Gordon, 2012). In a similar vein, her British counterpart, William Hague, showed an uncompromising tenacity against the double partition arguing that Kosovo could not be split along ethnic lines to resolve the conflict, categorically remarking that: '[T]he map is finished in Southeastern Europe' (cited by Radio Liberty, 2012). The irony here is that those fervent defenders of territorial status quo in the region were those who had more ardently pushed for territorial transformations in the form of Kosovo statehood only a few years earlier.

The consensus against partition amongst Western policy-makers, nonetheless, is far from being unanimous. Former Austrian Vice-President, Erhard Busek, has opened the door to the possibility of a double partition solution: 'I do not see why the international community would not agree on the division if Belgrade and Priština reached an agreement on the issue' (cited by B92, 2011). Off the record some international officers operating in Kosovo admit that 'the quicker solution [to consolidate Kosovo's statehood] is to change the borders. Partition is a bad word but a practical solution'.[6] Those opinions, however, are thus far rather uncommon amongst Western leaders.

Local Kosovo Albanian policy-makers are generally entirely opposed to the idea of north of the Ibar partition. For starters, such a move would contravene Kosovo's constitution which stipulates that 'the Republic of Kosovo is an … indivisible state (Article 1.1). The territorial integrity of Republic of Kosovo is intact, inalienable, indivisible and protected by all means provided in this Constitution and the law (Article 2.2)' (Constitution of the Republic of Kosovo, 2008, p. 1). Interestingly, the language used in the Kosovo Constitution is extremely similar to the Serbian constitution, which considers the Serbian territory as 'inseparable and indivisible' (Article 8). Once again, we are confronted with a paradox: the Kosovo Constitution would have never been enacted without the violation of the Serbian *Carta Magna* (Castan Pinos, 2015, p. 226).

At any rate, the idea of partition is emphatically rejected by the Kosovo leadership. In response to a letter by Serbian foreign minister, Ivica Dačić, calling for partition, Kosovo's foreign minister, Enver Hoxhaj, tweeted that 'Serbia's renewed ideas 4 border change are dangerous and unacceptable' (2017). In the same line of thought, PM Haradinaj, interviewed by the BBC on occasion of the tenth anniversary of Kosovo's independence expressed the idea that 'we are fully against dealing with borders, changing borders […] because that is why tragedies happen' (cited by BBC, 2018). Similarly, Kosovo government senior political advisor, Bashmir Xhemaj, asserted that 'territorial partition or exchange of territories[7] is totally unacceptable'.[8] The Kosovo government official also claimed that the debate around partition is 'a product for Serbia's own political consumption' that is fuelled by Belgrade elites.[9]

The position of the Serbian leadership is less clear-cut and more malleable than that of Kosovo officials or indeed the majority of Western diplomats. As Rossi points out, for Serbia a hypothetical acceptance of partition entails severe consequences, namely the recognition of Kosovo's independence and hence a violation of Serbia's own Constitution as well as the abandonment of Kosovo Serbs south of the Ibar, who represent roughly 60 per cent of the total Serb population in Kosovo (2014, p. 871). Despite these constraints, every single Serbian President (Tadić, Nikolić and Vučić) since Kosovo's independence was declared has hinted, typically in an inconspicuous fashion, the possibility of partition. The undisputed champion of this idea, which is presented as a pragmatic and realistic solution, is Ivica Dačić, Serbia's foreign minister since 2014 and the leader of the socialist party of Serbia.

In 2011, while Dačić was Serbia's interior minister he controversially stated that 'the only realistic solution is that places where Serbs live stay in Serbia and that the other part where the Albanians live secedes', adding that this was his opinion not the government's policy (cited by B92, 2011). Six years later, in 2017, Dačić insisted that a compromise in the form of a territorial partition 'through an agreement in which everybody wins and loses something' was the only option which would guarantee a lasting solution for the Serb-Albanian conflict (cited by Savić, 2017). Another member of the Serbian administration, defence minister Aleksandar Vulin, argued for a similar solution, that of a territorial 'permanent and firm delimitation between Serbs and Albanians' in Kosovo a year later (cited by *Gazeta Express*, 2018).

These declarations advocating for partition from high profile officials in the Serbian government epitomise the internal divisions that the Kosovo issue prompts in Serbia and the multi-faceted contradictions and complexities surrounding this territorial quagmire. What is perhaps more shocking about the pro partition statements is the fact that they are in stark contrast with the official policy which is based on 'conducting a peaceful, diplomatic and legal fight to preserve [Serbia's sovereignty over] Kosovo-Metohija in its composition' (Serbian Government, 2018). Belgrade's first contradiction is therefore between claiming the entire territory (official line) versus claiming sovereignty over the northern Serb-inhabited areas.

The Brussels Agreement and the Community of Serb Municipalities

Belgrade's approach suffers from a second contradiction: on the one hand it claims that it aims to preserve sovereignty (whether partial or full) and, on the other, it has been negotiating a settlement with Pristina and Brussels to establish a Community of Serbian Municipalities (ZSO[10]) which would take place in the framework of the Republic of Kosovo. That is, such agreement would necessarily result in the more or less explicit recognition by the Serbian government of the legitimacy of Kosovo's statehood. Belgrade's contradictions can be partly explained by factors exogenous to the Kosovo issue, namely its aim to become a member of the European Union. This objective seems to be, thus far, sabotaged by Serbia's reluctance to relinquish its sovereignty (claim) over Kosovo.

The rationale, from the Brussels perspective, appears to be rather straightforward. Given the fact that both Serbia and Kosovo have aspirations to join the club, the EU is in a position to use the old formula of conditionality in the form of the carrot of accession to exert leverage on both actors. One of the problems with this policy instrument is that the EU is not thrilled by the idea of 'importing' further problems[11] and perhaps as a result of this, the EU has begun with the most arduous criteria: the 'normalisation of relations'. In effect, this normalisation is the sacrifice, effectively a pre-requisite, demanded by the EU to Pristina and Belgrade so that they can continue with their 'European path'.

In the case of Serbia, this 'normalisation of relations' is specified in Chapter 35, under 'other issues', of the accession negotiations (European Council, 2015). A European diplomat admits that the term is deliberately polysemic and that its meaning fluidly evolves depending on the interaction between actors.[12] Since the margin of interpretation is extremely wide so is the margin of action, or at least, that is how the EU perceives it. While the term 'normalise' may be deliberately vague, a representative from the Kosovo government, Bashmir Xhemaj, interprets it in a very clear fashion when he asserts that 'normalisation of relations' means nothing more and nothing less than 'full mutual recognition and full diplomatic relations with each other'.[13] Dragiša Djoković, a Kosovo Serb and former MP in Belgrade, who entirely opposes Kosovo's independence, concurs nevertheless with this Xhemaj's conclusion in relation to the meaning behind 'normalisation of relations'.[14]

The concept may not be very precise but the EU has been extremely blunt when warning Serbia that 'the advancement of Serbia's EU accession negotiations ... will be measured in particular against Serbia's continued engagement towards a visible and sustainable improvement in relations with Kosovo' (European Council, 2015, p. 2). In other words, failure to 'normalise' relations with Pristina will more than likely result in the collapse of Serbia's accession negotiations (Elsuwege, 2017, p. 400).

In this context, the idea of the ZSO could be deemed as one of the most important carrots used by the European diplomacy, in addition to a vague and ill-defined promise of EU membership, to persuade Serbia to sit with the Kosovo administration. This objective was partially achieved when both parties signed the 'First Agreement of Principles Governing the Normalisation of Relations' (Government of Kosovo, 2013), which is commonly known as the Brussels Agreement, on 19 April 2013, under the auspices of the European Union. The agreement had immediate consequences, merely a week after it, on the 28 June, the European Council 'decided to open accession negotiations with Serbia' (European Council, 2013, p. 12). With the use of the carrot of accession in order to solve a seemingly protracted ethno-territorial conflict this was EU conditionality, the most effective tool of the Union's normative power, at its best. Or, at least, so it seemed.

In Kosovo, the agreement was met with two divergent reactions. Some actors, such as Kosovo's Prime Minister at the time, Hashim Thaçi, had argued that it represented a de facto recognition of Kosovo independence by Serbia (Vasovic and Pawlak, 2013). Others, however, viewed it as sell-out to Serbia, as an attempt to establish an entity resembling Bosnia's *Republika Srpska*, which would compromise Kosovo's sovereignty. In view of a member of the Social Democratic Party in Kosovo, Marigone Drevinja, 'we cannot allow an association [ZSO] to have executive powers, we [Kosovo government] would need their permission for crucial state matters and that would compromise our sovereignty. We do not want another *Republika Srpska* in Kosovo'.[15] Beha disagrees with both perceptions, claiming that the delegation of powers and provision of greater autonomy for Serbian municipality, could act instead as a dissuasion for the partition of Kosovo (2015, p. 104). For the Serbian government, the very fact that they had signed an agreement with Pristina represented an enormous sacrifice for, at least implicitly, it hinted at recognition and acceptance of the legitimacy of the Kosovo government and its state institutions (Economides and Ker-Lindsay, 2015, pp. 1035–1036).

The agreement triggered enthusiastic reactions from the media and EU policymakers such as former President of former European Commission, José Manuel Durão Barroso, who labelled it as a 'breakthrough' and 'historic' (European Commission, 2013). Despite Barroso's optimistic fervour, the agreement is rather a pre-agreement, which lacks solidity and is far from solving the territorial conflict over Kosovo. The evidence for this pessimistic conclusion is that more than five years after its signature little progress has been made in terms of the ZSO or indeed in relation to the 'normalisation of relations' between Belgrade and Pristina.

As for the specific content of the agreement, brokered by the former EU foreign policy chief, Catherine Ashton, most of its 15 articles deal with the problem of the north and how to accommodate the Serbian municipalities, both north[16] and south[17] of the Ibar. More specifically, the agreement defines the institutional structures, the legal provisions and the competences (economic development, health, education, urban planning) of this hypothetical Community of Serbian Municipalities (Kosovo Government, 2013). In exchange for these autonomy concessions, Serbia (and Kosovo Serbs) had to accept the authority of the Kosovo Police Force in the north as the only security structure, the full integration of Northern Kosovo courts into the state of Kosovo judicial system and the conduct of local elections under Pristina's (not Belgrade) umbrella (Kosovo Government, 2013). This police, judicial and electoral integration from Serbian to Kosovo structures has gradually been implemented since 2013.

Despite this partial 'success', five years after the agreement was signed optimism has somehow dissipated. While the European Commission states, in the 2018 reports on Serbia and Kosovo,[18] that 'progress has been made', they also acknowledge that both actors need 'to make further substantial efforts and contribute to the establishment of circumstances conducive to a comprehensive normalisation of relations' with each other (European Commission, 2018a; European Commission, 2018b). Interestingly, both the Serbian and the Kosovo reports, drafted by the European Commission, use the exact same words to describe a situation which is basically characterised by a lack of substantial progress.

Rossi's take is much more explicit and gloomy than that of the Commission as he stresses that, five years after the agreement, the so-called 'normalisation of relations' seems to have gone nowhere other than in the direction of a political deadlock (2018, p. 2). The deadlock has been undoubtedly aggravated by a diplomatic incident between both actors in March 2018, when a Belgrade senior official, Marko Djurić, the Director of the Office for Kosovo and Metohija, was arrested[19] in North Mitrovica by heavily armed members of the ROSU police while he was meeting with Kosovo Serbs to discuss matters related to the ZSO (MacDowall, 2018). KFOR Commander, Major General Salvatore Cuoci, admitted that the Kosovo Police operation had used 'brutal force', something which in view of the NATO commander, 'could have been avoided' (RTK, 2018).

The reactions of the Serbian President, Aleksandar Vučić, were unprecedentedly irate as he labelled the Kosovo government 'Albanian terrorists' and a 'bandit state' interpreting the incident as a provocation aimed at showing 'the power they [Kosovo authorities] have and the support of the West' (cited by B92, 2018a). Vučić also had words for the EU and EULEX, which he accused of participating in the operation, concluding that, under these circumstances, it was 'pointless to talk about the Brussels dialogue' (cited by B92, 2018a). The Serbian President's words epitomise the difficulty of implementing the agreement and the fact that any diplomatic misunderstanding has the potential of derailing it.

An additional complication for the ZSO and the Brussels agreement as a whole is the fact that the Kosovo government has recently raised the stakes by linking the creation of this autonomous structure with Kosovo's legal international recognition and UN membership. This strategy has been aired by Kosovo's Foreign Minister Enver Hoxhaj, who pointed out that the 'formation [of ZSO's] should take place in parallel with Kosovo's membership in the UN, when Kosovo gains legal status and full international recognition' (cited by B92, 2018b). The rationale behind Hoxhaj's statement is crystal clear: Kosovo's recognition by Serbia is a *sine qua non* condition for autonomy institutions for Kosovo Serbs. Whereas this approach may be positive for Kosovo strategically speaking, it also opens the door for a double mutual veto, paving the way for the perpetuation of the deadlock.

Finally, the capacity of the EU to shape policies in Belgrade and Pristina is dependent on several factors such as the continuity of the Union's strength and power of attractiveness as well as on the existence of a credible roadmap for accession. Internal troubles such as the Greek financial crisis or the British turbulent withdrawal from the Union have the potential to compromise the EU power to attract states. In the worst-case scenario, the carrot of EU membership may become a rotten carrot resulting in a decline of its appeal for countries in South-East Europe and beyond. The most direct consequence of that hypothetical scenario is that a loss of appeal would inevitably have damaging consequences in terms of the most important EU foreign policy instrument vis-à-vis candidate members: conditionality.

The other significant predicament is the lack of a specific time plan in terms of membership for accessing countries, particularly for those in

South-East Europe. As of 2018, this does not seem to be the case. In a report published in February 2018, the European Commission hints that Serbia could potentially join the club in 2025 as long as Serbia 'normalises' its relations with Kosovo (2018c, p. 8). For the latter the accession prospects appear even more remote as there are no specific dates or substantial steps mentioned other than ambiguously empty remarks on the advancement of 'Kosovo's European path' (European Commission, 2018c, p. 2). It seems clear that, for the EU, the tension between Pristina and Belgrade is a sensitive issue with a unique potential for 'explosiveness' not just for the parties involved but for the entire region.[20]

Mitrovica and its amalgam of frictional divisions

This book has primarily concentrated on the geopolitical aspect of the border transformations in Kosovo. There is, however, another dimension which deserves our attention: the consequences of those border transformations for local contexts. The city of Mitrovica is a useful illustration of how geopolitical and territorial transformations have a direct impact on local communities. The north of the city, mostly inhabited by Serbs and adjacent to other Serb-dominated municipalities,[21] has become the unofficial border between the hostile north and the rest of Kosovo. In particular, after the 1999 NATO intervention, the north of Mitrovica has become a de facto capital of an entity (Serbian municipalities in Kosovo) which, as explained previously, thus far lacks a legal status. It seems clear that the conflictual dynamics in the Kosovo in general and in the north in particular have consolidated the institutional importance of North Mitrovica.

The significance of the city is confirmed by the relocation of several key Serbian institutions, such as for instance, the University of Pristina, which was transferred from its original location (Pristina) to Mitrovica. Governmental buildings such as Telecom Srbija and the Government of Serbia office for Kosovo and Metohija, in addition to various schools and hospitals, have also been established in this part of the city. The institutional relocation has been coupled with the local institutional partition between the municipality of North Mitrovica and the Albanian-dominated south of the city. The effects of this urban partition are not hard to grasp; the development of a governance duality, where 'each side of Mitrovica has its own municipality and therefore two mayors and two local assemblies' (Castan Pinos, 2016, p. 132). Mitrovica may be one city geographically and spatially but, as Strömbom and Björkdahl put it, as a result of the entrenched division the city has become 'two worlds in [terms of] cognitive and actual reality' (2015, p. 29).

The deeper reflection is that cities are not immune to ethno-territorial disputes, quite on the contrary. Cities may not be the primary cause of the conflict but they are likely to suffer the deleterious effects of it. In effect, cities, such as Mitrovica, often transform into 'a battle zone for larger proxy wars initiated and orchestrated by agents whose interests extend beyond the municipal boundaries' (Calame and Charlesworth, 2009, pp. 11–12). As Chapter 1 analysed, rifts between Serbs and Albanians in Kosovo or indeed in Mitrovica did not emerge in the late 1990s as a result of the conflict between the Yugoslavian state and the KLA guerrilla nor due to NATO's intervention in 1999. The conflict and the subsequent intervention, however, contributed to reinforce the already existing divisions and frictions. The most tangible impact of this is the fact that both sides of the city experienced the ethnic cleansing[22] perpetrated by the 'other', that is by Serbs in the north and by Albanians in the south. Private properties and religious buildings (mosques in the north, orthodox churches in the south) were also destroyed, becoming collateral victims of the enclavisation process and the wider ethno-territorial conflict.

Mitrovica's main bridge[23] has become the paradigmatic image of division and of Mitrovica. The bridge has been blocked by different actors for a wide range of purposes. Originally, the French contingent of KFOR cut it off with barbed wire and permanent patrols to prevent ethnic scuffles between both sides. The fact that for a considerable period of time KFOR troops conducted passport check on the bridge contributed to reinforce the border dimension of Mitrovica as the demarcation line between the predominantly Serbian North and the mostly Albanian South. These prevention measures were not always successful, in countless occasions the bridge has been the flash point where groups from both sides of Mitrovica violently clashed. In 2008, for instance, in the context of Kosovo Serb protests against Kosovo's independence, a UN police officer died and several other were injured as a result of clashes with protesters (Attewill and Traynor, 2008).

In this context of ethnic conflict, enclavisation and urban segregation an actor deserves particular attention: the Bridge Watchers. This semi informal citizen-based group, now disbanded, made up of Serbs from North Mitrovica, established patrols at the bridge to, according to their accounts, protect the north of the city from Albanian mobs which would otherwise attack and rampage Serbian neighbourhoods. A senior UNMIK officer confirms that, at least during the 2004 Anti-Serbian riots, the Bridge Watch patrol prevented a mob of Albanian extremists from 'taking over their [North Mitrovica] neighbourhoods'.[24] There are also less flattering perspectives on the Bridge Watchers. The group has been regularly accused in the Western media of having connections with Serbian paramilitaries and of terrorising Mitrovica (Popham, 2008). Critics have labelled them as a 'gang of thugs' (Dziedzic, 2006), blaming them for being involved in ethnic-driven killings and ethnic cleansing (Morina, 2017).

After Kosovo declared its independence in 2008, the bridge has continued to be the focus of severe tensions. Barricades were erected by local Serbs to prevent the deployment of Kosovo's security forces to the north in 2011. Since 2014, gardens and more recently a parking lot which disenables any form of traffic interaction have become the new not-so-obvious barricades. At any rate, the metaphor of the dividing bridge is the perfect picture illustrating that there is a latent unresolved conflict in Kosovo. Over two decades after NATO's intervention, the issue of the bridge continues to pose a challenge to policymakers in Pristina and Brussels. In the 2018 report on Kosovo, the European Commission highlighted the necessity to address the bridge issue by stressing that the bridge 'should be opened without further delay or obstructions' (European Commission, 2018b, p. 48). Similarly to other aspects of the conflict in Kosovo, the bridge issue remains unsettled.

For locals, who hardly cross it, the bridge represents part of the everyday landscape, a physical reminder that 'the other' lives literally across the bridge (Castan Pinos, 2016, p. 132). Whereas crossing the main bridge is somewhat of a taboo and has a connotation of separation and estrangement, there are two smaller and recondite bridges east and west of the main one, which experience a much more intense level of crossing, according to the testimony of Italian KFOR troops[25] who regularly patrol the bridges. According to bridge-crossers[26] (from the northern side to the southern one) informally interviewed at the Eastern bridge for the purpose of this book, the chief reason to cross was to shop at malls and shopping centres located next to the bridge.

The segregation in Mitrovica is deeply entrenched and goes well beyond physical urban separation, institutional dualities and lack of interaction at the main bridge. The education system, for instance, is fully divided: Serbian pupils in North Mitrovica, as well as in other Serbian municipalities, attend schools, high schools and universities which follow the Serbian curriculum, as opposed to the Kosovo curriculum, which is the one mandatory for all other students. Other aspects of daily life such as sport, health and transport are also divided. It may be argued that such level of division is unsustainable in the long run.

However, the examples of Nicosia, Belfast or Beirut show that urban segregations have a capacity for resilience which defies normative anti-division discourses. This ability to survive is perhaps explained by the reproduction of patterns of division, such as physical segregation. The logic consequence is that social practices and interactions developed according to the segregation framework prompt their reification of division. Division, in other words, can easily become institutionalised and normalised. Once this occurs, segregation is the status quo.

Division may be justified by intersubjective fears and constructed threats but it may also be a product of *real events* which happened to *real people*. As explained earlier, both sides of the city have experienced violence, intimidation, displacement and even murder by their neighbours from the other side of the bridge. From the Serbian perspective, for instance, putting an end to division is perceived with scepticism because it is viewed as a vital threat not only because they fear it could jeopardise their presence in

Kosovo but also because it consolidates the Kosovo state. In view of Jaksić[27] 'the end of division is the end of Serbs [in Kosovo]'.

This leads us to an interesting yet controversial reflection. There is a quasi-irresistible normative temptation when it comes to urban segregation, particularly when this phenomenon occurs in non-Western regions. This temptation consists of exclusively focusing on division, treating it like the ultimate cause of the problem, disregarding that

> [U]rban segregation is perhaps above all a symptom, and a consequence of communal disputes. Therefore, by focusing primarily on division, one may mitigate the effects of the problem but neglect the fundamental causes that lie at the core of urban segregation.
>
> (Castan Pinos, 2016, p. 139)

In the case of Mitrovica, there are multidimensional processes, such as a recent history of mutual ethnic cleansing, empowerment/disempowerment dynamics and discontent of one of the communities towards the state, which serve to explain the symptom; division. The bottom line of the argument is that if our focus is, due to our normative prism, exclusively on eliminating division, we will solely be addressing the tip of the iceberg, neglecting essential structural elements.

Last but not least, politically-motivated public monuments are another element of urban ethnic segregation in Mitrovica. Some of these monuments are related to the 1998–1999 conflict, where each side narrate their version of the story emphasising victimhood and military heroics through monumental tangibles. Monuments to guerrilla fighters are generally erected as an embodiment of the Messiah narrative, a figure which represents a spotless saviour. In South Mitrovica, for example, there are numerous statues dedicated to Kosovo Albanian guerrilla fighters, such as the one dedicated to the Mitrovica-born KLA commander Safet Boletini 'Tigri', who was killed in action in 1999 (see Figure 5.3).

In North Mitrovica, only a few metres away from the bridge, a monument, decorated with Christian orthodox ornaments, remembers all the victims from the KLA killed in Mitrovica with their full names and the date of their passing. The recent conflict is not the only historical motive which displays divisive historical narratives in Mitrovica. The local authorities erected a ten-metre high[28] statue of Prince Lazar, the hero of the Battle of Kosovo, according to the 1389 Kosovo myth (see Chapter 1 for further details). This massive bronze sculpture (see Figure 5.3), whose forefinger points towards the place where the fourteenth century battle took place Kosovo Polje (and incidentally towards South Mitrovica), has significant political connotations. In a reassuring message to Kosovo Serbs with strong implications for contemporary times, Serbian government official, Marko Djurić, stated that 'Lazar is here to stay, because Serbs are here to stay' (Office for Kosovo and Metohija, 2016). In South Mitrovica, there are also

Figure 5.2 Statue of a KLA commander in South Mitrovica (2017).

Source: Gisela Gorbalán.

Figure 5.3 Prince Lazar in North Mitrovica (2017).
Source: Gisela Gorbalán.

commemorations of historical war heroes, embodying masculinity and belligerent bravado, in this case from a Kosovo Albanian perspective. The most illustrative example is the statue of Isa Bolletini, an Albanian nationalist from Kosovo who fought against the Ottoman Empire and participated in the Vlorë Albanian declaration of independence of 1912.

Finally, flags, one of the epitomes of banal reminders of nationhood (Billig, 1995, p. 41), constitute another tangible element of segregation between the two communities in Mitrovica. As explained in Chapter 4, the Albanian flag and to a lesser extent the 2008 established Kosovo flag, dominate official and private buildings in South Mitrovica, similarly to the rest of towns in Kosovo with an Albanian majority. These flags in Mitrovica and elsewhere are often accompanied by U.S., NATO and EU flags. In contrast, in North Mitrovica, like in the other Serbian municipalities of the north, the Serbian flag is omnipresent in lampposts and buildings. In this side of the city, the Serbian flag is also complemented by Russian Federation flags, illustrating that this local conflict has indeed very prominent geopolitical ramifications and vice versa, geopolitical disputes contribute to fuel the conflict in Kosovo and more visibly in Mitrovica.

The other potential border transformation scenario: Albanian unification

At the beginning of this chapter, a potential for further border transformation (double partition) was scrutinised. Partition of the north, however, is not the only scenario which would entail another redrawing of the recently redrawn boundaries of Kosovo. The additional potential border transformation comes in the form of unification between Kosovo and the Republic of Albania.

It could be argued that this ethno-territorial political project is rooted in history. In effect, the aspiration of uniting all Albanians, at that time divided in different Ottoman provinces, in a single polity was the main objective of the League of Prizren, a pan-Albanian nationalist organisation formed in 1878. This ambition was subsequently revived in different periods, including during World War II, when 'the Albanian fascist movement, Balli Kombetare, with the help of the Nazis, succeeded in establishing a greater Albania under German and Italian sponsorship' (Bardos, 2005, p. 33). As explained in Chapter 1, the pan-Albanian aspiration was later resuscitated by anti-Yugoslavia movements in Kosovo, particularly after 1968, and subsequently by the KLA guerrilla force during the late 1990s conflict with the Yugoslav security forces. Currently, the mere idea of Albanian unification causes panic amongst most Western policymakers but, as the following paragraphs will analyse, the project continues to attract support among ethnic Albanians in Kosovo, Albania, Macedonia and other areas in South-East Europe populated by Albanians. Since the Kosovo conflict and its borders are still unsettled, the idea deserves to be, at least, considered for critical scrutiny.

As seen in Chapter 4, despite the constant diplomatic support of the U.S. and other great powers such as the UK, France and Turkey, Kosovo remains in a legal limbo, unable to conclude the international legalisation of its secession as it faces unsurmountable obstacles towards UN membership. The inconvenient reality for Pristina and Washington is that without Russian and Chinese consent, Kosovo will never be able to make it into the UN club. Sadly for Kosovo, their sanction does not seem to be about to materialise in the foreseeable future, quite to the contrary. The options for Kosovo are therefore abridged, to say the least.

The first one is to continue gathering recognitions and battling in a quasi-Quixotesque fashion for UN membership. The obvious problem with this option is that the flow of recognitions has practically come to a halt, as Serbia's strategy of counter-recognitions is slowly beginning to bear fruit and UN membership is nowhere near the horizon. Additionally, the longer Kosovo continues being a parastate, the longer it will reproduce the practices of parastates and, as a result, the longer it will be trapped in the parastate logic. If Kosovo opts for this option, which is the one currently being pursued, it should probably abandon the idea of UN membership in the short- and mid-terms. Instead, it should conform itself with membership in relevant international regimes such as the WB, the IMF and FIFA among others. In other words, it can be one of the most successful parastates but it cannot overcome the fact of being a parastate.

The question is; how to overcome this political deadlock? The EU pressure to 'normalise' the relations between Pristina and Belgrade does not seem to be working very effectively. In addition, even if the negotiations were going smoothly (which they are not), it remains unclear whether this normalisation would end up in recognition by Serbia of its former province as a state or even less if this recognition would pave the way for Kosovo to obtain UN membership. In other words, the current path is marred by too many hypotheses and determinants, many of which are not even dependent on the agency of the actors involved. If this way out of the conundrum fails, there are two alternative solutions, both of which require further border transformations. The first option is a negotiation with Serbia which would probably require Kosovo to cede the north; that is, double partition in exchange for Belgrade's recognition. The Serbian government has hinted on several occasions that they would be open to that idea but as seen previously, this option is extremely unpopular amongst Kosovo Albanian policymakers and their Western counterparts.

The second alternative, the unification of Kosovo with Albania constitutes, similarly to double partition, a taboo which provokes anxiety amongst the international backers of Kosovo's secession.[29] The idea, however, enjoys wide popularity in Kosovo amongst ethnic Albanians: according to a 2010 Gallup poll, 81 per cent of Kosovo Albanians support the notion of 'Greater Albania'. This territorial project based on Albanian unification is also backed by 63 per cent of Albanians in the state of Albania and 53 per cent of Macedonian Albanians (Gallup Balkan Monitor, 2010, p. 47). Marigone Drevinja, a member of the Social Democratic Party of Kosovo, stresses the importance of the popular will regarding territorial issues: 'Kosovo should have the right to a referendum about vital matters', including that of unification with Albania.[30]

Despite its contentious character, the idea is not disconnected from Kosovo's political landscape. Vetëvendosje, a rising political movement that is the second most voted party in Kosovo's 2017 legislative elections, with 27.5 per cent of the votes, endorses this possibility as a viable option for Kosovo. A Vetëvendosje representative believes that 'as a country Kosovo should have the right to re-unify with Albania. Not because of nationalism but because of survival in a complex geopolitical situation. It [unification] would make things easier for us in terms of international recognitions'.[31] Vetëvendosje is, however, not the only actor which advocates for Albanian unification. Albanian Prime Minister, Edi Rama, controversially stated in 2015 that '[T]he unification of the Albanians of Albania and Kosovo ... is inevitable and unquestionable', adding that unification would happen within the EU or outside the EU framework (cited by Bytyci and Robinson, 2015).

More recently, an interesting development seems to have emerged. The idea of Albanian unification has begun being used as an instrument of discursive coercion by PM Rama as well as Kosovo President Hashim Thaçi. Both leaders have hinted, in interviews with Western media outlets, the possibility of Albanian unification as a second-best option in case their EU integration aims fail or indeed if their applications are excessively delayed (Macdowall, 2017; Crosby, 2017). The argument of unification as a last resort, that is, as an alternative in case independence fails to be fully legalised has also been justified through a card game metaphor by the Kosovo government political advisor Bashmir Xhemaj:

> [I]f the international community fails to solve the dispute, Kosovo cannot stay and wait forever. There will be attempts to find alternative solutions and the Albanian unification option is there, because we have the same culture, history and language and we share a land border. It is not our aim, we hope we won't have to play that card … but the card is there.[32]

It remains unclear, however, whether the unification threat has the potential to accelerate and reinvigorate Kosovo and Albania accessions or, on the contrary, could be counterproductive for their cause.

The furious reaction from the EU Commissioner for Neighbourhood Policy and Enlargement Negotiations, Johannes Hahn, who stressed that '[I]f someone thinks that such statements will put pressure on the EU, they're wrong.... Such statements which can be considered as interference in neighboring countries and implying changing borders, are not acceptable' (cited by *Gazeta Express*, 2017) seems to indicate that thus far the Albanian and Kosovo leaders' coercive strategy may have been counterproductive. On the other hand, it appears evident that the mere suggestion of border redrawing hits a raw nerve among European policymakers. The former head of the UNMIK mission, Søren Jessen-Petersen, warns that the unification 'solution' carries enormous dangers for Kosovo, namely the peril of falling out of favour with its international sponsors: 'Kosovo has received crucial support from Western states. If they go for this, they would lose American and European support and then they would be worse off'.[33] It is very important not to forget that without the financial, political, military and diplomatic support of its foreign backers Kosovo would have probably not been able to consolidate its partly-recognised state. For that reason, it is unclear whether Kosovo could afford the luxury of antagonising its, until this point, international allies.

From the EU and the U.S. perspective, the insistence on maintaining the border status quo is hardly surprising; any further border alterations would automatically translate into a manifest failure for Western policymakers.

The policy of granting statehood to Kosovo has been based on the understanding, perhaps ingenuous, that this border transformation would be the last and would put an end to ethno-territorial tensions in the region. Indeed, if instead of a containment, the Western-supported secession of Kosovo becomes a trigger generating further border alterations in the region itself, the whole EU and U.S. strategy for the South-East Europe region crumbles.

The imperative question is whether unification represents a way out of the conundrum or a return to actual conflict and a reinvigoration of ethnic nationalism in South-East Europe. For the EU, there is little doubt that it triggers the latter. As this section has discussed, some local Albanian leaders and activists entirely disagree with this conclusion and are pushing instrumentally or ideologically in that direction. As next chapter will show, one of the negative collateral impacts of the idea of 'Greater Albania' is that sovereignty-related conflicts involving Albanian populations may spill-over beyond Kosovo's borders, as occurred in Macedonia in 2001, shortly after NATO's Operation Allied Force intervention.

The contemporary discussions on double partition, on the one hand, and Albanian unification, on the other, challenge the postulates of Western policy makers who, as seen at the beginning of this chapter, argue that borders in Kosovo are 'set' and 'finished'. These statements seem to belong to the domain of 'wishful thinking'. Borders have a stubborn tendency of transforming, appearing, disappearing and reappearing. In Kosovo, and elsewhere.

Notes

1 Serbs south of the Ibar were the main victims during the riots of March 2004, which resulted in 19 people dead, nearly 1,000 injured, 730 homes from Serbs and other minorities destroyed and over 4,000 Serbs and members of ethnic minorities forced to flee their homes (UNSC, 2004, p. 6).
2 Dragiša Djoković, author interview, Mitrovica, 3 August 2017; Nemanja Jaksić, author interview, Mitrovica, 2 June 2014; Sladjana Miletić., author interview, Peć, 31 July 2012.
3 Nemanja Jaksić, author interview, Mitrovica, 2 June 2014.
4 Marigone Drevinja, author interview, Pristina, 4 August 2017.
5 William Ortiz, author interview, Pristina, 31 May 2014.
6 OSCE officer I, author interview, undisclosed location, 10 July 2012.
7 Xhemaj refers to the argument of transferring Northern Kosovo in exchange for Albanian inhabited towns in Southern Serbia's Preševo Valley.
8 Bashmir Xhemaj, author interview, Skype, 28 May 2018.
9 Bashmir Xhemaj, author interview, Skype, 28 May 2018.
10 In Serbian: 'Zajednica Srpskih Opština'.
11 European diplomat, author interview, Paris, 21 April 2018.
12 European diplomat, author interview, Paris, 21 April 2018.
13 Bashmir Xhemaj, author interview, Skype, 28 May 2018.
14 Dragiša Djoković, author interview, Mitrovica, 3 August 2017
15 Marigone Drevinja, author interview, Pristina, 4 August 2017.

16 Leposavić, Zubin Potok, Zvečan and North Mitrovica.
17 Those with a Serbian majority, that is, Gračanica, Novo Brdo, Ranilug, Partes, Klokot and Štrpce.
18 This and every single EU report and communication involving Kosovo, including the Stabilisation and Association Agreement, are accompanied by the following footnote: '[T]his designation is without prejudice to positions on status, and is in line with UNSCR 1244/1999 and the ICJ Opinion on the Kosovo declaration of independence' (European Commission, 2015; European Commission, 2018b). According to Krasniqi this rather bizarre formulation 'reinforces Kosovo's anomalous international status' (2014, p. 208).
19 The Kosovo authorities justified Djurić's arrest on the grounds that the entry of the Belgrade official was illegal. The Serbian government argues, however, that the visit had been communicated three times to the Kosovo authorities, following the ordinary procedures for this type of visits.
20 European diplomat, author interview, Paris, 21 April 2018.
21 Leposavić, Zvečan and Zubin Potok.
22 The only exception being Bošnjačka Mahala, a small mixed neighbourhood in North Mitrovica inhabited by Serbs, Bosniaks and Albanians.
23 Known by the locals as French Bridge or New Bridge.
24 UNMIK officer, author interview, Mitrovica, 1 August 2012.
25 Informal conversations with KFOR troops, held in June 2014 and July 2017. The soldiers also confirmed that, as of 2017, and despite the lack of interaction between both sides, the situation at the bridge is stable and peaceful.
26 Informal interviews with several bridge-crossers, July 2017.
27 Nemanja Jaksić, author interview, Mitrovica, 2 June 2014.
28 The statue itself is 7.5 metres high; the pedestal it sits on is 2.5 metres.
29 A prominent figure of the Vetëvendosje political movement complains that 'internationals' insist that the party should delete the unification idea from the party programme. Vetëvendosje activist, author interview, Pristina, 3 August 2017.
30 Marigone Drevinja, author interview, Pristina, 4 August 2017.
31 Vetëvendosje activist, author interview, Pristina, 3 August 2017.
32 Bashmir Xhemaj, author interview, Skype, 28 May 2018.
33 Søren Jessen-Petersen, author interview, Copenhagen, 9 March 2018.

Bibliography

Al Jazeera (2011, 27 July). 'Serbs torch border post in northern Kosovo'. Retrieved from: www.aljazeera.com/news/europe/2011/07/201172718229126278.html

Al Jazeera (2012, 16 February). 'Kosovo Serbs say 'no' to ethnic Albanian rule'. Retrieved from: www.aljazeera.com/news/europe/2012/02/2012215215056735916.html

Attewill, F. and Traynor, I. (2008, 18 March). 'UN police officer dies after Kosovo clashes'. *Guardian*. Retrieved from: www.theguardian.com/world/2008/mar/18/kosovo.serbia1

Bardos, G. (2005). 'Containing Kosovo'. *Mediterranean Quarterly*, 16(3): 17–43.

B92 (2011, 15 May). 'Partition of Kosovo only solution, minister says'. Retrieved from: www.b92.net/eng/news/politics.php?yyyy=2011&mm=05&dd=15&nav_id=74342

B92 (2018a, 27 March). 'That gang of terrorists – Vucic reacts to events in Kosovo'. Retrieved from: www.b92.net/eng/news/politics.php?yyyy=2018&mm=03&dd=27&nav_id=103793

B92 (2018b, 25 April). 'Pristina wants ZSO to be formed "when Kosovo joins UN"'. Retrieved from: www.b92.net/eng/news/politics.php?yyyy=2018&mm=04&dd=25&nav_id=104013

BBC (2018, 17 February). 'Kosovo PM Haradinaj "fully against" border changes'. Retrieved from: www.bbc.com/news/av/world-europe-43230529/kosovo-pm-haradinaj-fully-against-border-changes

Beha, A. (2015). 'Disputes over the 15-point agreement on normalization of relations between Kosovo and Serbia'. *Nationalities Papers*, 43(1): 102–121.

Billig, M. (1995). *Banal Nationalism*. London: Sage Publications Ltd.

Bytyci, F. and Robinson, M. (2015, 7 April). 'Albania and Kosovo to unite, inside EU or not: Albanian PM'. *Reuters*. Retrieved from: www.reuters.com/article/us-albania-kosovo-unification-idUSKBN0MY18L20150407

Castan Pinos, J. (2013) 'Assessing the significance of borders and territoriality in a globalized Europe'. *Regions and Cohesion*, 3(2): 47–68.

Castan Pinos, J. (2015). 'The Challenge to Territorial Integrity, Kosovo and beyond', in C. Gaitanides (eds), *Diversity in Europe* (pp. 220–236). Baden-Baden: Nomos Verlagsgesellschaft.

Castan Pinos, J. (2016). 'Mitrovica: a city (re)shaped by division', in E. O. Ciardha and G. Vojvoda (eds), *Politics of Identity in Post-Conflict States* (pp. 128–142). Abingdon: Routledge.

Constitution of the Republic of Kosovo (2008). Retrieved from: www.kryeministri-ks.net/repository/docs/Constitution1Kosovo.pdf

Crosby, A. (2017, 29 April). 'Here Are the Flash Points You Should Be Watching In The Balkans'. *Radio Liberty*. Retrieved from: www.rferl.org/a/balkans-flashpoint-to-watch-macedonia-serbia-kosovo-montenegro-bosnia/28456971.html

Djoković, D., author interview, Mitrovica, 3 August 2017.

Downes, A. (2001). 'The Holy Land Divided: Defending Partition as a Solution to Ethnic Wars'. *Security Studies*, 10(4): 58–116.

Drevinja, M., author interview, Pristina, 4 August 2017.

Dziedzic, M. (2006). 'Kosovo' in Durch, W. (ed.) *Twenty-First-Century Peace Operations* (319–388). Washington, DC: The Henry L. Stimson Center.

ECMI (2013a). 'Community Profile: Serb Community'. *European Center for Minority Issues*. Retrieved from: www.ecmikosovo.org/uploads/Serbcommunity1.pdf

Economides, S. and Ker-Lindsay, J. (2015). 'Pre-Accession Europeanization': The Case of Serbia and Kosovo'. *Journal of Common Market Studies*, 53(5): 1027–1044.

Elsuwege, P. (2017). 'Legal Creativity in EU External Relations: The Stabilization and Association Agreement Between the EU and Kosovo'. *European Foreign Affairs Review*, 22(3): 393–410.

European Commission (2013, 19 April). 'Statement by President Barroso on the agreement in the EU-facilitated dialogue between Serbia and Kosovo'. MEMO 13/353. Retrieved from: http://europa.eu/rapid/press-release_MEMO-13-353_en.htm

European Commission (2015). 'Stabilisation and association agreement between the European Union of the one part, and Kosovo*, of the other part'. Retrieved from: https://ec.europa.eu/neighbourhood-enlargement/sites/near/files/news_corner/news/news-files/20150430_saa.pdf

European Commission (2018a). 'Serbia 2018 Report'. SWD 152 final. Retrieved from: http://europa.rs/wp-content/uploads/2018/04/20180417-serbia-report.pdf

European Commission (2018b). 'Kosovo 2018 Report'. SWD 156 final. Retrieved from: https://ec.europa.eu/neighbourhood-enlargement/sites/near/files/20180417-kosovo-report.pdf

European Commission (2018c). 'A credible enlargement perspective for and enhanced EU engagement with the Western Balkans'. COM 65 final. Retrieved from: https://eeas.europa.eu/sites/eeas/files/communication-credible-enlargement-perspective-western-balkans_en.pdf

European Council (2013, 28 June). 'European Council 27/28 June Conclusions'. Retrieved from: www.consilium.europa.eu/uedocs/cms_data/docs/pressdata/en/ec/137634.pdf

European Council (2015, 30 November). 'Chapter 35. Other issues Item 1: Normalisation of relations between Serbia and Kosovo'. Retrieved from: http://data.consilium.europa.eu/doc/document/AD-12-2015-INIT/en/pdf

European diplomat, author interview, Paris, 21 April 2018.

Gallup Balkan Monitor (2010). 'Insights and Perceptions: Voices of the Balkans'. Retrieved from: www.esiweb.org/enlargement/wp-content/uploads/2009/02/2010_Summary_of_Findings.pdf

Gazeta Express (2017, 24 April). 'Hahn to Thaci and Rama: You can't pressure us with national unification statement'. Retrieved from: www.gazetaexpress.com/en/news/hahn-to-thaci-and-rama-you-can-t-pressure-us-with-national-unification-statements-172445/

Gazeta Express (2018, 6 February). 'Vulin says Serbia should seek partition deal with Kosovo'. Retrieved from: www.gazetaexpress.com/en/news/vulin-says-serbia-should-seek-partition-deal-with-kosovo-173581/

Gordon, M. (2012, 31 October). 'Clinton Urges Serbia to Accept Kosovo's Borders'. *New York Times*. Retrieved from: www.nytimes.com/2012/11/01/world/europe/clinton-urges-serbia-to-accept-kosovo-and-its-borders.html

Government of Kosovo (2013). 'First Agreement of Principles Governing the Normalisation of Relations'. Retrieved from: www.kryeministri-ks.net/repository/docs/FIRST_AGREEMENT_OF_PRINCIPLES_GOVERNING_THE_NORMALIZATION_OF_RELATIONS,_APRIL_19,_2013_BRUSSELS_en.pdf

Guardian (2010, 9 December). 'US embassy cables: Belgrade lays out Kosovo partition scenario to EU'. Retrieved from: www.theguardian.com/world/us-embassy-cables-documents/243273

Horowitz, M. and Weisiger, A. (2009). 'The limits to partition'. *International Security*, 33(4): 203–210.

Hoxhaj, E. (2017, 14 August). 'Kosovo is a multiethnic democracy w/ internationally recognised borders. Serbia's renewed ideas 4 border change are dangerous and unacceptable [Tweet]'. Retrieved from: https://twitter.com/Enver_Hoxhaj/status/897079590493016064

ICG (2008). 'Kosovo's First Month'. *Europe Briefing no. 47*. Retrieved from: https://d2071andvip0wj.cloudfront.net/b47-kosovo-s-first-month.pdf

Jaksić, N., author interview, Mitrovica, 2 June 2014.

Jenne, E. (2009). 'The Paradox of Ethnic Partition: Lessons from de facto Partition in Bosnia and Kosovo'. *Regional and Federal Studies*, 19(2): 273–289.

Jenne, E. (2012). 'When Will We Part with Partition Theory? Flawed Premises and Improbable Longevity of the Theory of Ethnic Partition'. *Ethnopolitics*, 11(3): 255–267.

Jessen-Petersen, S., author interview, Copenhagen, 9 March 2018.

Johnson, C. (2008). 'Partitioning to Peace: Sovereignty, Demography, and Ethnic Civil Wars'. *International Security*, 32(4): 140–170.

Kaufmann, C. (1996). 'Possible and Impossible Solutions to Ethnic Civil Wars'. *International Security*, 20(4): 136–175.

Kosovo's Ministry for Community and Return (2018). Retrieved from: http://mzp-rks.org/en/

Krasniqi G. (2014). 'Foreign Policy as a Constitutive Element of Statehood and Statehood Prerogative: The Case of Kosovo' in Keil S. and Stahl B. (eds) *The Foreign Policies of Post-Yugoslav States. New Perspectives on South-East Europe* (pp. 198–220). Palgrave Macmillan, London.

Landau, D. (2017) 'The quest for legitimacy in independent Kosovo: the unfulfilled promise of diversity and minority rights'. *Nationalities Papers*, 45(3): 442–463.

MacDowall, A. (2018, 26 March). 'Kosovo detains Serbian politician after 'illegal entry' into region'. Retrieved from: www.theguardian.com/world/2018/mar/26/kosovo-serbia-politician-marko-djuric

Macdowell, A. (2017, 18 April). 'Albanian prime minister: EU faces "nightmare" if Balkan hopes fade'. *Politico*. Retrieved from: www.politico.eu/article/albania-prime-minister-edi-rama-eu-faces-nightmare-if-balkans-denied/

Maloku, E., B. Derks, C. Van Laar and N. Ellemers (2016). 'Building National Identity in Newborn Kosovo: Challenges of Integrating National Identity with Ethnic Identity Among Kosovar Albanians and Kosovar Serbs' in S. McKeown *et al.* (eds) *Understanding Peace and Conflict Through Social Identity Theory* (245–260). Cham: Springer.

Mearsheimer, J. (2000). 'The Case for Partitioning Kosovo', in T. Carpenter (ed.), *NATO's Empty Victory: A Postmortem on the Balkan War* (pp. 133–138). Washington, DC: CATO Institute.

Miletić S., author interview, Peć, 31 July 2012.

Morina, D. (2017, 2 March). 'Mitrovica's Flashpoint Bridge Symbolises Kosovo's Divisions'. *The Balkan Insight*. Retrieved from: www.balkaninsight.com/en/article/mitrovica-s-flashpoint-bridge-symbolises-kosovo-s-divisions-03-01-2017

Office for Kosovo and Metohija (2016, June 28). 'Marko Đurić unveiled monument to Prince Lazar of Serbia'. Retrieved from: www.kim.gov.rs/eng/v369.php

Ortiz, W., author interview, Pristina, 31 May 2014.

OSCE officer, author interview, undisclosed location, 10 July 2012.

Popham, (2008, 23 February). '"The Bridge Watchers" terrorise Mitrovica'. *Independent*. Retrieved from: www.independent.co.uk/news/world/europe/the-bridge-watchers-terrorise-mitrovica-786166.html

Radio Liberty (2012, 25 October). 'British FM Says Kosovo Cannot Be Split to Resolve Disputes'. Retrieved from: www.rferl.org/a/uk-says-kosovo-cannot-be-split/24750959.html

Rossi, M. (2014). 'Ending the impasse in Kosovo: partition, decentralization, or consociationalism?'. *Nationalities Papers*, 42(5): 867–889.

Rossi, M. (2018, 19 April). 'Brussels Agreement Remains Kosovo's and Serbia's Best Hope'. *Balkan Insight*. Retrieved from: www.balkaninsight.com/en/article/brussels-agreement-remains-kosovo-s-and-serbia-s-best-hope-04-16-2018

RTK (2018, 7 May). 'KFOR ready to assist in Specialist Chamber's arrests'. Retrieved from: www.rtklive.com/en/news-single.php?ID=11391

Savić, M. (2017, 14 August) 'Kosovo Partition May Solve Historic Dispute, Serb Deputy PM Says'. Retrieved from: www.bloomberg.com/news/articles/2017-08-14/kosovo-partition-may-solve-historic-dispute-serb-deputy-pm-says

Serbian Government (2018). 'Kosovo is Serbia'. Retrieved from: www.srbija.gov.rs/kosovo-metohija/index.php?id=43376

Strömbom, L. and Björkdahl, A. (2015). 'Introduction–Governing contested issues in divided cities. Merging conflict resolution and public administration' in A. Björkdahl and L. Strömbom (eds) *Divided Cities: Governing Diversity* (pp. 15–40). Lund: Nordic Academic Press.

UNMIK officer, author interview, Mitrovica, 1 August 2012.

UNSC (2004). S/2004/348. Retrieved from: https://unmik.unmissions.org/sites/default/files/old_dnn/S-2004-348.pdf

Vasovic, A. and Pawlak, J. (2013, 19 April). 'EU brokers historic Kosovo deal, door opens to Serbia accession'. *Reuters*. Retrieved from: www.reuters.com/article/us-serbia-kosovo-eu/eu-brokers-historic-kosovo-deal-door-opens-to-serbia-accession-idUSBRE93I0IB20130419

Vetevendosje activist, author interview, Pristina, 3 August 2017.

Visoka, G. (2017). *Shaping Peace in Kosovo: The Politics of Peacebuilding and Statehood*. Cham: Palgrave Macmillan.

Xhemaj, B., author interview, Skype, 28 May 2018.

6 Kosovo beyond Kosovo

The collateral effects on other territorial conflicts

The previous chapters of this book have focused on several collateral consequences for Kosovo triggered as a result of the humanitarian intervention carried out by NATO in 1999. The current chapter will concentrate, instead, on the reverberations of this intervention beyond Kosovo's borders. As the chapter will show, these collateral effects include spill-over conflicts but also the instrumental use of Kosovo as a precedent by other secessionist movements worldwide. At any rate, two decades after the intervention, Kosovo continues to resonate beyond Kosovo in geopolitical discussions regarding the protection of civilians, the role of foreign actors in local conflicts and indeed, secession.

This chapter will focus on four particular cases (Macedonia, South Ossetia, Crimea and Catalonia) where the Kosovo legacy has played a significant role. There are, however, many other secessionist-driven conflicts where the effects of Kosovo's secession have been felt and conveniently *instrumentalised.*[1]

The Kosovo legacy: spill-over of the conflict into neighbouring Macedonia

In January 2001, roughly 18 months after the completion of NATO's 'Operation Allied Force', an armed conflict emerged in Macedonia, Kosovo's southern neighbour. A pro-Albanian guerrilla, the National Liberation Army (NLA), with close links to Kosovo's KLA, waged an insurgency against the fragile Macedonian state. Skopje had accused the group of having separatist aims. However, according to a communiqué from the group, its main objective was not secession but equal rights for Albanians in Macedonia: 'the NLA will fight until Macedonia constitutionally becomes a Macedonian-Albanian – or Albanian-Macedonian state.... We are in favour of preserving Macedonia's sovereignty and territorial integrity' (cited by European Stability Initiative, 2008). Political grievances from the Albanian community seemed to be the chief factor elucidating the armed rebellion. Some NLA statements, nevertheless, contradicted this constitutional spirit embracing aims which were clearly of a secessionist nature. For instance, a previous, more belligerent, NLA communiqué warned that: '[T]he uniform of the Macedonian occupier will be targeted until all areas with Albanian population are liberated' (cited by Wood, 2001).

It is estimated that 200 people, including 63 members of the Macedonia security forces and 64 members of the NLA, were killed and that up to 140,000 civilians became internally displaced persons (AIM press, 2001; Koktsidis, 2014). The Republic of Macedonia or FYROM[2] was until that point one of the areas that were least affected by the Yugoslavian wars that had devastated the region during the previous decade. In effect, Macedonia and Montenegro are the only republics that seceded from Yugoslavia in a peaceful manner. In the former case and despite its multi-ethnic composition, the country managed to avoid an ethnic crisis during its first post-independence decade and was even able to establish inter-ethnic power-sharing governments (Hislope, 2003, p. 130).

The 2001 armed conflict posed a serious challenge to the Macedonian social and ethnic fabric, that is, to the community relations between the Slavic-majority and the Albanian community (approximately 25 per cent of the population), which is concentrated on the north-west, on the border with Kosovo. The aim of this chapter is not to provide an exhaustive scrutiny of the conflict for this exercise would go well beyond the scope of this book. Instead, the purpose of the following lines will be to determine the influence and relevance of the Kosovo war in the armed conflict in Macedonia. In other words, to what extent was the 2001 insurgence in Macedonia fuelled by the conflict in Kosovo?

There are multiple elements which lead to the conclusion that the Macedonia conflict was indeed a spill-over, unintended consequence from Kosovo. One of the most conclusive arguments that support that hypothesis is the nature and composition of the main protagonist of the insurgency: the NLA. It must be noted that in Albanian the name of this insurgent group – *Ushtria Çlirimtare Kombëtare* – is practically identical to that of the KLA – *Ushtria Çlirimtare e Kosovës*. Coincidentally or not, in Albanian the abbreviation of both groups is the exact same: UÇK. The connection between both groups, however, is much more intimate than simply sharing an abbreviation and having a similar name.

According to Mincheva, whilst most of the cadre of the KLA reinvented themselves as policymakers through the Democratic Party of Kosovo (PDK), some of its fighters decided to continue with the armed struggle across the border: in Serbia's Preševo Valley[3] and in Northern Macedonia (2008, p. 49). A report from the BBC claimed that the militant transfer from one conflict to the other was straightforward 'perhaps most, of its [NLA] members did fight in Kosovo, in the KLA' (2001). The paradigmatic example of this militant transfer is the Supreme Commander of the NLA, Ali Ahmeti, who was one of the key military figures of the KLA. The fact that they share the abbreviation and that most NLA militants had fought for the KLA is not the only connection between the Kosovo and the Macedonian conflicts.

Weapons, the other necessary ingredient for violent conflict, did also flow in abundance from Kosovo to north-west Macedonia. This epitomises a double failure for KFOR/NATO, Kosovo's security provider in the aftermath of the intervention. On the one hand, the arms flow indicates that NATO failed to establish successful border checks which would halt the transfer of weapons beyond Kosovo. The Kosovo-Macedonia border was therefore beyond porous for armed fighters and weapons. On the other hand, and perhaps more worryingly, it also illustrates NATO's inability to successfully disarm its key strategic ally in the Kosovo conflict, the KLA. In the view of Hislope, the link between both insurgencies is overwhelmingly encompassing: '[W]hat Kosovo added to the internal conditions of Macedonia were the indispensable elements of war-making – arms, logistical support and strategy' (2003, p. 130). Going a step further, Carpenter points out that the NATO intervention in 1999 provided pan-Albanian insurgents with an operational base to wage war across borders, laconically concluding that the Macedonian conflict was 'the fruit of that U.S.-NATO policy' (2002, p. 21).

Last but not least, a great deal of scholars agree with the notion that NATO's intervention in Kosovo operated as a catalyst for pan-Albanian nationalism, encouraging Albanian territorial claims in Macedonia and more generally reinvigorating the idea of 'Greater Albania' (Judah, 2001; Carpenter, 2002; Baros, 2003; Hislope, 2003). As seen in the previous chapter, the idea of Greater Albania is openly supported by a major political party in Kosovo, Vetëvendosje, and hinted at as a second-best strategy, in case EU integration fails, by the political elites in Pristina and Tirana. The much-feared (by Western policy-makers) promotion of ethnonationalism in the region constitutes yet another collateral effect of NATO's humanitarian intervention in Kosovo.

The armed conflict between the NLA and the Macedonian government formally ended in August 2001, eight months after it began, with the signature of the Ohrid Framework Agreement. The agreement addresses the issue of rights for the Albanian community, including linguistic rights and equitable representation, while clearly upholding Macedonia's territorial integrity (OSCE, 2001). The EU played a crucial role, with the use of its normative power, in terms of forcing the parties to settle their disputes through a negotiation (Björkdahl, 2005, p. 278) and NATO supervised the disarmament of the NLA guerrilla. The country has since incorporated Albanian parties in coalition governments and in March 2018, the Macedonian Parliament adopted a law providing the Albanian language with official status 'over the entire country' (Marusić, 2018). Ethno-national tensions, including violent incidents, have nonetheless not disappeared. In April 2015, for instance, a group of armed men led by Kosovo Albanians and claiming affiliation to the NLA took control of a police station to demand the establishment of an Albanian state in Macedonia (BBC, 2015). Some weeks later, clashes between a Macedonian Albanian armed group and Macedonian security forces in the northern city of Kumanovo resulted in 22 people killed; 14 militants and eight police officers (BBC, 2015).

A final reflection with regards to the crisis in Macedonia is needed. It should be noted that in stark contrast to the support enjoyed by the KLA from countless Western policy makers, the NLA's rebellion was universally condemned. The same actors who had two years earlier provided diplomatic, financial and military assistance to the KLA rebellion against Yugoslavia, including an intervention which would eventually empower the rebels, were unequivocally labelling the NLA insurgents as terrorists. Ministers from all major European powers, as well as Javier Solana, the High Representative from the EU, unambiguously supported the Macedonian government and denounced the terrorist character of the NLA (Kolstø, 2016, p. 176). This is particularly fascinating when bearing in mind that, as argued previously, many NLA militants had previously fought in Kosovo with the KLA. Judah's explanation for this clearly differentiated approach to pro-Albanian insurgencies is that the spread of the conflict to Macedonia was a 'doomsday scenario' that had the potential to spread across the region, a scenario which was 'unfolding – not despite NATO's involvement in the region, but indeed because of it' (Judah, 2001, p. 7). In other words, NATO's intervention had added combustible fuel, not water, into the ethno-territorial fire of the region.

An inescapable discussion: does Kosovo constitute a precedent?

As argued above, the first, most immediate collateral effect of Kosovo's intervention did occur in Macedonia, and to a lesser extent in Southern Serbia, in the form of a violent conflict of an ethno-territorial nature. This 'aftershock' is the most important collateral impact produced by Kosovo in terms of an armed conflict. There have been, however, other aftershocks albeit of a more discursive nature. One of them is the contested issue of the precedent for other secessionist conflicts around the globe.

There are two dichotomic, mutually exclusive, narratives around the issue of whether Kosovo constitutes a precedent or not. One of the versions asserts that Kosovo is a *sui generis* case with unique conditions and therefore it cannot be used as a precedent. The alternative interpretation ontologically contradicts the former by asserting that Kosovo is indeed a precedent. The stakes are extremely high for the very reason that there are serious political implications concerning the question and, even more so, the answer. If the latter case did hold water that would necessarily imply that the interveners had paved the way for unilateral boundary redrawing, violating the territorial integrity of a state in the name of a flexible understanding of the self-determination principle (and possibly geopolitical interests).

Before further engaging with this divisive discussion, it is important to point that prior and after Kosovo's unilateral declaration of independence those who supported the idea tirelessly insisted that Kosovo could not be viewed as a precedent. UN Special Envoy, Martti Ahtisaari, clearly stated that 'Kosovo is a unique case that demands a unique solution. It does not create a precedent for other unresolved conflicts' (UNSC, 2007, p. 4). As seen in Chapter 3 this unique solution is a euphemistic formula which stands for (foreign supervised) independence. Ironically, the fact that it explicitly mentions that the Kosovo case 'does not create a precedent' could be seen as an indication that there was a fear that Kosovo could, indeed, be potentially used as a precedent. The main justification for this uniqueness is the fact that Kosovo was put under UN administration thus denying Serbia governance over Kosovo as a result of 'Milosevic's actions' (UNSC, 2007, p. 4). Critics could argue that this reasoning may be considered a circular argument, or *petitio principii*, logical fallacy. In other words, to support the Kosovo independence argument as a result of the fact that Kosovo was under UN administration could constitute a self-fulfilling prophesy because without the NATO intervention, the UN administration would, more than likely, not have taken place. To put it simply, the UN administration originated as a result of an international intervention and, consequently, those who intervened contributed to make it *sui generis*.

This idea of uniqueness of the case is also replicated by Kosovo's independence declaration itself, whose preamble insists on the idea that Kosovo is 'not a precedent for any other situation' (cited by BBC, 2008). Likewise, the U.S. State Department, in the communication that formally recognised Kosovo as a state, a day after independence was declared in Pristina, emphasises that 'Kosovo cannot be seen as a precedent for any other situation in the world today' due to the 'unusual combination of factors' which led to Kosovo's independence (U.S. State Department, 2008). Interestingly, amongst the listed factors, the U.S. State Department communication cites the break-up of Yugoslavia, ethnic cleansing of Kosovo Albanians and the prolonged UN administration (U.S. State Department, 2008) but it fails to mention a decisive element: NATO's intervention. Without such intervention, Kosovo would have, arguably, been less unique and more similar to other secessionist-driven conflicts.

This is precisely Ker-Lindsay's argument who contends that the uniqueness claims are 'spurious' because the dynamics of the Kosovo conflict are not dissimilar to other secessionist conflicts around the world (Ker-Lindsay, 2010, p. 107). The main difference, in Ker-Lindsay's view, is that the international community, particularly the United States, did not pressure the parties to accept a compromise acceptable to both but pushed for a solution (independence) which satisfied one actor (the secessionist one) while fully alienating the other (Ker-Lindsay, 2010, p. 107). Another key dissimilarity is that while secessionist conflicts, violent or otherwise, are generally met with indifference from the international community, the Kosovo conflict triggered an international armed response which eventually paved the way for the secession of the territory.

Recapitulating, when delving further into the conditions, listed by Ahtisaari and the U.S. State Department among others, which make Kosovo unique, we find two main reasons. The first is that the territory had been administered by the UN. As stated previously, this argument suffers from a circular argument fallacy: it was under UN administration because NATO intervention made it that way and therefore its uniqueness in a way derives from the actions of those, like the U.S. State Department, who claim Kosovo is unique. The second argument is that Kosovo was oppressed by Serbia/Yugoslavia, which committed gross violations of human rights. This suggestion obliquely implies that Kosovo's secession is legitimised due to moral reasons, that is, by the fact that the territory was a victim of human rights violations by the host state.

This has broad implications which are connected to the Remedial Right Only theory. The core idea of the theory is that secession can be justified, as a last resort, if the encompassing state causes serious and persistent harms to the seceding group (Buchanan, 2004; Seymour, 2007). The main predicament of the theory is that it opens the door to justifying secessions, and hence the violations of states' territorial integrities, on moral grounds. In other words, the theory and its application in Kosovo[4] can potentially pave the way to a precedent in which self-determination outweighs territorial integrity, when injustices have been committed against a particular population/minority. The way the Kosovo conflict was managed may open a Pandora's box that many states, particularly those affected by secessionist challenges of their own, may regret. As the next sections will show, some of them, even European Union member states, have been anxious about the possibility of a 'Kosovo contagion'.

The bottom line of this discussion is that whether or not Kosovo constitutes a precedent in legal terms, Kosovo has become a precedent, or at least an argument, in the political domain. As Borgen puts it: '[D]espite the declarations and best intentions, just saying something is 'unique' may not be enough to prevent a shift in state practice' (2008, p. 464). In this case, this practice consists of the use of Kosovo as a precedent by a multiplicity of actors, state and non-state. In the same vein, James Fearon claims that the one-off 'special exception' argument used in the case of Kosovo leaves many questions unanswered, for example: '[H]ow many one-time exceptions or special circumstances can be declared? Does doing this increase the demand for exceptions?' (2004, p. 413). As next section will show, other actors, namely Russia, immediately made use of this exceptional argument for sovereignty-driven conflicts where its national interest was at stake.

Kosovo as a pretext: separatist conflicts in Georgia

The case of Georgia, and its secessionist regions of South Ossetia and Abkhazia, illustrates the fact that Kosovo may constitute a double (political) precedent: not only in terms of secession but also in terms of humanitarian intervention. Both regions had declared independence in 1991 and 1992 respectively, but their secessionist aspirations had been largely ignored, including by Russia, until Kosovo declared its independence in 2008.

The Russian government has an intricate relationship with Kosovo's independence. On the one hand, it has steadfastly supported Belgrade, using the argument that both NATO's intervention in Kosovo and the subsequent unilateral independence of this territory were illegal, thereby seriously compromising the legal pillars of the international system (Hughes, 2013; Averre and Davies, 2015). On the other hand, the Russian government has used Kosovo as a pretext to first justify and subsequently recognise and support the secessions from South Ossetia and Abkhazia (Borgen, 2008; Summers, 2011) and later the annexation of Crimea. In 2006, for instance, the Russian President, Vladimir Putin, anticipated that a potential independence of Kosovo would legitimise the secessionist claims of the two Georgian breakaway regions: '[I]f someone thinks that Kosovo can be granted full independence as a state, then why should the Abkhaz or the South-Ossetian peoples not also have the right to statehood?' (Kremlin, 2006). In between the lines, Putin was admitting that an independent Kosovo would constitute a precedent which could potentially lead Russia to recognise South Ossetia and Abkhazia. It is therefore not too far-fetched to argue that the collateral effects of Kosovo were reaching, in a poisonous fashion, the Caucasus region.

For their part, the leadership from the South Ossetia and Abkhazia have reiterated on several occasions that Kosovo was a precedent for their cause. They had, for instance, been lobbying their case with Russian policymakers turning 'the Kosovo impasse to their advantage' (Ó Tuathail, 2008, p. 683). In the context of the 2010 ICJ *advisory opinion*, analysed extensively in Chapter 4, Abkhazia's late President Sergei Bagapsh stressed that: '[T]he decision of the International Court once more confirms the right of Abkhazia and South Ossetia to self-rule. And from a historical and legal point of view, Abkhazia and South Ossetia have much more right to independence than Kosovo' (cited by BBC, 2010). Kosovo had become the main argument for justifying the secession of these two territories. At the other side of the spectrum, former Georgian President Mikheil Saakashvili had expressed his 'tremendous worry' that Kosovo would damage his country's territorial integrity. Interestingly, such concerns were shared by the Head of European diplomacy at the time, Javier Solana, who had acknowledged, back in 2006, the potential negative effects that the Kosovo precedent could have for Georgia, in relation to territorial matters (Lobjakas, 2006).

The 'negative effects' that Saakashvili feared and Solana referred to did not take long to materialise. Barely five days after Kosovo's independence declaration, on 22 February 2008, the Russian President, Vladimir Putin, escalated his denunciation of such unilateral move, which had the blessing of the most prominent Western states, by denouncing that

> [T]he independence of Kosovo is a terrible precedent.... And undoubtedly, it may entail a whole chain of unpredictable consequences.... Ultimately this is a stick with two ends, and one day the other end of this stick will hit them on their heads.
>
> (cited by B92, 2008)

The 'unpredictable consequences' turned out to be fairly predictable as the Kosovo precedent was becoming reified through discourse and subsequently through practice and policy. A few weeks after Kosovo's unilateral declaration of independence, in April 2008, a Russian presidential decree authorised the establishment of direct relations between Russia and the authorities from Abkhazia and South Ossetia (Allison, 2008, p. 1147). Needless to say, this was a crucial step in the direction of full recognition.

The diplomatic crisis escalated into a short, five days, yet full-scale, interstate war in August 2008, when after a series of border skirmishes the Georgian army bombed and invaded South Ossetia, in an attempt to exert territorial control over the region. The incursion caused numerous deaths including South Ossetian civilians and Russian peacekeepers.[5] Saakashvili's plan fully backfired as Russia instantly responded, with a full-scale intervention involving aircraft, tank columns and even destroying key targets in Georgia proper (King, 2008). The five-day war had critical consequences in relation to territoriality: on 26 August of that same year, the Russian Federation recognised the independence of South Ossetia and Abkhazia.

President Medvedev's[6] statement announcing the recognition of both breakaway regions deserves close attention because of the strong reverberations from Kosovo. For starters, there is a reference to Kosovo; Medvedev claims that Russia had been committed to a negotiated settlement with Georgia 'even after the unilateral proclamation of Kosovo's independence' (Kremlin, 2008). In addition, the language used in the statement stems clearly from the parlance of humanitarian intervention; it includes for instance references to 'devastated villages', refugees and civilians killed as a result of Georgia's invasion (Kremlin, 2008). The statement details the reasons justifying Russia's intervention in South Ossetia, which is presented as a moral endeavour whose main aim was to 'put an end to the eradication of the Abkhaz and Ossetian peoples' (Kremlin, 2008). Likewise, the secession of these territories is justified with the rationale that 'all the hopes for the peaceful coexistence of Ossetians, Abkhazians and Georgians in a single state' had been dashed by Georgia's ruthless behaviour and consequently granting these breakaway regions with statehood 'represents the only possibility to save human lives' (Kremlin, 2008).

This statement shows that Russia seems to have mimicked in South Ossetia, possibly in a deliberate fashion, the arguments, the language and even the practice carried out by the West in Kosovo. By practice, I refer to the foreign military intervention, justified with moral arguments, in a secessionist conflict favouring the separatist armed rebels with the final result of the violation of the territorial integrity of the host state. The model implemented and to a certain extent mimicked from the West is that of unilateral humanitarian[7] intervention, based on the postulate of 'illegal but legitimate' that was repeated like a mantra to justify the Kosovo intervention. The final result also includes the creation of parastates whose survival largely rests upon the support from their international backers; Russian support in the case of South Ossetia and Abkhazia and the U.S. when it comes to Kosovo.[8] In the view of Kemoklidze,

> the moral justification cited in support of the recognition of Kosovo-that after suffering 'genocidal violence' at the hands of the Serbs, the Kosovar Albanians could no longer reside peacefully side by-side with the Serbs in a single political entity-has (unintentionally) created suitable political conditions' for secessionism to triumph in Georgia.
>
> (Kemoklidze, 2009 p. 122)

In conclusion, the reaction from the Kremlin could be interpreted not just as a reassertion of its regional power and near abroad interventionism as some authors have claimed (Allison, 2008; King, 2008; Ó Tuathail, 2008) but also as a tit-for-tat or *quid pro quo*, to punish the U.S. and its allies for altering the borders in South-East Europe. The intervention in South Ossetia can be viewed as an opportunity where 'Russia was paying back the USA and EU in their own coin' (Hughes, 2013, p. 1012). All the more so, Russian interventionism in Georgia was the empirical demonstration that the 'stick with two ends' (prompted by Kosovo) that Putin made reference to in February 2008 was not simply a rhetorical figure but a tangible reality with tangible consequences.

Kosovo as a legitimation: Crimea

The instrumental use of the Kosovo precedent for the purpose of justifying Russia's interventionism in its 'near abroad' did begin in Georgia but it did not end there. The 'stick with two ends' unleashed by Kosovo had also a prominent role in the Crimean annexation,[9] reintegration according to the Russian government perspective, by Russia, which occurred amidst the political crisis of early 2014 in Ukraine.

As protests, many of them of a violent character, erupted in several cities in Ukraine, the Russian government conducted military drills on the border with Ukraine. In Crimea and the federal city of Sevastopol, where Russia's Black Sea Fleet was legally stationed,[10] Russian military intelligence officers, popularly known as little green men,[11] dressed in military gear took over the most strategic buildings of the Peninsula in a quasi-bloodless operation[12] (Yuhas, 2014). One of the pivotal features of this shadowy take over was the expulsion of all Ukrainian soldiers from Crimea (Herzenhorn *et al.*, 2014). In this context of political uncertainty, a self-determination referendum, deemed illegal by the Ukrainian authorities, was held in 16 March to determine the territorial future of the peninsula. The results of the contested referendum showed that a vast majority of the voters (96 per cent with an 82 per cent turnout) did cast their ballots in favour of the peninsula becoming a part of the Russian Federation (Kremlin, 2008). This would seem to indicate that the border transformation in Crimea, similarly to Kosovo, enjoyed wide support amongst the local population.

Scholars have provided a wide range of divergent explanations regarding Russia's intentions behind their seizure of Crimea. Russia's seizure of the peninsula has been interpreted as an 'improvised gambit' triggered by Russia's fear of losing its naval base in Sevastopol (Treisman, 2016, p. 48), as the empirical evidence that Russia, under Putin, was embracing an ethno-nationalist ideology (Teper, 2016, p. 393), as clear expression of Russian neo-imperialism (Galeotti and Bowen, 2014) or as Putin's defensive response to the West's post-Cold War expansionist approach (Mearsheimer, 2014, p. 85).

Most of these contradictory interpretations are not incompatible with the idea that Kosovo provided a vital source of legitimation for the Russian seizure of Crimea. Two days after the referendum, on 18 March, Russian President Vladimir Putin, in a celebratory speech addressed to members of the Duma and other authorities used the Kosovo precedent argument extensively; he spoke about it for three minutes and 13 seconds (YouTube, 2014). During this time, Putin highlighted the 2010 ICJ *advisory opinion*, including a direct citation from it: '[G]eneral international law contains no prohibition on declarations of independence' (ICJ, 2010; Kremlin, 2014). He reminded his audience that Kosovo was 'a precedent our western colleagues created with their own hands in a very similar situation, when they agreed that the unilateral separation of Kosovo from Serbia', denouncing the fact that 'things that Kosovo Albanians … were permitted to do, Russians, Ukrainians and Crimean Tatars in Crimea are not allowed' (Kremlin, 2008). It seems quite evident that in addition to using the Kosovo case to justify the Russian seizure of Crimea, the aim of the Russian President was also to highlight the double standards of Western states 'with regards to the territorial integrity/self-determination dichotomy' (Castan Pinos, 2015b, p. 231). The rationale is straightforward: if norms are compromised by the West with impunity, these very norms can also be twisted by Russia in the name of 'protection of civilians' and national interest.

Russia's takeover of Crimea can therefore also be understood as a challenge to the U.S. normative hegemony. In other words, Crimea may be

Figure 6.1 Mural in North Mitrovica linking Crimea and Kosovo[13] (2014).
Source: author.

just the tip of the iceberg of a much more intricate process aimed at undermining the geopolitical status quo, characterised by U.S. unilateralism, which emerged after the collapse of the Soviet Union and the ensuing end of bipolarity. At this point it is imperative to refer to Burke-White's claim according to which:

> [F]or most of the past 70 years, and certainly since the early 1990s, the United States has been able to lead the international legal system, often in cooperation with Europe. It defined the rules, the exceptions to those rules and often the enforcement of those rules.
>
> (Burke-White, 2014, p. 66)

Bearing this in mind, the core idea of my argument is that Russia is not only reasserting its relative and absolute power by boosting its military might but also by questioning the Western-based legal-normative foundations of the post-Cold War era.

The message sent by Russia from Crimea appears to be quite clear: the West does no longer have the monopoly when it comes to defining rules or, perhaps more importantly, the monopoly to bend them. In a nutshell,

Kosovo did confirm the Russian fear according to which 'the most powerful Western states will flout Westphalian norms in pursuit of their special interests' (Foot, 2003, p. 17). Kosovo was also the useful pretext so that Russia could start flouting those norms itself, in the name of its national interest but also in the name of a precedent midwifed by the West.

There is a final facet, concerning the different status of Kosovo and Crimea, which is worth mentioning. Whilst, as Chapter 4 explained, Kosovo's legal status is unsettled primarily due to its difficulties to obtain UN membership, the border transformations in Crimea are by all means a *fait accompli*. The crux here is that annexations, unlike secessions, do not need international legal validation[14] to make them successful, the only necessary requirement is the will and the capacity of the host state to effectively control the incorporated territory. Russia has steadfastly proven to have both.

Kosovo as an inspiration: Catalonia

The seismic waves of Kosovo's controversial secession did not only reach post-Soviet territories such as South Ossetia, Abkhazia and Crimea. Its effects were also powerfully felt in Catalonia, a stateless nation recognised as an autonomous community by the 1978 Spanish Constitution, which has in recent years posed a serious threat to Spain's territorial integrity. The conflict between the Catalan government and the Spanish authorities escalated to an extremely critical situation on 1 October 2017, when the former organised an independence referendum without the consent of the latter. Madrid's clumsy and unsuccessful attempt to prevent the referendum by force, deploying thousands of riot police from the national and the paramilitary police, led to widespread state-fueled violence throughout Catalonia. The referendum and the symbolic[15] independence declaration of 27 October were met by a Spanish crackdown which led to the suspension of the Catalan autonomy, the imprisonment of several members of the Catalan government, accused of violent rebellion, and prominent leaders of the civil society. In addition, several Catalan policymakers, including former Catalan President, Carles Puigdemont, went into exile in different European states. As hinted above, my argument is that this conflict was also influenced by Kosovo's secession as well as by the ICJ *advisory opinion* regarding its legality issued in 2010.

In the view of Wilde, this ICJ *advisory opinion* on Kosovo's independence was of imperial importance for secessionist movements, not least because the document seems to imply that unilateral declarations of independence are not illegal if conducted by a nonstate actor:

> [T]he finding that the prohibition on violating territorial integrity is applicable only to states – and not also to nonstate actors – is relevant to all situations in which substate groups aspire to achieve independence.... Thus, an act that would be illegal if conducted by another state

> is not illegal if conducted by a nonstate actor. All substate groups in the world are now on notice that, according to this view, no international law rule bars independence declarations.
>
> (2011, p. 304)

Indeed, this detail did not go unnoticed for Catalan secessionists. According to Alexandre Miquel, a political communication expert working for an influential pro-independence civil society organisation (Òmnium Cultural), the ICJ *advisory opinion* 'brought hope to Catalonia because for us it opens the door to the possibility of seceding through a unilateral declaration [of independence] in a fully legal manner'.[16] This idea bears strong similarities to the reaction of Catalan pro-sovereignty leaders who, in the wake of the ICJ opinion, drew parallels between Catalonia and Kosovo and called on the Spanish government to recognise the independence of this territory (*Catalan News*, 2010). Two years earlier, the Catalan Vice-President at the time, Josep Lluís Carod-Rovira, had sent a letter congratulating the Kosovo Prime Minister 'on the achievement of Kosovo's independence' a day after it was proclaimed (cited by Arenas and Riba, 2008). That same year, numerous Catalan city halls passed motions supporting Kosovo's independence.

The presence of Kosovo in parliamentary debates has been persistent in Catalonia, both as a useful valid precedent according to the pro-secession parties but also as a dangerous example in the eyes of pro-unionist parties. Albert Rivera, leader of the pro-union party Ciudadanos, for instance has consistently criticised pro-secession parties for attempting to pursue the unilateral 'the Kosovo way' (cited by CCMA, 2011). The debate over the parallelism between Kosovo and Catalonia also reached the European Parliament when three pro-independence MEP's[17] sent a written question to the Commission in September 2012. In their parliamentary question, they explicitly referred to Kosovo and the ICJ *opinion*, generously[18] interpreting its conclusions with Catalonia's right to secede:

> The International Court of Justice's opinion on Kosovo's unilateral declaration states that the democratic principle is above territorial integrity and, therefore, state law. Therefore, does the Commission believe that it must define a democratic and transparent road map for a possible Catalan independence process?

As the sovereignty-driven conflict was escalating in Catalonia so were the references to Kosovo. In a white book (on Catalonia's national transition) drafted by the Catalan government in 2014 to scrutinise Catalonia's possible seceding scenarios, the Kosovo unilateral precedent is mentioned four times and deemed as of 'interest' for a 'new state which seeks to integrate in the international community' (Catalan Government, 2014, p. 129). Subsequently, in 2016, former Catalan President Carles Puigdemont evoked

Kosovo's UDI in an ordinary session of the Catalan Parliament which ended up in a discussion about Kosovo between pro-secession and pro-unionist MP's (Sastre, 2016). During the uncertain post-referendum period in October 2017, while the Catalan president was mulling over the possibility of proclaiming independence, the ghost of Kosovo (and Yugoslavia) once again appeared on the scene. According to pro-unionist MP Rivera, '[Catalan] Separatism is paving the way for the Kosovo way. I never expected that Yugoslavia would become an example to emulate' (Rivera, 2017).

Interestingly, the parallels between Catalonia and Kosovo have also been established by the Serbian government. The day Catalonia symbolically declared independence, on 27 October 2017, Serbia's Foreign Minister, Ivica Dačić contended that '[T]he path of Kosovo and Catalonia is the same' with the exception that in the latter case, unlike in Kosovo, no great powers had supported the secession of that territory (B92, 2017). Dačić, similarly to Putin in relation to Crimea, uses the Catalan case to highlight the double standards of the West when it comes to the principle of territorial integrity. On the other hand, in an interview with a Spanish newspaper *El Pais*, Ramush Haradinaj, Kosovo's Prime Minister, denied any similarity between both cases arguing that 'establishing any analogy is ludicrous' because *inter alia* Kosovo was born in the context of Yugoslavia's disintegration, Milošević repression and a bloody war (cited by Sánchez-Vallejo, 2018).

The unaddressed question is if that is indeed the case and Kosovo can in no way be equated to Catalonia (or the Basque Country) and therefore it is not a valid precedent, why does Spain stubbornly obstruct EU common foreign policy by not recognising Kosovo? The Spanish sabotage is illustrated, for instance, by the fact that the Spanish PM at the time, Mariano Rajoy, denied attending an EU-Western Balkans summit in Sofia due to the presence of Kosovo representatives in May 2018. This is particularly shocking when taking into account that the Serbian PM, Ana Brnabić, did attend the summit.

According to the Spanish official version, Madrid's refusal to recognise Kosovo's independence is based upon reasons exclusively related to international law. In the eyes of a senior Spanish diplomat:

> [T]he Spanish thesis stems from international law, which does not authorise the unilateral declaration of independence. [UNSC] Resolution 1244 does not contemplate this. The resolution must be the framework to resolve this issue. Our position is not determined by the internal situation in Spain.[19]

This last point is, of course, not uncontroversial. The internal situation, namely the secessionist challenge that Spain faces in Catalonia and to a lesser extent the Basque country, is a determinant factor that accounts for Spain's non-recognition of Kosovo.

According to Ferrero-Turrión 'Spain's concerns over the Catalonia issue has had a crucial impact on its position' (2017, p. 52). In the same vein, Catalan pro-secession activist, Alexandre Miquel, contends that it is crystal clear that the chief reason behind Spain vehement opposition to recognising Kosovo is that 'they [Spanish government] are afraid of our [Catalan] unilateral declaration of independence'.[20] Pristina's policymakers and diplomats are well aware of Spain's 'internal issues' and the fears those issues trigger regarding a potential contagion from Kosovo. Haradinaj's statement emphasising that 'we will never recognise Catalonia's independence' (cited by Sánchez-Vallejo, 2018) epitomises Kosovo's acknowledgment that the main impediment to obtain Madrid's recognition is Catalonia. Further enhancing this argument, an active European diplomat has acknowledged that Spain's intransigence when it comes to Kosovo has little to do with Kosovo itself and is instead eminently caused by its internal troubles with Catalonia.[21] In a more surreptitious manner, Kosovo government official, Bashmir Xhemaj, claims that Spain and the other four EU member states' refusal to recognise Kosovo's independence 'continue to withhold the recognition of Kosovo for their own domestic reasons, which have nothing to do with Kosovo and its legitimate case for statehood and recognition'.[22]

More generally, it is possible to argue that the Spanish government's anxieties related to the fear of 'losing Catalonia' have effectively conditioned, and arguably compromised, the bulk of its foreign policy. This appears evident when it comes to Spain's relationship vis-à-vis Brussels. Whilst Spain tends to align itself with constructive integrationist postulates in the EU, when it comes to Kosovo's recognition it has adopted an inflexible stand that literally sabotages the dominant position of EU members states regarding Kosovo. This hardline approach is atypical for Spain and can hardly be explained in light of international law or ideological alignment with Belgrade.

As explained in Chapter 4, Spain is one of the five EU members that has thus far refused to recognise Kosovo. Together with the Russian and Chinese likely vetoes at the UNSC, the non-recognition of these five member states is one of the key impediments for Kosovo's UN membership. In addition, their refusal to recognise Kosovo hits a raw nerve: it impedes the EU from speaking with a unified coherent voice rendering its preferred adjective 'common' as null and void when it comes to its 'foreign policy' in South-East Europe. Out of the five non-recognisers in the EU, Spain is the state with more political weight and it is also the one with a more inflexible position. In EU diplomatic circles there is the common understanding that if Spain would abandon its veto, the other four member states would follow suit.[23] The Spanish government fears that Kosovo could become a precedent for Catalonia reifies and consolidates the argument that Kosovo constitutes a precedent. By treating it like a precedent, they make it so.

In Catalonia, but as seen previously, also in the post-Soviet space, the legacy of Kosovo extends well beyond its borders. The lesson here is that indefatigably claiming the case does not constitute a precedent, as Western policymakers have done since 2008, is not sufficient to impede that it becomes reified through discourse, practice and policy as, indeed, a precedent. Kosovo has been and continues being a pretext, a legitimation and an inspiration for those who aspire to challenge the border status quo.

Notes

1 For instance in Bosnia's *Republika Srspka*, an autonomous entity (mostly inhabited by Bosnian Serbs) with ample powers and competences whose President, Milorad Dodik, has recurrently hinted at the possibility of this entity's secession. According to Saša Bižić, a local journalist from Banja Luka (the capital of the autonomous entity), 'Kosovo's secession encouraged politicians and people [in *Republika Srspka*] to become more vocal about their intentions to secede from Bosnia'. Saša Bižić, author interview, Banja Luka, 28 July 2017.

2 FYROM stands for Former Yugoslav Republic of Macedonia. This is, at the time of this writing, the country's official name in international organisations such as the UN and the EU. Locally, however, the term 'Republic of Macedonia' is widely used. The dispute over the name involves Macedonia and its southern neighbour, Greece. The name dispute predicament goes well beyond the scope of this book.

3 Serbia's Preševo Valley is mostly inhabited by Albanians. A similar yet smaller insurgency was fought by another offshoot of the KLA, the UÇPMB, in 2001. The group was able to exert control over territory for a short period, until the Yugoslavian army was able to retake the area (with NATO's explicit blessing) from the pro-Albanian rebels.

4 The applicability of the remedial rights theory to Kosovo has been contested by several authors. One of the objections is that minorities suffered abuses at the hands of the secessionist armed groups (the KLA), during and after the conflict, and these violations of human rights invalidate the legitimacy of Kosovo's secession on moral grounds (Summers, 2011; Castan Pinos, 2015a).

5 The Russian peacekeeping force had been deployed in 1992, in the aftermath of the Georgian–Ossetian war (1991–1992), under the auspices of the Sochi Agreement (Ó Tuathail, 2008, p. 677).

6 President Dmitry Medvedev replaced Putin on 7 May 2008. He was in office for one term, until 7 May 2012, when Putin was reelected President of Russia and Medvedev became Prime Minister.

7 Needless to say the 'humanitarian' adjective can be disputed in the case of Russia's intervention in South Ossetia. As Chapter 2 showed, that very adjective can also be challenged in the case of NATO's intervention in Kosovo.

8 The chief difference lies between Kosovo and the Georgian breakaway regions is the fact that whilst Kosovo has managed to be recognised by approximately 110 UN members (see Chapter 4 for further details), Abkhazia and South Ossetia have (as of 2018) only been recognised by Russia, Nicaragua, Venezuela, Syria and Nauru.

9 Interestingly, the Russian government has followed a very different approach towards the self-declared Republics of Donetsk and Lugansk, in Eastern Ukraine. Despite the direct and indirect support that it provides to these two parastates, Russia has, as of 2018, not recognised their independence (as it did with South Ossetia and Abkhazia in 2008) nor integrated them into the Russian Federation (as it did with Crimea in 2014).

10 The Kharkiv pact, an international agreement signed by Ukraine and Russia in 2010, allowed Russia to deploy 25,000 soldiers in the peninsula.
11 In Russia, perhaps with some degree of irony they are referred to as 'Polite Green Men'.
12 A Ukrainian soldier died.
13 The text reads: Kosovska Mitrovica. Kosovo is Serbia (in Russian). Crimea is Russia (in Serbian).
14 Evidence for this is the fact that UNGA resolution 68/262, which upheld Ukraine's territorial integrity and deemed the 16 March referendum illegal, has no legal effects whatsoever despite the fact that it was passed with a solid majority: 100 states voted in favour, 11 against and 58 abstained (UN, 2014).
15 It was symbolic for two reasons. It was not published in the official gazette of the Catalan Parliament and therefore it did not become law. In addition, the Catalan government did not take any initiative, such as taking control of the territory, borders and other strategic infrastructures, to make the declaration effective.
16 Alexandre Miquel, author interview, Barcelona, 14 July 2017.
17 Ana Miranda (from a Galician pro-independence party), Ramon Tremosa and Raül Romeva. Romeva later became the Catalan Foreign Secretary (2016–2017). As of 2018 he is in preventive detention, accused, like other members of the Catalan government, of *inter alia* violent rebellion.
18 The ICJ *opinion* does not state that 'the democratic principle is above territorial integrity and, therefore, state law'. As explained in Chapter 4, the main point of the *opinion* is that: '[I]nternational law does not regulate the act of making a declaration of independence, which should be regarded as a political act' (ICJ, 2010, p. 27).
19 Spanish diplomatic source, author interview, Belgrade, 2 July 2012.
20 Alexandre Miquel, author interview, Barcelona, 14 July 2017.
21 European diplomat, author interview, Paris, 21 April 2018.
22 Bashmir Xhemaj, author interview, Skype, 28 May 2018.
23 European diplomat, author interview, Paris, 21 April 2018.

Bibliography

AIM Press (2001, 30 December). 'What do the Casualties of War Amount to?'. Retrieved from: www.aimpress.ch/dyn/trae/archive/data/200112/11230-003-trae-sko.htm

Allison, R. (2008). 'Russia Resurgent? Moscow's campaign to "coerce Georgia to peace"' *International Affairs*, 84(6): 1145–1171.

Arenas, S. and Riba, T. (2008, 21 February). 'El govern felicita Kosovo per carta per la independència'. *El Punt Avui.* Retrieved from: www.elpuntavui.cat/politica/article/238477-el-govern-felicita-kosovo-per-carta-per-la-independencia-.html

Averre, D. and L. Davies (2015). 'Russia, humanitarian intervention and the Responsibility to Protect: the case of Syria'. *International Affairs*, 91(4): 813–834.

B92 (2008, 23 February). 'Putin: Kosovo is a terrible Precedent'. Retrieved from: www.b92.net/eng/news/politics.php?yyyy=2008&mm=02&dd=23&nav_id=47916

B92 (2017, 27 October). 'Catalonia, same as Kosovo; but no big powers are behind it'. Retrieved from: www.b92.net/eng/news/politics.php?yyyy=2017&mm=10&dd=27&nav_id=102669

B92 (2018, 2 March). 'FM's plea to another country to reconsider Kosovo decision'. Retrieved from: www.b92.net/eng/news/politics.php?yyyy=2018&mm=03&dd=02&nav_id=103618

Baros, M. (2003). 'The Macedonian Conflict and International Law: Self-Determination or Self-Defence?'. *International Peacekeeping*, 10(3): 60–78.

BBC (2001, 20 March). 'Who are the rebels?'. Retrieved from: http://news.bbc.co.uk/2/hi/europe/1231596.stm

BBC (2008, 17 February). 'Full text: Kosovo declaration'. Retrieved from: http://news.bbc.co.uk/2/hi/europe/7249677.stm

BBC (2010, 22 July). 'Reaction in quotes: UN legal ruling on Kosovo'. Retrieved from: www.bbc.com/news/world-europe-10733837

BBC (2015, 10 May). 'Macedonia blames Kosovans for deadly Kumanovo clashes'. Retrieved from: www.bbc.com/news/world-europe-32680904

Bižić, S., author interview, Banja Luka, 28 July 2017.

Björkdahl, A. (2005) 'Norm-maker and Norm-taker: Exploring the Normative Influence of the EU in Macedonia'. *European Foreign Affairs Review*, 10(2): 257–278.

Borgen, C. (2008). 'Introductory note to Kosovo's Declaration of Independence'. *International Legal Materials*, 47(4): 461–466.

Buchanan, A. (2004), *Justice, Legitimacy, and Self-Determination*, Oxford: Oxford University Press.

Burke-White, W. (2014). 'Crimea and the International Legal Order'. *Survival*, 56(4): 65–80.

Carpenter, T. (2002). 'Kosovo and Macedonia: The West Enhances the Threat'. *Mediterranean Quarterly*, 13(1): 21–37.

Castan Pinos, J. (2015a) 'The challenge of separatism and its weak reverberation in the Americas'. *Central European Journal of International and Security Studies*, 9(3): 98–115.

Castan Pinos, J. (2015b). 'The Challenge to Territorial Integrity, Kosovo and beyond', in C. Gaitanides (ed.), *Diversity in Europe* (pp. 220–236). Baden-Baden: Nomos Verlagsgesellschaft.

Catalan Government (2014). 'Llibre Blanc de la Transició Nacional de Catalunya'. Retrieved from: www.gencat.cat/eapc/revistes/RCDP/Documents_interes/RCDP_54/05_19Llibre_blanc_Sintesi.pdf

Catalan News (2010, 24 July). 'Catalan nationalist parties react to the international recognition of Kosovo's independence'. Retrieved from: www.catalannews.com/politics/item/catalan-nationalist-parties-react-to-the-international-recognition-of-kosovos-independence

CCMA (2011, 13 April). 'El Parlament rebutja tramitar la proposició de declaració d'independència presentada per Solidaritat'. Retrieved from: www.ccma.cat/324/El-Parlament-rebutja-tramitar-la-proposicio-de-declaracio-dindependencia-presentada-per-Solidaritat/noticia/1151286/#

European diplomat, author interview, Paris, 21 April 2018.

European Parliament (2012, 21 September). 'Parliamentary Questions'. Retrieved from: www.europarl.europa.eu/sides/getDoc.do?pubRef=-//EP//TEXT+WQ+E-2012-008324+0+DOC+XML+V0//EN

European Stability Initiative (2008). 'Issues: The 2001 Conflict'. Retrieved from: www.esiweb.org/index.php?film_ID=4&id=311&lang=en&slide_ID=21&function=print

Fearon, J. (2004). 'Separatist Wars, Partition, and World Order'. *Security Studies*, 13(4): 394–415.

Ferrero-Turrión, R. (2017). 'Spain' in Ker-Lindsay, J. and Armakolas, I. (eds) *Lack of Engagement? Surveying the Spectrum of EU Member State Policies towards Kosovo* (pp. 51–54). Pristina: Kosovo Foundation for Open Society.

Foot, R. (2003). 'Introduction', in R. Foot, J. Gaddis and A. Hurrell (eds), *Order and Justice in International Relations* (pp. 1–23). Oxford: Oxford University Press.

Galeotti, M. and Bowen, A. (2014, 21 April). 'Putin's Empire of the Mind'. *Foreign Policy*. Retrieved from: http://foreignpolicy.com/2014/04/21/putins-empire-of-the-mind/

Herzenhorn, D., P. Reevell and N. Sneider (2014, 22March). 'Russian Forces Take Over One of the Last Ukrainian Bases in Crimea'. *New York Times*. Retrieved from: www.nytimes.com/2014/03/23/world/europe/ukraine.html

Hislope, R. (2003). 'Between a bad peace and a good war: insights and lessons from the almost-war in Macedonia'. *Ethnic and Racial Studies*, 26(1), 129–151.

Hughes, J. (2013). 'Russia and the Secession of Kosovo: Power, Norms and the Failure of Multilateralism'. *Europe-Asia Studies*, 65(5): 992–1016.

ICJ (2010). 'Accordance with International Law of the Unilateral Declaration of Independence in Respect of Kosovo, Advisory Opinion, I.C.J. Reports 2010'. Retrieved from: www.icj-cij.org/files/case-related/141/141-20100722-ADV-01-00-EN.pdf

Judah, T. (2001) 'Greater Albania?'. *Survival*, 43(2), 7–18.

Kemoklidze, N. (2009). 'The Kosovo Precedent and the Moral Hazard of Secession'. *Journal of International Law and International Relations*, 5(2): 117–140.

Ker-Lindsay, J. (2010). *Kosovo. The Path to Contested Statehood in the Balkans*. London: I.B. Tauris.

King, C. (2008). 'The five-day war managing Moscow after the Georgia crisis'. *Foreign Affairs*, 87(6): 2–11.

Koktsidis, P. (2014). 'From deprivation to violence? Examining the violent escalation of conflict in the Republic of Macedonia'. *Dynamics of Asymmetric Conflict*, 7(1), 1–29.

Kolstø, P. (2016). *Media Discourse and the Yugoslav Conflicts: Representations of Self and Other*. Abingdon: Routledge.

Kremlin (2006, 31 January). 'Transcript of the Press Conference for the Russian and Foreign Media'. Retrieved from: http://en.kremlin.ru/events/president/transcripts/23412

Kremlin (2008, 26 August). 'Statement by President of Russia Dmitry Medvedev'. Retrieved from: http://en.kremlin.ru/events/president/transcripts/1222

Kremlin (2014, 18 March). 'Address by President of the Russian Federation'. Retrieved from: http://eng.kremlin.ru/news/6889 (accessed 2 April 2014).

Lobjakas, A. (2006, 4 October). 'Georgia: Solana Fears Kosovo 'Precedent' For Abkhazia, South Ossetia'. *Radio Liberty*. Retrieved from: www.rferl.org/a/1071802.html

Marusić, S. (2018, 14 March). 'Macedonia Adopts Albanian Language Law Amid Scuffles'. Retrieved from: www.balkaninsight.com/en/article/macedonia-passes-albanian-language-law-amid-tension-03-14-2018

Mearsheimer, J. (2014). 'Why the Ukraine crisis is the west's fault: The liberal delusions that provoked Putin'. *Foreign Affairs*, 93(5), 77–89.

Mincheva, L. (2008). 'Counter-terrorism Strategies in the Balkans: Risk Assessment of the Regional Conflict Potential and Recommendable Counter-Terrorism Policies', in I. Prezelj (ed.) *The Fight Against Terrorism and Crisis Management in the Western Balkans* (pp. 47–56). Amsterdam: IOS Press.

Miquel, A., author interview, Barcelona, 14 July 2017.

Ó Tuathail, G. (2008). 'Russia's Kosovo: A Critical Geopolitics of the August 2008 War over South Ossetia'. *Eurasian Geography and Economics*, 49(6), 670–705.

OSCE (2001). 'Framework Agreement'. Retrieved from: www.osce.org/skopje/100622?download=true

Rivera, A. (2017, 14 October). 'El separatismo prepara el terreno para la vía Kosovo. Nunca pensé que Yugoslavia fuera ejemplo a seguir. Qué locura' [Tweet]. Retrieved from: https://twitter.com/albert_rivera/status/919125502396452864?-lang=bg

Sánchez-Vallejo, M. (2018, 29 April). 'No hay ninguna analogía posible entre Kosovo y Cataluña, establecerla es un sinsentido'. *El Pais*. Retrieved from: https://elpais.com/internacional/2018/04/29/actualidad/1525015344_341405.html

Sastre, D. (2016, 4 May). 'Puigdemont evoca en el Parlament la independencia unilateral de Kosovo'. *El Mundo*. Retrieved from: www.elmundo.es/cataluna/2016/05/04/5729c4d846163f54568b4603.html

Seymour, M. (2007). 'Secession as a Remedial Right'. *Inquiry: An Interdisciplinary Journal of Philosophy*, 50(4): 395–423.

Spanish diplomatic source, author interview, Belgrade, 2 July 2012.

Summers, J. (2011). 'Kosovo: From Yugoslav Province to Disputed Independence,' in J. Summers (ed.) *Kosovo – A Precedent?: The Declaration of Independence, the Advisory Opinion and Implications for Statehood, Self-Determination and Minority Rights* (pp. 3–52). Leiden: Martinus Nijhoff publishers.

UN (2014). 'General Assembly Adopts Resolution Calling upon States Not to Recognize Changes in Status of Crimea Region'. Retrieved from: www.un.org/press/en/2014/ga11493.doc.htm

UNSC (2007). 'Report of the Special Envoy of the Secretary-General on Kosovo's future status'. S2007/168.

U.S. Department of State (2008). 'U.S. Recognizes Kosovo as Independent State'. Retrieved from: https://2001-2009.state.gov/secretary/rm/2008/02/100973.htm

Teper, Y. (2016). 'Official Russian identity discourse in light of the annexation of Crimea: national or imperial?'. *Post-Soviet Affairs*, 32(4): 378–396.

Treisman, D. (2016). 'Why Putin Took Crimea: The Gambler in the Kremlin'. *Foreign Affairs*, 95: 47–54.

Wilde, R. (2011). 'Accordance with International Law of the Unilateral Declaration of Independence in Respect of Kosovo'. *The American Journal of International Law*, 105(2): pp. 301–307.

Wood, P. (2001, 29 December). 'Macedonia: Step back from the abyss'. *BBC*. Retrieved from: http://news.bbc.co.uk/2/hi/in_depth/world/2001/review_of_2001/1703711.stm

Xhemaj, B., author interview, Skype, 28 May 2018.

YouTube (2014). 'Putin Justifies Russia's Annexation of Crimea (with English subtitles)'. Retrieved from: www.youtube.com/watch?v=uS8hbmoc15c

Yuhas (2014, 13 April). 'Ukraine crisis: an essential guide to everything that's happened so far'. *Guardian*. Retrieved from: www.theguardian.com/world/2014/apr/11/ukraine-russia-crimea-sanctions-us-eu-guide-explainer

Conclusion

In the post-Cold War era, humanitarian intervention and secession/territory seizure have become important features of geopolitical struggle for power and influence. The behaviour of great powers and their discourses often clash as a result of these phenomena, exposing an astonishing propensity towards double standards. For instance, while Serbia's territorial integrity was unreservedly violated by the U.S. and its allies, the very same states that decisively contributed to Kosovo's unilateral secession were appalled – to the extent of imposing economic sanctions against Russia – when Ukraine's territorial integrity was undermined by Russia in 2014.

It appears clear that the strategy of promoting secession in hostile (and weak) states has gained momentum, becoming an instrument *à la mode*. Likewise, humanitarian interventions, that is, armed operations justified on moral grounds (i.e. protection of civilians) against states perceived as rogue by a particular great power, have also become effective geopolitical tools. Kosovo superbly epitomises both trends: intervention and secession promotion. In this South-Eastern European parastate, the U.S. and its transatlantic allies illegally intervened in an internal conflict between a state and a secessionist insurgent group, the KLA, becoming de facto the latter's air force. The intervention, framed as humanitarian, generated a multiplicity of collateral effects, one of them being Kosovo's unilateral secession.

NATO presented the operation as a 'last resort'. However, as Chapter 2 has argued this was very far from being the case. To claim that NATO exhausted all diplomatic options would display a total ignorance of the content of the Rambouillet (non)Agreement. Rambouillet can hardly be considered a textbook example for a negotiated settlement. Instead, it appeared that the priority was to intervene to impose what former NATO SACEUR, General Clark, defined as 'the political will of the NATO nations on the Federal Republic of Yugoslavia' (2001, p. 418). The ludicrous military conditions laid out on Appendix B, which asked Yugoslavia to relinquish its sovereignty allowing NATO to literally take over the entire country, illustrate that there were alternatives to waging war. It also illustrates Gibbs' argument according to which external intervention was indeed one of the chief causes of the conflict (2009, p. 1).

The NATO intervention in Kosovo was above all a war, though decorously referred to by its supporters as humanitarian intervention. War was therefore a choice and the preferred option was far from being the 'armed surgery' operation that the proponents had envisioned. During Operation Allied Force campaign, NATO and most of the Western press used the euphemistic jargon which was later reproduced in other Western-led wars such as 'surgical strikes', 'legitimate targets' and the infamous 'collateral damage' when there were 'mistakes' in the form of civilian casualties. The prosaic reality clashes with such euphemistic terms – the idea of a clean war corresponds more to an illusion or a conceptual construct by NATO rather than to an empirical reality. As Rynning eloquently points out:

> [W]estern militaries pretend to fight the war that Western societies expect – war not as war but armed surgery to deliver us painlessly from evil. Ultimately, of course, this modern, liberal expectation that war can be controlled makes it easier to choose war.
>
> (Rynning, 2018)

One of the most immediate collateral effects of the 1999 humanitarian intervention was the fact that the 78-day bombing campaign directly caused hundreds of civilian victims – both Serbs and Kosovo Albanians – and indirectly thousands by aggravating the conflict. As Chapter 2 showed, from 80 per cent to 87.5 per cent of the victims of the conflict died during or after Operation Allied Force. If protecting civilian lives was the chief aim of the operation, it is not too far-fetched to argue that the intervention was, empirically speaking, an astounding failure. NATO did not manage to prevent ethnic cleansing either, quite on the contrary. The NATO-led operation did trigger Milošević ethnic cleansing of Kosovo Albanians which, according to Chief Prosecutor and author Carla del Ponte 'began under the cover of NATO airstrikes' (Del Ponte and Sudetic, 2009, p. 275).

In addition, as Chapter 3 explains, the departure of Yugoslavian security forces and subsequent deployment of NATO (KFOR) troops exposed over 200,000 Kosovo Serbs and Roma to reversed ethnic cleansing. The former, who had been used as a political instrument by Milošević, had become easy targets for the victorious side after the end of NATO bombing campaign. They had turned into Kosovo's new victims, although their ordeal was not as well documented in the West as the torment previously suffered by the Kosovo Albanians. The interveners, UNMIK and KFOR, that is the UN and NATO, systematically failed to protect vulnerable groups like Serbs and Roma from vengeful crimes, as explained in Chapter 3. In some cases, such as in March 2004, widespread ethnic-fuelled acts of violence were committed under their guard and those very institutions whose presence and legitimacy in Kosovo stemmed from their role as 'protectors of civilians' were too incompetent, too frightened or perhaps too concerned about the stability of their mission to act decisively to prevent crimes against unarmed civilians.

The humanitarian intervention operation conducted by NATO in Kosovo was *prima facie* a war based on moral imperatives. It would be naïve, however, to deny that there were national and geopolitical interests at stake. Even former British PM Tony Blair admitted, in 1999, that the operation was 'guided by a more subtle blend of mutual self-interest and moral purpose' (cited by Kaiser and McGuire, 1999). This admission is of paramount importance because, according to one of its pivotal advocates and implementers, the national interest dimension is part of the equation of humanitarian intervention. The question is: do both *ingredients* cohabitate harmoniously in a balanced fashion or does one of the two – namely national interest – take preponderance in detriment to the other? In Kosovo, the self-interest dimension of the interveners was more than self-evident before (Rambouillet), during and particularly after the intervention.

The war or humanitarian intervention against Yugoslavia had substantial collateral effects in political and geopolitical terms. For starters, it fundamentally altered the territorial status quo in South-East Europe and, in turn, the balance of power in the region. Therefore, the intervention had serious power implications which went far beyond the humble and modest goal of 'protecting civilians'. As Chapter 4 has argued, one of the most tangible impacts of the intervention has been the creation, under the auspices of international institutions, of a new de facto state, or more precisely parastate. This new entity was born in February 2008 after a unilateral declaration of independence which was drafted, supported and even encouraged by the U.S. and some of its European allies.

While it is crystal clear that Serbia has, since the Kumanovo agreement of 1999, lost its sovereignty over the territory, it is less clear who is in charge of that sovereignty two decades after the intervention and a decade after the UDI proclaimed by the Kosovo Assembly. Kosovo's sovereignty is, indeed, curtailed by an amalgam of actors including the EU, the U.S. and NATO. Chapter 4 has argued that despite the period of 'supervised independence' formally coming to an end in 2012, Kosovo's sovereignty continues to be undermined by the international actors who made that independence possible in the first place. One of the illustrations of this foreign interference in Pristina's internal affairs is the enormous influence the U.S. embassy exerts on Kosovo's politics, for instance, when it comes to *help* electing Prime Ministers and Presidents.

Tentatively, another collateral effect would be the fact that the *success* – in the sense that the mission managed to expel the Yugoslavian security forces from Kosovo and transform the political realities of the territory – of Operation Allied Force emboldened the United States and its allies to engage in military adventurism elsewhere. It is worth remembering that the Kosovo operation occurred in a context when the *unipolar moment* was experiencing its golden age. Kosovo illustrated that the West's military might was able to make a significant geopolitical difference with very little political cost.

Kosovo has indeed been praised as a triumph and as 'a success of liberal interventionism' (*Independent*, 2008). One of the key champions of this idea is undoubtedly Tony Blair, the founding father of the 'Doctrine of the International Community', which was born during Operation Allied Force. This doctrine, which epitomises Western self-righteousness, is succinctly defined by the former British PM in his memoirs as 'intervention to bring down a despotic dictatorial regime' (Blair, 2010, p. 248). This is, in effect, the very doctrine that Blair, Bush and other Western leaders applied in Iraq in 2003 and their successors in Libya in 2011. Kosovo therefore operated as a catalyst for Western-led military interventions in the early twenty-first century. As Blair himself admits 'Kosovo had not diminished my appetite for such intervention where I thought it essential to resolve a problem that needed resolution' (2010, p. 246).

Chapter 5 has questioned whether Operation Allied Force 'resolved a problem' or rather created new ones. From the perspective of Western interveners, borders in the region are clear and set after Kosovo's secession. The caveat is that Kosovo's statehood, and particularly its consolidation through UN membership, is proven to be tremendously problematic due to a wide range of factors *inter alia* Serbia's continuous opposition to Kosovo's secession and Russian and Chinese vetoes at the UNSC. If this deadlock becomes permanent, Kosovan and Albanian leaders have both begun to think alternative possibilities, such as the unification of both territories, which involve the redrawing of the political boundaries of South-East Europe. What this potential illustrates is that, two decades after NATO's intervention, we may not have seen all its collateral effects. Some of them may still be in the gestation period and may manifest themselves in the future.

Another unresolved issue is what this book has labelled as 'the problem of the north', that is, the hostility and alienation of Kosovo Serbs, particularly those living in the four Serbian municipalities in the north towards the institutions of the Kosovo state. Chapter 5 has argued that the partition of the four northern municipalities and its reintegration into Serbia constitutes yet another potential for border redrawing in the region. This possibility is regularly hinted at by high profile figures in the Serbian government. The European Union has attempted to tackle the threat of partition as well as the hostile relationships between Pristina and Belgrade through a negotiated settlement, popularly known as the Brussels agreement, signed in April 2013. The key buzzword of this Brussels initiative is the 'normalisation of relationships' between both capitals. Despite EU efforts, both coercive and co-optative, little progress has been made, particularly since 2014, and therefore the deadlock continues.

The EU's attempts to solve the problem(s) in Kosovo have encountered a myriad of difficulties. One of them, remarkably, is largely internal. Despite the fact that numerous European leaders have insisted that Kosovo was a unique case and consequently it did not constitute a precedent for other secessionist conflicts, five EU member states refuse (as of 2018) to recognise Kosovo's independence. In a more or less surreptitious fashion, a wide range of actors, including European diplomats, admit that this refusal has little to do with Kosovo itself and is rather connected to these countries' own domestic issues. The epitome of this is Spain, a *non-recogniser* state which has endured a serious secessionist challenge stemming from Catalonia. The problem is that, as Chapter 6 has argued: '[T]he Spanish government fears that Kosovo could become a precedent for Catalonia reifies and consolidates the argument that Kosovo constitutes a precedent'. The discrepancy within the EU in relation to recognising Kosovo or not affects the coherence and credibility of the bloc's 'common' foreign policy.

The problem with this debate is that repeating that Kosovo does not constitute a precedent has not deterred many actors from thinking – and acting – otherwise. One of the most prominent counter-productive collateral effects of the intervention in Kosovo – and the subsequent Western support for secession in this territory – has been the provision of dialectic ammunition to the West's contemporary geopolitical foe, Russia. Moscow has indeed used its particular interpretation of the 'protection of civilians' Western formula to intervene in Georgia in 2008 and Ukraine in 2014. In both cases, the Kosovo precedent has been invoked as a justification. As a result, it would be possible to argue that the intervention in Kosovo has, to a certain extent, been an element contributing to the emboldenment of Russian foreign policy and this, in turn, has been a key factor in the deterioration of the relations between Moscow and the West. Thus, it is rather evident that the collateral effects of the Kosovo intervention have transcended Kosovo itself. In geopolitical terms, NATO's war in Kosovo has escalated the tensions between Moscow and Washington by generating mutual distrust and establishing a perilous interventionist precedent.

The practice of humanitarian intervention, as the Kosovo case shows, involves many more dimensions than the repeated mantra, and excellent selling point, of 'protection of civilians'. This moral imperative may very likely be accompanied by motives of a less altruistic nature, including foreign interference, hegemony-consolidation, geopolitical alterations of the balance of power and imperialism. It is worth remembering that this practice involves war, an instrument nasty and brutish but seldom short. While the so-called 'air campaign' lasted 78 days, the NATO troop deployment which followed the bombing has lasted for two decades and it is still ongoing. Scholars have tended to discuss the desirability of humanitarian intervention from a moral and legal perspective, largely neglecting a scrutiny of its effects. This book is a humble attempt to fill this gap. One of the lessons of Kosovo is that it is important to consider the implications of intervention, not least because many of them are undesired, long-term, collateral and sometimes counter-productive. In other words, it is essential not to be naïve about humanitarian intervention for this practice inevitably generates collateral effects which, on some occasions, may make the remedy worse than the disease.

Bibliography

Blair, T. (2010). *A Journey. My Political Life.* London: Random House Ltd.

Clark, W. K. (2001). *Waging Modern War.* New York: Public Affairs.

Del Ponte, C. and C. Sudetic (2009). *Madame Prosecutor. Confrontations with Humanity's Worst Criminals and the Culture of Impunity.* New York: Other Press.

Gibbs, D. (2009). *First Do No Harm: Humanitarian Intervention and the Destruction of Yugoslavia.* Nashville: Vanderbilt University Press.

Independent (2008, 17 February). 'Leading article: Kosovo: a triumph for intervention'. Retrieved from: www.independent.co.uk/voices/editorials/leading-article-kosovo-a-triumph-for-intervention-783279.html

Kaiser, R. and McGuire, M. (1999, 23 April). 'Blair unveils bold intervention doctrine'. *Chicago Tribune.* Retrieved from: http://articles.chicagotribune.com/1999-04-23/news/9904230097_1_blair-third-world-debt-cold-war

Rynning, S. (2018). 'Zero civilian casualties: why the face of Western war gives us a false idea of conflict'. *The Conversation.* Retrieved from: http://theconversation.com/zero-civilian-casualties-why-the-face-of-western-war-gives-us-a-false-idea-of-conflict-93090

Index

Page numbers in *italics* denote figures.